This book by Harsha Singh is a masterly *upadesh* for the seekers of spiritual advancement. Being a quasi-autobiographical work, it is imbued with deep insights and that rare authenticity. Here Harsha provides a road map and milestones for one's spiritual advancements. For sceptic beginners he provides the scientific foundation and deep insights from Buddhist, Hindu and Judaic philosophical masters.

This beautifully written book also provides to the readers radiant glimpses of the joy of epiphanic moments of a seeker's journey.

—Vijay Kelkar
Chairman, Thirteenth Finance Commission, India;
President, Indian Statistical Institute, Kolkata

This book builds a path forward on how to be a great achiever with a heart of gold. It has substantive depth and wisdom, and combines modern and traditional practices. I have seen the author live what he advocates and highly recommend it to the new age managers and entrepreneurs.

—Ajay Singh
Chairman and Managing Director, SpiceJet Limited

In his circle of friends, Harsha Vardhana Singh is known for being so positive and loving that they speak of a Harsha Effect: bringing out the better angels of all their natures. Drawing on his highly successful career and deep spiritual learning, he has given us a manual to help us find peace in our busy lives and generate our own Harsha Effect.

—Arvind Subramanian
Chief Economic Advisor, Government of India

Small Steps Concentric Circles

A RATIONAL MIND'S
GUIDE TO SPIRITUAL GROWTH

SMALL STEPS CONCENTRIC CIRCLES

HARSHA VARDHANA SINGH

Foreword by HH the Dalai Lama

First published 2018

ISBN 978-81-8328-380-9

Published by
Wisdom Tree
4779/23, Ansari Road
Darya Ganj, New Delhi-110 002
Ph.: 23247966/67/68
wisdomtreebooks@gmail.com

Printed in India

To

Aghoreshwar, my Baba who gave me all,
Guru Baba who softly takes me ahead across my concentric circles,
Suryadev Ram Baba (Anil Ji) whose compassion lights the way

Contents

Foreword

Whether you are a believer or not, or whether your philosophy on the origin of existence resonates well with the theory of creator or of karma, the essence is that we all seek happiness and yearn to find clarity over complicated philosophical issues that continuously linger within. As humans, we have this marvellous human intelligence with an ability to explore and understand reality in ways no other creature on earth can. Therefore, whether it concerns a religious matter or others, we should always apply our intelligence and ability to thoroughly investigate things to ensure that our actions and practices conform with reality. The purpose of spiritual practice is to bring more peace and happiness for oneself and others. Genuine peace and happiness will arise if compassion becomes one's central practice and if its application is combined with the wisdom of discernment. Extreme self-centeredness, and lack of respect and concern for others' well-being will not bring a genuine sense of achievement in you.

Whether you are a religious believer or not, the practice of love, compassion, discipline, mindfulness and so forth, are all common values that anyone, with or without any religious allegiance, can practise to add meaning and beauty to life. I call this approach 'secular' and the practice of ethics in this context as 'Secular Ethics.' According to the Indian understanding, the word secular entails no disrespect, but rather respect for believers and non-believers alike. For our own mental and physical well-being, we need to practise these basic ethical values since they by themselves are not religious values or teachings.

In a world with people from varied spiritual backgrounds and upbringing, no particular religion is suitable for everyone. Given this reality, it is important for us to develop respect for all the religious traditions for their immense benefit in answering the spiritual needs of the people of the world. Due to their diverse philosophy, inclination, upbringing and intellectual vigour, different people have different spiritual experiences. In his book *Small Steps Concentric Circles,* Harsha Vardhana Singh shares his own spiritual experience, which I hope the readers will find interesting and useful.

—The Dalai Lama

Prologue

I have led a double life—two lives very different and distinct.

Born in Delhi, India's capital city, I studied in educational institutions amongst the best in the country. My next stop was the University of Oxford as a Rhodes Scholar. After completing my PhD in economics there, I worked for about thirteen years in international organisations in Geneva (Switzerland) before returning to India to join the newly formed Telecom Regulatory Authority of India (TRAI). Back home, I interacted with a wide range of stakeholders in a fast evolving policy, business and technological context. At TRAI, we converted the old prevailing system into a modern one, changing mindsets and expanding opportunities for people, evolving regulatory systems that were essential for fundamental reform. In 2005, I was back in Geneva as a very senior official in an international organisation where intense and difficult forward-looking discussions take place in a challenging international environment. After eight years in this position, I am a part of international think tanks and a professor at reputed universities in more than one country.

In this part of my life, I have interacted with a whole range of leaders, key decision-makers and others in a large number of countries, extending across the diplomatic community, politics, business, farmers, government officials, academia, NGOs, media, international institutions, intellectuals and those dealing with common concerns every day. I have worked with top bosses and seen several others at close quarters in India and abroad, including during the ongoing shift in global economics and soft power, with growing aspirations of people coexisting with major economic and social problems across the world. Most of my working life has been in the West, travelling to many parts of the world and interacting with people from over a hundred countries. I have led a modern life and been trained in modern techniques to deal with issues and concerns relating to modern societies. I am an integral part of modern society.

My other life has been completely different. Growing up in a very spiritual family, I was often in the company of holy men. My maternal grandfather was a sadhu (Hindu monk), whom, in my early years, I visited in the village for about a couple of months every year. Sadhus visited my paternal and maternal grandfathers' village homes often and I interacted closely with them. This interaction, however, was not limited only to my village life. Sadhus and other holy men were often guests in my father's home in Delhi too. I spent long hours with these persons of different spiritual persuasions, fascinated by their lifestyles and stories, absorbing their thoughts, and sometimes amazed at the special events that occurred around them. In hindsight, I see that this was good preparation for the next phase of this 'other' life when I met a most exceptional spiritual leader from the city of Varanasi. He was my father's spiritual guide or guru, in the formal traditional framework, having initiated him as a spiritual disciple. I called him Baba, a common Indian term used for sadhus and other spiritual persons. Without being so anointed, he was the leader of an ancient spiritual order, which he reformed to become more of a part of society. His spiritual practices were accompanied with major social work, including successfully treating a large number of lepers with alternative medicine. He combined compassion, a practical approach to everyday life and deep spiritual practices. I found him immensely charismatic, affectionate and highly considerate.[1] I was drawn to him and became an informal part of his acolytes. Very slowly, I walked the road of spirituality with like-minded people, many of whom were sadhus. From time to time, I lived with them, I thought like them, immersed in their world, a world very different and difficult to conceptualise for those who have not seen it intimately. This would become clear from the very few books written by those who have lived as sadhus.[2] As I became more integrated in this life, I had some unusual and exceptional experiences and insights. This life took me along a very uncommon path, different from the urban or modern society, or even rural Indian society and, of course, starkly different from the western world where I have lived for quarter of a century.

In the beginning, these two streams of my life were distinct and independent of each other. On occasions, there were conflicts when certain aspirations of the modern, normal life felt like breaching the fundamental principles of spiritual objectives. Likewise, living a simple life of a quasi-sadhu, I sometimes missed the modern conveniences, comforts and approaches. But each life had its own attractions, commitments and even compulsions for me and I grew up living in two very different worlds. This had some interesting consequences.

I had a number of questions in my mind about motivations, objectives, methods and the basis for our progress in life. In my life, I was seeking two apparently opposite objectives. One was to succeed in conventional ways, to perform well in studies or my job, to obtain material comforts, to promote the opportunities for my family and to be appreciated for my substantive worth. The other was to find inner peace and greater understanding of the world around us, to know the great unknown.

I have experienced first-hand a number of events that would be considered as miracles. They were way beyond the realm of usual occurrences. Most of these were from Baba, but strangely, I too started getting insights and glimpses that were exceptional and far removed from normal occurrences in the world around me. Some were experiences commonly associated with a spiritual journey, some indicated events which were to happen at a later date, while others were like flashes of understanding about some larger reality. I did not comprehensively understand them but very much wanted to do so. It made me an intense seeker of a larger reality through books and discussions with people, while continuing normally with my dual-carriage life. I read extensively on spirituality and on simplified scientific explanations to achieve greater understanding of these phenomena. I found many interesting overlaps among these books, but there were many unanswered questions. The pace of my apparent insights outstripped any understanding that I could get from my dedicated efforts. Though my comprehension has increased immensely, I continue to walk the road to fully understand the source of these experiences, paradoxically complex yet simple, depending on the level of detail we wish to focus on. This experience has given me a sense of perspective much wider than usual, a framework to better understand events, both ordinary and extraordinary.

Another interesting development occurred en route this journey. Very often I found that even during formal lunches or dinners, and much more during informal discussions, a large variety of people would suddenly change track and raise spiritual issues relating to decision-making, managing the stress of life or to discuss some spiritual experiences. Though diffident at first, I increasingly found myself trying to address these issues. Long, intense conversations followed. Over the years it happened repeatedly, something like what the baseball player Yogi Berra described as 'déjà vu all over again'.

My discussions had mixed results. Several treated my views with seriousness, even asking me to teach them some simple techniques to better address anxiety or agitated state of mind. Others were less enthusiastic and perhaps even amused to consider a spiritual outlook to address their concerns. For them, spirituality was by definition a non-logical way of looking at things. Being from the modern world, some with immense conventional success while others aspiring to it, they were deeply uncomfortable with any frame of reference that took them towards a different paradigm. In my conversations with them, I started developing a framework that was logical but anchored on insights that were based on lives and understanding of spiritual masters. My own experiences with Baba proved highly valuable in this context, as did my extensive professional and social interactions with high achievers and leaders in the fields of business, politics, international diplomacy, government and social projects. I saw that they all used and embodied certain spiritual principles in their actions. In each area of operation, the high achievers emphasised these principles for decision-making. My most difficult moments helped me develop a much deeper understanding of this framework. The most recent of these was a period from late October 2009 to mid-January 2010, a period which my wife spent in the ICU, fighting death daily for almost three months. I have thus seen that whether it is to cope with difficulties or to make progress in material life, the way forward was through the application of spiritual principles.

This view may appear to be inconsistent or simply wrong if we consider spiritual outlook or principles as being limited to only non-material aspects. My experience, my double life, has shown me that the scope of spiritual principles is far wider than conventionally understood. It covers a wide spectrum ranging from logical and positive thinking at one end, to methods like meditation and breathing exercises that help develop such abilities, and goes on to the other end of the spectrum with metaphysical phenomena and experiences that are completely other-worldly.

This structure has helped me to better understand and evolve a more consistent view of my double life, with extensive overlap between experiences which earlier seemed to be on the opposite ends of lifestyle spectrum. More importantly, this has helped me better achieve my goals in both the material and spiritual life, and I have seen that a number of others have also benefited from these ideas. Many persons, both spiritually oriented and those who consider themselves very practical and a-spiritual, have encouraged me to share my thoughts more widely through books or lectures. In this context, I want to specially mention the encouragement from Clara Berger, an energy therapist based in Geneva. I have, thus, attempted to address a thirst amongst all of us for practical methods to achieve material success with a positive attitude and peace of mind. My numerous conversations have shown that normally people search for simple and practical ideas that are not esoteric, not other-worldly, and can become part of our everyday life to address the material aspirations and concerns faced by most of us. I am very much a part of this group and consider myself fortunate to have experiences which provided me with a relevant perspective to increasingly address these concerns. It is a journey, but a journey that improves us materially and spiritually.

This book is an effort to explain some of these methods to make progress in this journey. My focus is to provide tools and concepts that can be used practically in life to address a variety of situations, enabling the suggested methods to become a part of daily life. The idea is to equip ourselves with simple tools to deal with both the issues we face every day and the major concerns that may arise in particularly trying moments. While in large part this book aims to provide practical insights for the material world, people may find deeper relevance or utility in the concepts covered by the other parts of the spiritual spectrum. Therefore, I also go into a number of these other concepts and methods. In some cases, this helps us to see the overlap between these different parts of the spiritual spectrum, or to understand various options for sequential or stage-wise progress within the spiritual framework. For me, the most beautiful and relevant aspect is that we could be in contact with our deeper reality or power at any point in this spiritual spectrum, with our efforts being manifested in different ways depending on which part of the spectrum we may be traversing.

The ideas expressed in this book are a result of conversations or personal experiences during the good and bad times in life. Therefore, I have written this book as a story with conversations among different characters. The focus is on the thoughts and messages contained in the questions and the responses by characters in the book rather than a wholesome portrayal of the characters themselves. In effect, these conversations reflect the multiple processes of internal search to understand and make progress towards material and spiritual objectives. While most of the thoughts in this book are based on actual conversations and the characters are based on real people, I have used artistic licence to change situations and characters. For those who may recognise themselves, I request their indulgence to pardon me for any transgressions.

One lesson that may come across when reading self-help books is that many of them provide similar or overlapping ways of making progress. Still we find a thirst for greater knowledge or means of addressing our everyday concerns. A reason may be that 'the common person' dealing with common concerns, weaknesses and desires seeks simple methods that convert high level or somewhat esoteric self-help concepts into meaningful or tangible action points to practically apply them as part of daily life. I belong to this category of 'common man' with several weaknesses and shortcomings, as well as an aspiration to cope with them, to try to enhance the positive and mitigate the negative in myself through practical spiritual steps in the material world. This book is an attempt to provide such methods and hopefully make it easier for people to make deeper progress in their material and spiritual journey in life.

Thus, my effort has been to simplify difficult concepts through methods or techniques that can be adopted in daily life. Much of my focus is on the part of the spiritual spectrum that deals with objectivity, logic and clear perception of issues. There is considerable interest also in meditation and related practices, as shown by vast self-help literature on the subject. I have shared a simple meditation technique which has helped a number of people who have tried it. An interesting aspect of this technique is that it can be adapted to suit both an a-spiritual perspective as well as a spiritual one. Further, I have addressed some issues that arise normally in making meditation practices a normal part of our daily life, including some caution that must be exercised with certain practices. I have also discussed metaphysical aspects but very briefly, because they belong to that portion of spiritual spectrum which is both deep and usually treated with the highest level of cynicism. Moreover, in my experience, it is a by-product of a spiritual journey rather than the main focus, namely, being in touch with a strong energy force within us and developing calm and peace of mind to address our daily concerns. However, since it could arise as a by-product, I have discussed some aspects which we may need to understand better.

I wanted to write this book as a story so that people could relate to some of the conditions or thoughts which arise when we deal with everyday events. However, the subject matter involves addressing many deep and substantive thoughts and therefore, the story as such is dominated by the conversations which deal with these diverse issues. Thus, in addition to simplifying and converting larger concepts into manageable and practical methods, I have provided a few quotations from other writers to illustrate some points and also referred to certain books which could be of interest. In particular, I have discussed certain key lessons from three bestsellers. This is to look at some of the points that may require emphasis for people with different persuasions, and to consider a number of common questions that arise in the minds of people when they seek greater peace of mind and understanding while going about their daily tasks. The discussion provides a basis to more comprehensively reflect in our life some important points made in these books. I have been highly selective and the references of books I mention are not exhaustive, but merely illustrative. It also reflects a large conceptual overlap amongst different writings.

This book is a labour of love and I owe a debt to all my loved ones: To Baba, whose incomparable affection and caring objectivity showed the amazing depth of his all-encompassing spiritual love that was felt by so many, yet each experienced it as being specially focused on the person; my spiritual guide Guru Baba, whose steady, patient and comprehensive care has provided solutions, insights, progress and contentment for me; his deeply compassionate wife Gururatnaji whose spiritual energy, affection and commitment to provide support for those in need are always a source of great confidence and joy; Anil Baba (Suryadev Ram), who has given me care and spiritual support whenever I needed it most, like a compassionate spiritual family member from the depth of time; my parents whose spirituality was reflected in their love and daily life; my wife Veena, who has epitomised evolving high spirituality and great support for me, especially when I walked the more difficult parts of the road in life; my children KetakiRuchika, Aabir and Anandamayee; sister Vibha and brother-in-law Vir and their children, Sukriti, Irfan, Jaba and Ankit; Uncle Das, Donny and Rupa—their love and support helped me develop a positive attitude; my Rakhi-sister Parul Subramanian, whose patience, generosity and caring epitomises the essence of spirituality, and a number of kindred spiritual souls whose deep spiritual energy and light strongly reflect the same source as my own, significantly helping me in my progress. All these special persons in my life have been my teachers, with Parul also helping to improve this book immensely. I also want to thank all others who have enriched me with their affection, patience, guidance and tolerance. Primary amongst these are Shobit Arya, my publisher, who embodies spirituality and depth of vision in his daily behaviour and my editors who did a superb job of improving the text while retaining the message. I owe a debt of gratitude to all these who have helped me grow towards increasingly understand the overlap in my double life.

References

1. Ram, Aughar Harihar. *Oasis of Stillness: Life and Teachings of Aghoreshwar Bhagwan Ramji, A Modern Day Saint of India*. USA: Aghor Publications, 1997.
2. For example, Rampuri. *Autobiography of a Sadhu: A Journey into Mystic India*. USA: Destiny Books, 2005.

1

Still, on the Move

What a journey, thought Ananda as he settled into a comfortable seat on the plane. He was not thinking of the flight from Geneva to New Delhi. It was a much longer journey, starting in his childhood, meandering across several nations, a long time spent in India and Geneva, ending on the picnic spot at Combloux, France. With a strong sense of achievement, he again looked at the paper summarising the ideas he had shared with Benedict and Francis at Combloux. The pattern was so much clearer now.

He felt very happy at the thought of meeting Vadya on his return home, hoping to find some quiet moments to share his new perspectives. He thought of their two daughters, Juhi and Joy. How long before he could discuss his insights with them, he wondered. Perhaps a long time, but then one should never underestimate the children of the present generation. Unknown to him, he was smiling widely when he thought of his daughters. The air hostess passing him smiled back at him. She realised he was immersed in a joyous thought and wanted to add some more spirit to it.

'Can I offer you something to drink, sir? Some champagne, water or juice?' she asked.

Ananda's first thought was to pick up a glass of water, as he recalled the advice of veteran travellers that one should hydrate oneself on flights. However, when he extended his hand towards the drink trolley, he changed his mind and picked up a glass of champagne. I deserve to celebrate a bit and relax with champagne, thought Ananda. He sipped his champagne and decided to watch a film on the in-flight video. He wanted to watch a comedy, but he had seen all of them on the flight to Geneva. It was quite an achievement for someone who normally did not watch movies. Did personalities change when you are not linked to Earth? he mused as he looked at other options. He settled to watch a new version of a film he had liked very much, *Karate Kid*.

He was enjoying the film, identifying in different ways with the characters when it hit him all of a sudden: This meeting of two different worlds he saw in the film, wasn't it the story of his own life? And he froze, his mind alert.

'Being still and doing nothing are two very different things,' said the teacher of the Karate Kid, one of the two main characters. How interesting, thought Ananda.

Wasn't this the message he too sought to convey when he taught people a simple form of meditation? Yes, he would remember this line for future use. It was a very simple expression of a very powerful idea. He took out his mobile phone, punched the keys to record the dialogue and sent it to himself as a text message, saving it as a draft in his messages folder. He now started watching the film with greater attention. Soon, the teacher said something else that he felt addressed him directly as if he were a character in the film. 'There is only one person you need to learn how to control,' pronounced the teacher. Ananda recalled using exactly the same words in his conversation with Benedict and Francis during the picnic at Combloux. Something like the words of

Leo Tolstoy: 'Everyone thinks of changing the world, but no one thinks of changing himself.'

Ananda's thoughts went to his drive from Geneva to Combloux. Benedict was driving and his old friend, Francis was telling him about their recent experiences. It was a long drive as Benedict had decided to show Ananda some scenic spots in the area, even taking difficult mountain roads to do so. Meanwhile, Francis had talked almost non-stop and seemed to be missing out no detail.

Francis and Benedict's quest seemed much like his own or that of Marie whom he had met a few months ago, but who had since become a part of the larger family he and Vadya had built over time. Well, well, it is only Vadya who has built this family with her deep affection for all and unstinting efforts to make people feel welcome. I am merely a beneficiary of Vadya's goodness, basking in the goodwill and positive feelings she is able to generate, thought Ananda with some amusement, pride and even guilt.

His attention shifted back to the film. He admired the teacher and the wonderfully crafted scenes. Francis, too, had been a teacher to Benedict, and Ananda had tried to be one for Marie. The path was not easy, as it had not been for the Karate Kid. But the Kid had managed to succeed, to validate the teacher's training. Was there to be a sequel to this new *Karate Kid* film, in the same way that we all have sequels in our own lives?

Ananda thought about the time early in his life when he had started developing an interest in the larger picture of life. It began with some visions that had disturbed him initially. The visions had continued, and over time, he became more comfortable with them, even enjoying the new insights emerging from them.

He did not get these special glimpses at will, but at the most unexpected moments, always partial and incomplete. Often, he would see a blurred image or even a moving picture, so much like a hallucination which sometimes offered a completely new insight. He was fascinated when the different parts of the picture would slowly reveal themselves, like a solution to a jigsaw puzzle. He felt these experiences had helped him to deal with his life with greater understanding, even though many among his family and friends treated him as impractical.

The experience had given him a strong urge to explain his unusual perceptions to people.

With some self-indulgence and a sense of his own importance, he thought, after all, my parents have named me 'Ananda', which means 'joy' or 'bliss'. I want joy both for myself and others. He realised his thoughts were egotistical and a little pompous, a fact that troubled him.

Often, when he started talking on the topic he lost the audience within a few minutes. It had been very disappointing in the beginning, but later he started choosing his audience with greater care. Ananda's desire to draw people into seeing the larger picture had given him so much happiness that often he became fully immersed in the effort. Vadya had to keep reminding him of the children and other worldly responsibilities.

Ananda was lucky to have a wife who so indulged him. He was convinced that Vadya, his wife, was far ahead of him in the spiritual quest, balancing with great calm and effectiveness the unusual requests of her husband and the multiple tasks involving family and friends.

His experience showed that there was no dearth of people looking for peace of mind while focusing on material objectives, without disrupting their daily lives. Ananda felt he could try to share his insights and walk the path with each of them if necessary. However, whenever Ananda discussed the spiritual aspects of life, he felt a need to simplify. Every time he had mentioned the spiritual path to others, they thought of religion or prayers, or God. The discussion would become other-worldly, cut off from the reality of everyday life. Ananda aspired to simplify the issues, to link his thoughts with normal daily experiences, using tangible and manageable concepts. He had been seeking a simple way, something which was feasible and could become part of everyday life in the same way as giving up smoking or making efforts to live a healthier life.

Ananda recalled several occasions when his friends had made fun of him. He smiled indulgently as he thought of some who he was particularly fond of. They were globally recognised for being exceptionally good at their job, sought everywhere for their expertise, their views were discussed worldwide and their presence always made a difference. They were evolved souls with great capacity to see the larger picture, Ananda thought. But they had their sights elsewhere.

Ananda was aware that he was not the first person to seek a simpler way. Throughout history, there had been great thinkers, social reformers, spiritual giants, people whose ideas had spawned major movements with huge followings, people who were capable of and did achieve the task of changing lives and thought processes, and yet, Ananda was looking for a simpler way. Perhaps this search was for someone who had glimpsed the larger picture, even an incomplete one. The discussion at Combloux had helped him progress in this quest.

The beautiful surroundings of Combloux had added a new dimension to his perspective. He looked at the piece of paper again with satisfaction, recalling how with a rush of clarity he had seen a stage-wise process for spiritual pursuit. It was as if some mental adrenaline had enhanced his insight to provide answers to a question that had been with him for most of his adult life. He was now able to see how one could walk the path of balancing material achievements with spiritual progress. It had been a long journey. Something like the progress in scientific understanding of deeper realities. He picked up the book he had read in Geneva and mouthed the short passage flagged in it:

> From Wheeler's emphasis on analysing the universe in terms of information, to the recognition that entropy is a measure of hidden

> information, to the reconciliation between the Second Law of Thermodynamics and black holes, to the realization that black holes store entropy on their surface, to the understanding that black holes set the maximum for the amount of information that can occupy a given region of space, we've followed a winding road across many decades and traversed an intricate web of results. The journey has been full of remarkable insights, and has led us to a new unifying idea—the holographic principle.[1]

This journey of evolving scientific understanding and conjecture described in the book felt almost personal to Ananda. So similar to his own journey, with increasing glimpses of a larger reality. He, too, had been looking for a depth of understanding which provided simple steps that could be replicated even in the spiritual context. His discussion with Francis and Benedict had provided him the basis to clarify such steps.

He knew that in science the advances were far more accessible to the practitioners and once discovered, took much less time to show effect than the efforts required to make personal progress in life. The latter needed persistence and patience because usually success comes in small steps as we address different challenges in our journey. With appropriate steps, the scope of success keeps expanding. Something like the ripples in a pond when a stone is thrown in it, the waves progressing to cover an expanding area with their concentric circles. Ananda's journey had been to find some ways of making the personal journey amenable to practical small steps across the concentric circles of multiple objectives. This trip to Combloux had been good for that.

Leaning back in his seat, lost in thought, Ananda switched off the video to catch the few hours of sleep he would get on the flight. His thoughts drifted to his first meeting with Francis some years ago, outside the Intensive Care Unit of a well-known hospital in Geneva. He still felt uncomfortable about it because he had been discourteous to Francis. It was perhaps the stress of Vadya fighting for her life at the ICU. Ananda had grown a lot during those extremely difficult times, experiencing both the huge human potential and extreme helplessness. In those twelve weeks at the ICU, he had met two very special persons: Dr Ritz, the doctor in charge of the ICU, and Francis. What a journey, he thought again, lost in thought about his experiences in the past few years.

References

1. Greene, Brian. *The Hidden Reality: Parallel Universes and the Deep Laws of the Cosmos.* USA: Vintage Books, 2011, pp 311-312.

2

Ananda and Francis

Francis walked back to his car after dropping Ananda off at the airport. He always felt more complete after spending time with Ananda. They complemented each other with their diverse backgrounds but common interests, even though Ananda always seemed so different, almost other-worldly. No, not almost, but definitely other-worldly. He seemed unconnected with the practical world. Later, Francis saw that Ananda always seemed to land on his feet, claiming that this was due to his larger perspective, a vision beyond the normal world. It was good that he decided to get to know Ananda better.

With a start, Francis realised that he was still sitting in his car in the parking lot after having paid for the parking. It was necessary to get out in time for the payment to remain valid. He drove back to his office and went to the cafeteria for his morning coffee. As he sat at a table near the window, he thought of his first substantive question to Ananda long ago: Spirituality in India is very old and it must have developed in its villages. Do the Indian villagers have concerns and issues similar to us, like ambition, a desire to promote themselves, acquisitiveness, competition and jealousy?

He vividly recalled Ananda's response, as if he was still sitting across the table from him, 'They have the same concerns, with one important difference. Their emphasis on how to address each situation tends to be different from what we see here. They emphasise what I call the "Triple A" aspects of life.'

Francis had noticed a tendency in Ananda to pontificate, sounding professorial and esoteric as he came up with acronyms such as 'Triple A'. Francis had just smiled with a quizzical look in his eyes, tilting his head a bit to indicate his incomprehension of this 'Triple A'. Ananda had got the message. After sipping some water to settle himself, he had explained, '"Triple A" is for Attitude, Analysis and Action. These three are crucial for developing appropriate perspectives and taking useful decisions in life. If our "attitude" is positive and we show sensitivity towards others, that provides us with a good foundation for progress. We need to build on this by "analysing" objectively the main features of any situation and the likely interaction with others, to make us better aware of the implications of our actions. We can then choose the relevant "action", based on these two As. Actions based on a positive and sensitive attitude towards others, after objectively examining the options, are usually more cooperative or less selfish. This "Triple A" differs across people and even societies, changing the way in which people address their concerns.'

'Why should we be sensitive or positive towards others?' Francis asked. 'Is that not unnatural, when we normally focus on our ego?'

Ananda shook his head vigorously from side to side. It was interesting how intense the gesture for disagreement was in the Indian mannerism. 'No, Francis. In our brain, compassion and caring for others is as normal as greed, ego, lust, fear or avarice. In fact, research has shown that it is often a far more normal behavioural attribute than others. Whichever of these so-called natural attributes we emphasise, those will increasingly become an important part of our mindset. Try it and see for yourself.'

'I am sure to fail,' ruminated Francis. 'I will not succeed in being positive all the time.'

'Do not give up without trying. And have a positive attitude. Think like the famous inventor, Thomas Alva Edison, who said, "I will not say that I failed a 1000 times. I will say that I discovered 1000 ways that can cause failure." Whenever you succeed to have a positive attitude, think of it as an achievement. Whenever you fail, think of it as an instance where you have learnt something that should be avoided. Whenever you feel low, look up at the light bulb and think of Edison, the man who invented the bulb,' encouraged Ananda.

'Is there any evidence from Indian villages that shows such a positive attitude?' asked Francis.

'Yes, Francis. There are several such examples mentioned in the 2012 baccalaureate speech at the University of Pennsylvania that was given by Nipun Mehta.[1] He decided to walk throughout India with his spouse and get to know its people and their views, and to contribute whatever could be done through positive actions at a basic level. It is a very interesting speech, which is worth reading in any case, but it clearly shows a difference of perspectives and viewpoints between India's urban and rural areas. Let me share a small part of it.'

> On our walking pilgrimage, we noticed that those who had the least were the ones most equipped to honour the priceless. In urban cities, the people we encountered began with an unspoken wariness: 'Why are you doing this? What do you want from me?' In the countryside, on the other hand, villagers almost always met us with an open-hearted curiosity, launching straight in with: 'Hey, you don't look local. What's your story?'

> In the villages, your worth wasn't assessed by your business card, professional network or your salary. That innate simplicity allowed them to love life and cherish all its connections.
>
> Extremely poor villagers, who couldn't even afford their own meals, would often borrow food from their neighbours to feed us. When we tried to refuse, they would simply explain: 'To us, the guest is God. This is our offering to the divine in you that connects us to each other.' Now, how could one refuse that? Street vendors often gifted us vegetables; in a very touching moment, an armless fruit-seller once insisted on giving us a slice of watermelon. Everyone, no matter how old, would be overjoyed to give us directions, even when they weren't fully sure of them. And I still remember the woman who generously gave us water when we were extremely thirsty. Much later only we learnt that she had to walk ten kilometres at 4 am to get that one bucket of water. These people knew how to give, not because they had a lot, but because they knew how to love life. They didn't need any credit or assurance that you would ever return to pay them back. Rather, they just trusted in the pay-it-forward circle of giving.

Lost in this past conversation, Francis looked out of the window and stared at the cherry tree. He recalled how he would earlier look at those trees in full bloom but not notice their beauty. He used to take the wonderful scenery for granted. It was Ananda's exuberance each time he saw flowers and trees in full bloom that had made him realise the bounties of nature that surrounded them. 'Triple A', excitement with natural beauty, seeking and finding positive attributes in people, a willingness to pick himself up after a fall to once again seek emerging horizons, Ananda had shared all this with him. The most valuable of course were their deeper spiritual discussions that had enabled him to go towards his internal resources.

Francis remembered his initial meeting with Ananda at a hospital in Geneva, when Ananda had been edgy and somewhat irritable, wanting to return quickly to the ICU. At that time, he did not think that they would become such good friends, almost like alter egos. How life changes when we give it time and opportunity to bloom. Just like the cherry tree outside the window. He realised that his experience with Benedict had been similarly enriching on the long road they had travelled since their initial meeting.

References

1. Mehta, Nipun. *Paths Are Made By Walking*. USA: Baccalaureate speech at the University of Pennsylvania, 13 May 2012. (http://www.upenn.edu/almanac/volumes/v58/n34/bacc-mehta.html)

3

Benedict and Francis

'I want to have greater material success. I know I should be more competitive to achieve it but that makes me tense. I want to be happy without any tension. I deserve to be happy. I know I am a good person. Perhaps that is why I have so many issues to sort out about my feelings and behaviour. Sometimes, the tension becomes difficult to deal with.' The young man was baring his heart out to his somewhat older lunch companion.

It was a small Italian restaurant near their office and since the two were regular customers, a corner table was available to them whenever they ate there together. A quick phone call to inform the restaurant and the table was theirs. They normally arrived for lunch earlier than most customers and their conversation centred on work, family, where the next holiday was being planned and any interesting current news. Today, all of a sudden, the conversation had turned to personal aspirations and concerns, a much deeper interaction. Benedict, the younger man, was willing to reveal his vulnerable side to Francis.

'Benedict, I have usually found you happy. Why is it that you feel so dissatisfied today? Is there some problem in office?' asked Francis, as he kept his glass of red wine back on the table. He noticed that Benedict had stopped eating and was looking at him with a strange expression on his face. Francis wondered whether he had said something that disturbed Benedict. That could not be the cause of the sudden change in the conversation, could it? He had been enjoying his wine and the delicious risotto for some time now, and Benedict had done most of the talking. It must be something at office which was bothering Benedict.

Benedict was tapping on the table, the middle and index fingers of his right hand targeting the checks on the red and white tablecloth alternately. He did not seem to be aware of this and was looking down intently at his pizza. He normally ate pizza for lunch, choosing one among the three he liked most in the restaurant. His reasoning was that this allowed him to relax by not exercising his mind too much in deciding what to choose for lunch. His condition at that moment, however, could not have been less calm. He was absent-mindedly tapping the red and white squares, totally lost in thought as he gazed at his plate of half-eaten pizza. He looked up slowly and crossed his hands in front of his chest. Francis had read somewhere that this gesture was the body language of someone who felt defensive or even perhaps vulnerable.

'No, nothing happened at office. It is just me. I was thinking that you never lose your cool in any situation, and I keep getting upset almost every week. I have read so many books to calm me down, but it just does not work. I cannot leave my material pursuits and I find my mind remains far from the so-called Zen state. I am young and I have so much to achieve. How can I do so and be happy at the same time?' asked Benedict.

Francis took a sip of his wine and spoke softly to ensure that no one else heard, 'You know, I also have my material objectives, my desires and aspirations, my responsibilities and disappointments. I too have tensions. Everyone does. So don't worry. This will pass. We all have our good and bad days.'

'I am not talking about a few good and bad days. I want to feel peaceful and happy and not lose my cool or get disturbed every other day. Look at yourself. You seem to be contained and do not get easily disturbed as most of us do. How do you manage this? You have progressed in the material world as well, in fact, better than most of us. How do you manage this combination of being good with people and also successful at work?' Pouring more wine for himself and Francis, Benedict posed his question. Perhaps, he was trying to indicate that he was making ordinary conversation. But the expression on his face gave away how keen and anxious he was to get a serious and adequate response.

Francis was hoping to order dessert soon but realised that the gravity of this conversation far outweighed the importance of satiating his desire to have *marron* vermicelli with vanilla ice-cream, the dessert he always looked forward to as a fitting end to any meal.

'Some of my demeanour is perhaps just part of my natural temperament. But it is always possible to work on oneself. There are some very useful books that can help. One way ahead could be to read some of these books and then discuss them with a friend who you feel could help you further. Of course, it should not become an obsession. Rather, it should be like any other activity, such as learning a new language. I have myself benefited from such a process. If you wish, I would be happy to discuss any such matter with you, over lunch or otherwise. Why not begin by giving some time to yourself for a bit of introspection and then take it from there?'

Benedict seemed relieved, 'I would very much like to do that. Francis, thank you for offering to discuss this further with me. This is really generous of you and I feel better already. I will come back to you in a few days.'

Francis sensed an immediate change in Benedict's mood. So he went on to suggest, 'There are some discussion groups too, where people meet to know more about spiritual practices and learn about each other's experiences. Would you like to go to one which is to be held next week?'

Benedict first hesitated and then agreed to accompany Francis.

'Benedict, you will need to be patient at the event. There will be a lecture followed by a question-answer session. The ideas may seem heavy to begin with, but it will be useful to stay connected. It becomes simpler, if we stay connected.'

Benedict nodded, almost absent-mindedly, as they got up to leave the table.

4

Group Discussion

Benedict reached the location of the Discussion Group early because it took him only fifteen minutes to drive there, much less than he had anticipated. It was in France, very close to where he stayed, near the Geneva airport. The venue was a large, old house located opposite a school. Francis had told him to park in the parking lot at the school. He parked and then waited in his car, hesitating to go in alone. In fact, he was feeling very uneasy now and wondering whether he was doing the right thing. In the past, he had refused to attend such gatherings because he considered them a waste of time. He saw himself as an objective and practical person, who had no time for such esoteric pursuits. It was perhaps a moment of great weakness during his lunch with Francis when he agreed to accompany him to the event. He felt a sense of inadequacy, even insecurity, as the time for discussion approached. He again wondered whether he had made an error of judgment. Lost in thought, Benedict did not realise that someone was knocking at his window. He felt more than heard it and looked to his left where Francis was smiling and tapping on the glass. He stepped out of the car and greeted Francis.

'I am really sorry, Benedict. I did not realise you would be reaching so early. Apologies for making you wait. Come, let us go in and meet whoever has arrived. You will like these people. It is a good group, open-minded, positive and keen to get greater insights into their special areas of interest. Today, we have a speaker who will dwell on certain interesting spiritual insights from the East, which were emphasised at that time in various parts of the world. These ideas date back to a time much before Christ was born, about 500 years earlier.'

They entered the big house with a large garden and a variety of flowers and trees. The flowers and trees needed some attention, but the lawn was very neat and had a sweet smell of freshly cut grass. There was a circle of cane chairs in one corner of the garden and a couple of small round cane tables with glass tops stood within easy reach. Plastic glasses and plates were kept on two large tables placed about ten feet apart, together with bottles of wine, fruit juices, potato chips and peanuts. Francis and Benedict took a glass of red wine each and joined those who were already sitting. Introductions were made by Francis, and Benedict was welcomed by all. The conversation was about the forthcoming elections in Switzerland. The group comprised international civil servants and locals, new arrivals and long-time inhabitants of Geneva and its environs. They were biding their time before the arrival of the speaker for the day, who was running a bit late. Being a non-resident, the speaker had lost his way and was receiving instructions on the phone from the host. He was due to arrive soon.

Ian, a South African, who had left his country two decades ago, raised his glass to greet Benedict and said, 'Welcome. I take it this is the first time you have joined this group. We have a very interesting speaker coming today. His name is David. He is a philosopher from England and a really fascinating person who has travelled extensively to various parts of the world. The tradition at these talks is that the main discussant refers to two books that relate to the topic of his lecture, so that people can do some follow-up reading. Let us see which ones David recommends. There he is, coming this way with the host of today's discussion.'

Benedict looked up and saw two men, tall and slim-built, walk briskly towards the circle of cane chairs. They looked like brothers, both of medium-height, with straight brown hair, parted in the middle. It was uncanny. One could be easily mistaken for the other, if you did not pay attention to the cheekbones or the colour of eyes. It was interesting to learn that these two had never met before.

The host now addressed the group, 'Good evening everybody. For those of you who do not know me, I am your host, Julian. I welcome you to the session today. With me is David, our speaker for this session. David and I are meeting for the first time today, but I have heard a lot about him from my sister and am very keen to hear him. So without any delay, David, the floor is yours.'

David looked around and started speaking softly, 'Good evening everybody. My apologies for being so late. I hope this delay gave you a chance to know each other better.' As people smiled, he continued softly, 'I was told about this group by Julian's sister in Paris. She suggested that I share some of my experiences with you. I am stretching it when I use the term "experiences", because what I will share with you today will be a combination of experiences, perceptions, ruminations and perhaps, also biases. I have tried to be objective in what I am going to share with you. Yet, my own perceptions and my admiration of the genius of some prominent social reformers, who existed much before Christ, may have affected my views. I have been awestruck by these personalities, who had the courage to question highly established ways of thinking and come up with new, and to some extent, relatively simple answers to complex questions. I hope what I share with you today will interest you. It's about a part of the world that I visited to recapture what I had read while studying for my higher degree in England. Please feel free to ask me questions at any time during my talk.'

Benedict eyed David sceptically. Was David being humble when he admitted to bias, or was he just covering his tracks, in case he came up with some incredulous claims? Benedict wondered if he could slip out on some pretext.

He was slightly taken aback as David's voice suddenly began to rise, driven by a new energy, 'My story begins with two interesting books and how I got inspired after reading them. I know I am supposed to recommend two books in the course of my lecture, so though I will mention these two books here, I will only recommend one of them.'

Ian raised his hand and asked, 'Then why mention the one which you will not be recommending?'

'Oh, already there are queries. I like this. To answer your question, referring to a book without recommending it is again part of my story, but I feel that you may gain more specific insights on my topic today through the other references.

'The story begins with my reading of Bertrand Russell's book, *Mysticism and Logic*[1]. In fact, it begins with his essay on this topic within the book, bearing the same title. This is a difficult topic that requires some re-reading to absorb and feel comfortable with the points made by Russell. When I read the book, one viewpoint of Bertrand Russell's came across very clearly and generated immense curiosity in me. It was a statement, which I would like to quote.'

Saying this, David took out a few pages from his pocket and continued, 'Bertrand Russell, the great philosopher and a highly-trained and rigorous mind says in this essay that, and I quote:'

> While fully developed mysticism seems to me to be mistaken, I yet believe that, by sufficient restraint, there is an element of wisdom to be learned from the mystical way of feeling, which does not seem to be attainable in any other manner. If this is the truth, mysticism is to be commended as an attitude towards life, not a creed about the world. The metaphysical creed, I shall maintain, is a mistaken outcome of

> emotion, although this emotion, as colouring and informing all other thoughts and feelings, is the inspirer of whatever is best in man.[2]

David went on, 'When I first read this passage as a young man in the 1960s, flushed with the idealism of youth, it had a profound impact on me. I thought how wonderful it would be to know more about mysticism and use it to bring forth in me what is best in man. Fortunately, a friend presented me with a book, which is my first recommendation in this talk. It was a book by Christopher Isherwood, titled *Ramakrishna and His Disciples*.[3] It is the story of a great Indian mystic and Isherwood has written it with a high level of devotion, knowledge and clarity. I fancied myself to be a bit of a philosopher at that time, who had an objective and trained mind. So I was drawn to what Isherwood said in the book. He asked the reader to approach Ramakrishna with the same curiosity one might feel for any highly unusual human being. Someone like Julius Caesar, Catherine of Siena or even Leonardo da Vinci.

'Being an Englishman, I was struck by what Isherwood had to say in the first few chapters of the book. Again, I will have to quote the crux of the message'. Saying this, David picked up the paper again and read aloud:

> The British in India at that period must have seemed strange, paradoxical beings to any detached observer. They were imperialists with bad consciences. They were...public benefactors who were nonetheless ceaselessly engaged in piecemeal conquest of a nation. [...] Many were altruistic, many were heroic, many were deeply devout and felt they had accepted voluntary exile in this savage and unhealthy land in order to do God's work among the benighted. What almost none of them seem to have been aware of was that they were in the most religious country in the world; and in the presence of a spiritual culture which made their own sectarianism seem provincial indeed.[4]

'I was hooked. After reading this, I just had to travel to India. I checked with friends which part of the country I should visit first.

Some friends suggested that I take a couple of months and travel across the entire length—from the north to the south of India. I wanted to narrow the search a bit and spend more of my time reading about Hindu philosophy, the country's ancient history and its present-day society in India. The mind just boggled at the wealth and complexity of this society. So I decided to take it in small steps.'

David waited then to see if there were any questions. Benedict felt very self-conscious and avoided looking at him. No one raised a hand, so David continued, 'My reading showed some fascinating aspects about great spiritual leaders who preached 350 to 500 years before Christ. In fact, I found two leaders who did not emphasise God in their teachings. They focused more on individual behaviour. These great teachers were erstwhile princes, who had given up all luxury to become monks. They had large followings and both established or extended organised religions, different from Hinduism, which was prevalent in India even then. The period in which they lived overlapped, and interestingly, they roamed around in the same geographical area, largely in the eastern part of India, the so-called Gangetic plain. The two leaders were Gautama Buddha who established Buddhism, and Mahavira, who was the last in line of the great teachers of Jainism—a religion based on a long-established philosophical stream for which Mahavira provided a much firmer footing. They are both considered divine by their followers.

'I decided to begin my trip by visiting a place which both had been to—Nalanda in Bihar. The place had another attraction for me. Nalanda had been one of the most famous early universities in India. From fifth century to twelfth century AD, it embodied a pinnacle of learning. Even before that, Nalanda had long been a focus of attention for great rulers, who added large buildings to draw monks and philosophers to this intellectual crucible. The monks were not only engaged in regular religious or mystical practices but also actively participated in the intellectual search for answers to the larger mysteries of life.

Nalanda was actually a seat of competing philosophies and education even before the University was established. It was also close to Varanasi, a city that both Buddha and Mahavira visited. Varanasi, one of the holiest cities of the Hindus, has long been considered a place of very high spiritual practice and energy. My itinerary, thus, revealed itself. First Nalanda and then Varanasi.'

David paused to pour some water into a tall glass kept for him and heard a query raised by a lady on his left, 'Hi. I'm Christina, a lawyer by profession. Can you please tell me why you are recommending the book by Isherwood?'

David put down his glass and smiled, 'Happy to meet you Christina. Like a good lawyer, you ask the right questions. In my view, the book contains a great depth of knowledge on several aspects of mystic India, which can come only through experience, or having received this knowledge from others who have experienced it. While being contemporary, it reflects a very old tradition—a long continuing lifestyle and viewpoints of those preceding even the two great spiritual masters whom I mentioned. It also illustrates many of the elevated thoughts and insights that would have stemmed from the experiences of these masters. It shows a side of mystic India that is relatively recent, yet connected with an everlasting way of spiritual life, which formed the basis of the quotation I read from Isherwood.'

'Thank you. I just wanted to know more about the book,' explained Christina.

David nodded, 'I know. It's very good to address any doubts that arise at the right time. Since I am talking about this book and regular Indian society, I want to make a quick diversion to touch upon something which both mystic India and normal everyday life teach you.'

David started smiling as if recalling some amusing incident, 'Since I just mentioned the importance of timely action, I should also think about how to introduce the quality of patience. It is amusing that the part of India where I started my travels has the same word for "yesterday" and "tomorrow". People distinguish the past or future tense based on the context of the statement. This view of time perhaps helps to inculcate patience, but has its good as well as bad points.'

'What are the good and bad points? I do not want to take you away from your lecture, but could you please give some indication?' asked an old man who was sitting next to Christina. 'Oh, I am John, a retiree staying in this village,' he added.

David addressed the old man, 'To sum up, my view is that we must have a combination of PPT—Patience, Persistence and Timeliness. All three need discipline, which involves avoiding laziness. Without strong discipline it is not possible to implement PPT in our life.'

'Can you give us an example of someone who showed such qualities?' asked John.

'Yes, of course. I will tell you about someone linked to Nalanda University. His name was Naropa, a great intellectual and saint of the tenth and eleventh century. Naropa became the Dean of Nalanda University at a young age, while concurrently being a senior faculty member at another eminent university at Vikramsheela—perhaps the only person to have achieved such a great honour. Seeking benediction and spiritual lessons from his master, Naropa had to undergo severe tests and many disturbing experiences. He persevered for over twelve years. That required immense discipline, patience and persistence, along with timely and appropriate response to the situations he faced. Each experience was to teach him to free his mind from preconceived notions and habitual thinking.'

'Can you suggest a book to read on this?' asked John.

'Yes, absolutely. You should see for instance a book by Herbert Guenther on the life and teaching of Naropa.[5]'

Benedict raised his hand and spoke with some hurry, 'Are you emphasising it is important not to be lazy?'

David answered, 'Avoiding laziness is an important part of discipline and persistence. I will continue with the example from Naropa's life. At Nalanda University, Naropa was highly respected for his high spiritual training and knowledge. However, he gave it all up when he felt that it was merely theoretical and not meaningful or substantive enough. One of the greatest logicians and intellectuals of his time, he became one of the greatest mystic achievers, a veritable saint of the highest order. His teachings to his Tibetan disciple and spiritual successor, Marpa, were the basis that made Marpa the key person to spread many major aspects of Buddhist practices to Tibet, including Vajrayana and Mahamudra.'

'You mean Marpa, the spiritual master who taught one of the greatest Tibetan Buddhist masters, Milarepa?' asked Julian. 'This Naropa, the Great Master, is he the same one who gave the six yogas of Naropa to help attain enlightenment in an accelerated manner? I have heard about them.'

'Yes. This is the same great mystic. However, as I just mentioned, he faced several problems when he was searching for the great spiritual Master Tilopa to request him to become his teacher. I think that a quotation can better illustrate my point. I read this in a short book online.' Saying this, David fished out another paper from his other pocket and started reading:

> Enduring many hardships he—Naropa, travelled east, but he did not find Tilopa. He was about to give up because it was too difficult and he did not have any strength left. Then he heard a voice that told him that laziness is the work of demons. Only if he gave up laziness, would he meet Tilopa and get enlightened.
>
> From this point on, every event and everything told in connection with Naropa's life story are actually teachings on the path to enlightenment. They describe exactly what Tilopa taught Naropa and what is necessary for someone to reach enlightenment. The first thing one has to give up is laziness, because otherwise one has no chance of reaching enlightenment; there is no enlightenment combined with laziness.[6]

'So one has to remain disciplined and exercise patience, persistence and timeliness. This discipline requires us not only to avoid laziness, but also to stay focused and alert by taking action in a timely manner,' said David. 'Now, without being lazy on my part, I will move towards the rest of my lecture.

'Coming back to its main thrust, I want to recall the aim of my lecture today. You will remember that during my visit to India, I wanted to study mysticism so that I could bring out the best in myself. During this quest, I read about Nalanda, Varanasi and Sarnath—places where Buddha had preached. I travelled to these places and further, met several people to discuss key mystical aspects. I saw what Isherwood had meant when he said India was very old and had a deep spiritual tradition. For instance, I saw that in India people were so keen to perpetually keep the divine presence in their lives, that they often gave their children names linked to the Divine. In this way, every time they called out to their child, they took the name of God. For me, of course, it was very different.'

Benedict, who had been mainly studying the expressions of others, suddenly became interested and asked, 'What do you mean by different?'

'I had to make special and persistent efforts to even catch a glimpse of this new way of thinking, had to go beyond reading to actually make it a comfortable part of my understanding. It was a combination of reading and discussing with a number of persons, together with quiet thinking on my own that opened some new ways of looking at events and experiences in life. I saw that this gave me a mystical way of looking at practical aspects, but I also realised that no extent of knowledge or understanding can take us forward in a meaningful way without specific action on our part to live the concept.'

Seeing that Francis was trying to catch his attention, David raised a quizzical eyebrow in his direction. Francis spoke quickly, as if he felt guilty for taking up the time of the lecturer, 'I feel that knowledge and understanding are very important for our progress.'

'Yes, they are, but with a caveat,' David explained. 'Knowledge and understanding only have the seeds to provide a basis for greater insights; they tell which steps to take for improving ourselves, preparing us to be more content. The fact that we may have a potent framework of understanding does not automatically lead to progress or improvement if appropriate actions are not taken. The relevant steps on the path, the actions required, have to be your own.

'With respect to action, it is impossible to miss an interesting dichotomy in India. The prevailing majority view is that the Divine is all-pervasive, and that events take place due to the will of the Divine. However, much importance is also given to individual actions and efforts. Their whole theory of Karma is based on individual action. Progress in both the material and the spiritual world is based on this.

'Another interesting point is that the scope of what is considered to be "action" can be very extensive, much beyond the types of activities which we consider as "action" in our Western understanding of the term. For instance, in India, devotion to the Divine is in itself considered a form of individual action, as is an act of philanthropy, usury or even goodwill. The majority view in India can be summarised as follows: Situations in our life are created by the Divine for us to face, but we ourselves decide which of the possible actions we choose to respond to our situation. Depending on our choice, we will face the associated results of that action. Combined with this, there is also a sentiment one hears very often in India: Only our own effort is for us to make. The result of our effort is not within our control, and we should not worry about it.

'It is their ability to change the identity of an entire society utterly steeped in religion, that makes the genius of Buddha and Mahavira most impressive. Their brilliance is spellbinding when we consider how revolutionary their effort was, preaching as they did about four- to five-hundred years before Christ. They fundamentally changed the basic premise of a good life—from prayer to action.

'Let us take forward these apparently conflicting concepts, namely the omnipresence and all-importance of the Divine and the importance of our own actions. These two thoughts are present in every search for peace and progress in life. In many cases, we seek to address our worries by seeking the blessings of the Divine through prayers. In Indian society, there is a lot of emphasis on prayers and visiting holy places or temples. Even at the time of Buddha and Mahavira, such activities were given an emphasis. Normally, people would consider their efforts at prayer and visiting places of worship as adequate to progress spiritually or to address their worries in life. However, while they had one part of their life fully focused on prayers and spiritual practices, their actions remained as egotistical or avaricious as ever. There was, thus, a dichotomy in their efforts to seek Divine blessings to be content and their own everyday actions. If we simplify what these two great teachers did in this context, we find that they focused on only one of these two aspects. Both emphasised only the importance of our actions for progress in dealing with the tensions and worries in life.

'In this framework, you do not need to focus on the pervasive presence or any other facet of the Divine. You only need to consider your own actions and make sure that these are good in the conventional sense that we all define as "good" in our world.'

Benedict raised his hand and asked, 'What do you mean by "good"?'

David noticed how tense Benedict looked. So he lowered his voice a bit and said encouragingly, 'This is a very good question, which I will be addressing soon. At present, I would seek your indulgence to continue with the flow of the present argument.'

Saying this, David continued, 'Both Mahavira and Buddha extended the scope of our efforts or "action" by giving importance to all types of actions such as thinking, perception, concentration or focus, speech, intent and views. If all these actions are good, there is non-attachment, and thus, no emphasis on feeding one's own ego or acquisitiveness. That would bring forth all that is good in man, a la Bertrand Russell.'

'In his eight-fold path, did Buddha not distinguish between action and views or thoughts?' asked Julian.

'Yes, that is so,' agreed David. 'Action is the physical expression of thought. This is the way we all look at action. But consider for a moment, the common thread that runs through the many aspects emphasised in the eight-fold path. You will find that everything is a result of us releasing our energy to perform the task—be it thinking, or be it physically expressing our thoughts through our acts. At the basic level of energy, at the deeper spiritual levels, these thoughts are all actions, interlinked and contributing to each other. As Buddha said, "What we think, we become". I think that the eight-fold path could be seen as an effort to separate these different expressions of energy in conventional terms, to keep things easy to understand.

'Let me now explain my understanding of the key change brought about by these two masters, both of them providing ways to address tensions and problems, which you will agree are always a part of life. Their way was to address all issues through the extended scope of "right action". This is, of course, very subjective and also an immense objective.'

'In my view, however, their aim was actually much larger. Take Buddha, for example. I feel that through his framework, Buddha was fundamentally changing the way of thinking for society itself. I think he was confident that following "good" or "right" behaviour would make people more evolved and perhaps, subsequently even take life to a more complex and elevated Divine path. It is worth noting that the advanced disciples of the Buddha were actually trained in ritualistic practices involving interaction with various forms of the Divine.

'I think that Buddha was a very practical person, in addition to being a truly great mystic. He devised a practical path for the common man without any focus on an all-powerful God. Though paradoxical, it actually helped people walk the path to the Divine. He wanted people to get out of their earlier mindset, which said that by focusing on God or prayer, the relevant action for spiritual upliftment had already been taken. Otherwise, we end up under-emphasising our own actions and our interaction with others. I want to share with you my own understanding of this apparent paradox, i.e. follow a path without the Divine to actually reach the Divine. In this approach, if we succeed in embodying the wide scope of "good" actions in daily life, then even without focusing on God, we can ultimately know or reach God. This is a two-way causality, which in my opinion, Buddha saw clearly.' Raising a piece of paper David said, 'Let me explain this with a picture.' The paper had a diagram with two circles and arrows connecting them.

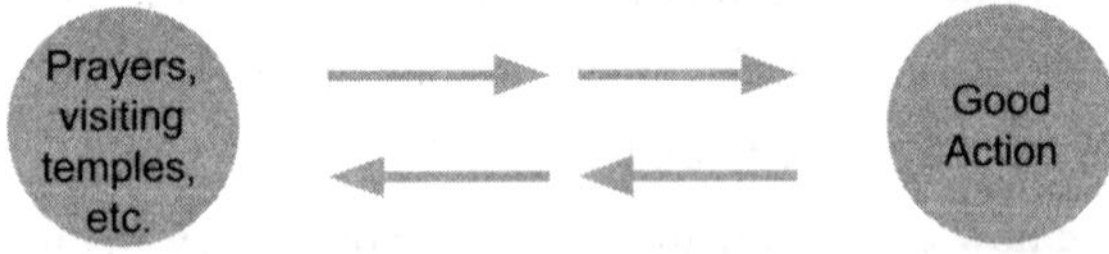

'Look at these two circles. The first one represents prayers and other usual spiritual activities; and the second one represents the good actions or behaviour which I have been talking about. The arrows from the first circle to the second one depict the normal perception that if we focus on prayers, spiritual practices and other similar practices, then progress on the spiritual path would help us to know the Divine better. It will hopefully also change our behaviour, making us less selfish, more compassionate and calmer, less egotistical and much happier. However, this causality does not normally happen because once we finish our prayers or spiritual practices, our other actions remain self-oriented and acquisitive. So the answer lies in directly affecting the second circle, namely our own behaviour. The basic issue is: Do we build the base for greater contentment and happiness, and does this lead to higher spiritual achievement, once we manage to adopt good behaviour?

'The perspective of two-way causality is that with progress in "good actions", we also progress towards spirituality and knowing the Divine. This is indicated by the arrows going from the second circle towards the first one. In my opinion, this alternative view of spiritual achievement is based on embodying good behaviour as our normal behaviour. Once good behaviour becomes our normal behaviour, we start embodying spiritual attributes and so travel on the spiritual path. This helps us to progress towards the Divine, the essential source of peace and happiness.

'Like Buddha, Mahavira also emphasised right or good actions, only the scope of the relevant actions in his case was very wide. To simplify, right actions would cover faith, thought, knowledge and personal conduct, similar to the extended scope of action we saw in the case of Gautama Buddha. To keep right conduct, Mahavira specified certain forms of behaviour, which included non-violence, truthfulness, chastity, non-stealing and non-possession or non-attachment. The practice of non-acquisitiveness or non-attachment had to be a very concrete and deliberate part of daily life rather than just a mindset. Mahavira's path too, therefore, kept God out of spiritual practice. Progress for a person was seen only in terms of one's own actions.'

Benedict noticed a somewhat stout man seated to his left, who seemed to be getting a little uneasy the last few minutes. He then suddenly raised his hand and said, 'Hi, I am Laurence from Geneva. David, do you mean to say that these two persons established major religions during their time, but did not focus on God, the key necessity for religious or spiritual endeavour? You mean God was missing in their frame of reference?' Saying this, he sat down as quickly as he had got up to ask his question, while continuing to stare at David for an adequate response.

Then Julian asked a question, which was on the minds of some other guests too, especially those who went to meditation classes with him, 'You know that spiritual groups keep emphasising meditation, chanting and prayers. How can you then say that the teachings focus only on the second circle in your picture and not on prayers or meditation?'

Picking up his glass of water for a sip, David nodded at Laurence and Julian, 'Thank you for these questions. Both relate to the fundamental issue we need to address, namely that a religious or spiritual movement normally involves an all-powerful Divine or activities perceived as being linked to a spiritual frame of mind. Though this is not universally so, but from the practices we have seen, for example, at Buddhist camps and meetings, we know that spiritual methods are an integral part of the Buddhist processes too. Then why am I saying something which appears to be so obviously incorrect? I have reached my conclusions based on my understanding of these two masters, after seeing them in the context of various other spiritual movements in India. In my understanding, the manner in which the spiritual masters provide guidance can be summarised by modifying a very famous slogan by Karl Marx. In 1875, Karl Marx said: From each according to his ability, to each according to his need. I feel the principle used by spiritual masters is "to each according to his ability, to each according to his need."

'Before I take this further, a small digression is necessary. We need to be clear about two concepts: Spirituality and religion. Spirituality is a philosophy or the search for truth, while religion is an organised practice of that philosophy. As I learned more about Indian spiritual thought, I saw that Hinduism had not been the only spiritual tradition in India. Hinduism derives its spiritual basis from the Vedas. I was also introduced to Shramana Philosophy—an Indian spiritual tradition, which according to some predates the Vedas; of course, there is another view that this philosophy is also encompassed in the Vedas. According to Shramana philosophy, primacy was given to personal actions as they form the basis for spiritual progress, which in turn would free the soul from the cycle of rebirth. Reincarnation and the cycle of rebirth were an essential part of Shramana thinking, but an omniscient and all-powerful God was not. Thus, the objectives of these efforts were wholly spiritual, even if the emphasis on God was missing.

'Gautama Buddha and before him, Mahavira were the highest examples of Shramana philosophy. An interesting point, however, is that God was not completely missing from their frame of reference. It is noteworthy that in Jainism, a person can become a God through his own actions, gaining salvation and freedom from rebirth. In Buddhism, there is a concept of the primordial Buddha, an entity who is not the creator but the originator of all things. There are also Gods, who are less potent than an almighty would be. So the concept of Godhood existed even in these philosophies, but different from the all-powerful God.'

Julian again raised his hand and interrupted David's flow of thoughts, 'David, you have still not answered our query. Could you please clarify the importance of meditation and similar practices?'

'I am just coming to that, but with some prior explanation that will give us the relevant perspective. While there may be different views, I feel that both these teachers believed focusing on God may divert us from the important task of spiritual evolution. Since they felt that each individual has to make spiritual progress based on one's own actions, they went straight to the point, focusing on individual actions and examining the nature of actions that would lead to spiritual evolution. Mahavira said, "Instead of finding out an imaginary God, try to become a God, the highest stage of mankind." In addition to good conduct, he stressed on the need for careful analysis. In fact, he emphasised on plurality or multiple possible perceptions of truth. His view was that each person is able to observe some aspects of the truth, and one needs to consider different views, positions and possibilities to get the whole truth.'

'Plurality of truth!' exclaimed Benedict. 'How does that help us?'

'One way would be that in our personal interactions, we consider the possibility that we may not be the only one with the correct viewpoint. What the other person is saying may also be true or valid. This helps us approach issues with an open mind and limits conflicts. That too would be part of good action,' explained David.

'Another feature of this expanded scope of truth becomes important when we consider which steps we need to take to make progress. My simple point in emphasising the primacy of good action can be seen in terms of an important premise. A teacher's knowledge of the Truth is usually larger than what any teacher decides to tell the disciple, and the spiritual teacher may decide to reveal only a limited part of the larger Truth to keep things simple and manageable. The teacher's decision would be based on the intent to provide the practitioners with the most efficient and bare minimum way to reach their spiritual goals: To each according to his ability and need. This guidance is like a journey through a corridor, leading up to a large room. Upon reaching the room, we may see that the available space is much larger than we may have imagined. Travelling through this corridor may be the easiest way to reach the room—a larger reality. Any other path to this larger reality may be complex and thus, these tougher methods may be reserved only for the advanced disciples. Also, for most of us, if the goals are sequential, such as travelling through the corridor to reach the room, we may be able to understand and appreciate the higher levels of reality more easily once we achieve the specific initial goals. The point I am making illustrates this general principle. Hence, once the goal of internalising the larger scope of good actions is achieved, it prepares us for our spiritual evolution. It provides us with the ability to reach the larger Truth and become aware of the actions that would take us towards it.

'I have already mentioned some aspects of Mahavira's teachings encompassing actions, attitude, logical thought and lifestyle. Similarly, in Buddhism, there is emphasis on morality or good conduct, mental tranquillity and knowledge or spiritual insight. Like in Mahavira's framework, here too, logic and careful analysis play a very important role for achieving spiritual progress. But these efforts, based on analytical or logical thought, have to be combined with appropriate individual effort or action to make progress.'

Benedict, who had been looking uncomfortable for some time, now interrupted the flow of the lecture, 'David, all this detail seems very difficult to incorporate in life. You need to be a monk to follow these ideas.'

'That is not the case,' replied David. 'A lot of people leading normal material life embody such principles, albeit to different degrees. We are all travellers on this road. The point I want to focus on is that both these teachers recognised that our normal life was full of tension, though what we all seek is happiness and zero tension. According to them, such objectives require a practical framework of action, and that is what they tried to provide by combining appropriate personal actions, based on a logical thought process. For most people, involved as they are with their daily material concerns, an important way to achieve progress is through good action. If we do not practice good action, then any other practice, however elevated, does not prove very useful.'

'You have still not addressed the point about meditation that has given several of us a great way of being more peaceful,' asked Julian. Several other heads also nodded then to concur.

'Meditation is important to address any issues which arise in our mind; it is at a much deeper level than our actions. Meditation helps us experience inner peace. However, the key point is that without good action, it would be impossible to get results, even if you meditate or follow any other practice. So, the most important part of the sequence, for all those involved in daily chores, is to focus on good action. This is the fundamental level at which spiritual effort has to take place. Everything else is supplementary, existing only as a means, to enable us to do good action.'

'David, you also claim that good action leads to spiritual progress. How does that happen?' continued Julian.

'Focusing on good action is not just to initiate or ensure success of this process aimed at inner calm and happiness. It also develops attributes like compassion and goodwill towards others, which are essential for a spiritually evolved person. Therefore, with good action we become more and more like a spiritually evolved person. This process of conversion is precisely the process of spiritual evolution.

'The essence of goodness is to project our energies and concern towards others through compassion. Over time, this positive attribute, which is the basis of good action, helps us do away with our mental delusion, overriding ego and selfishness that lead to such delusions. Once we develop compassion through good action, our daily routine itself becomes like meditation. This process takes us a long way along the spiritual path, where we get deeply connected to the Divine, with devotion reflected in our daily behaviour. Interestingly, this is also one of the key messages in the major Hindu spiritual book—the Gita, in its explanation of karma yoga and the progress we make towards a mindset of bhakti or devotion. It is interesting that two very different spiritual perspectives, one from the Gita and another from Shramana philosophy, give us the same result, namely an emphasis on our actions, and within that on good actions.'

'What do you mean by that?' asked Benedict.

'The Gita emphasises an omnipresent, all-encompassing and most supreme God and that we should make an offering of all our actions to God, all actions being, thus, selfless. In contrast, Shramana philosophy does not have any such all-powerful God. The spiritual thrust of these two sources cannot be more different. Yet, both of them give us the same conclusion, namely that we should focus on actions. So, in terms of practical lessons for us, they are equivalent.

'Another interesting difference could be that a thought process with all-encompassing Divine is based on deep faith, while one without reliance on the Divine is based only on application of objective evaluation and logic combined with the basic thrust of spiritual thought: Good action.

'Let us now consider the importance of meditation. When positive or compassionate action is not possible, we need to enable ourselves by other means such as meditation, prayer and introspection. However, it makes immense sense to focus on good action even without any additional supporting efforts,' explained David.

'An interesting feature of good action is that it covers activities much beyond what we conventionally link with action here in the West. The value of this method is that without following any specific religion or spiritual practice, we can progress towards greater contentment in our life. We can address tension better, which is a normal part of our life.'

Benedict's attention was now fully on the speaker. He asked, 'Do you mean that we should be willing to face tension and that we will generate tension if our actions are not good?'

David nodded and began explaining, 'If our actions are not good, they will create dissatisfaction and discontentment among those affected. Due to this, and also, our own realisation that we have acted negatively, we will feel uneasy. With time, this discomfort will make us lose our calm. Without being calm, we cannot be content. Two Cs are very important for maintaining a happy state of mind. We need to be calm in order to prepare the conditions for being content. When calm, we are in a frame of mind that helps us assess a situation in a logical way. This helps us choose the appropriate action and lays the foundation for being content on a sustained basis. Lack of calm agitates the mind, prevents us from selecting the correct action based on a clear and objective analysis, making it virtually impossible to be content.

'Taking a cue from these thoughts, my messages today can be summarised in the following points.' He then distributed a page with several points emphasised as key messages. Benedict squinted his eyes and started reading them.

- The best way to deal with tensions is through our actions and the thoughts leading to those actions. Therefore, we need to focus on appropriate actions and the thoughts underlying the actions.
- We alone are responsible for our actions. In fact, our actions are normally the only part that we control in any situation or event.
- We always have a choice among a set of actions available to us. This choice should be made based on a careful assessment of the various options.
- To conduct such an assessment, we need to apply a logical framework of thought to reach our decisions. Make as clear and objective an assessment as possible, then choose the action to be taken.
- Truth or the correct way of looking at a situation may be wider than what we think. So, we need to keep an open mind.
- Our actions must be good actions. This helps us narrow the appropriate choice among different actions.
- Choose actions which are good because if our actions are not good, their consequences will generate further tension in our life, at present or later.
- If we take good actions, we enable ourselves to better deal with the tensions in our life.
- The content of actions—good or bad—is important because it helps us develop personal attributes reflecting the nature of our actions.
- Good actions develop within us attributes essential to gain inner calm and happiness.
- Being calm is required, if we are to be content and objective in any situation.
- This can be developed through sustained application of effort

with Patience, Persistence and Timeliness (PPT). And of course, meditation.

'I want to now quickly conclude my lecture because we must leave some time for questions and answers. I want to finish this part of the interaction by sharing with you my fascination with the fact that Mahavira and Buddha emerged at about the same time period, with their very profound ideas. I wanted to learn whether this was a period when large-scale changes in spiritual thought were occurring in other parts of the world too. Further reading showed that this was indeed the case. Within about a period of 500 years, which is not a long period in the frame of history, similar and very major changes in spiritual thought were taking place largely in Asia and in parts of present-day Europe. This brings me to my second book for reference. It is Karen Armstrong's *The Great Transformation*[7]. This is an important piece of work to understand the sweep of changes in spiritual efforts occurring across vast portions of humanity, around the time period that I have covered in my lecture. Going through it can show how similar and overlapping such thoughts can be, even though large distances separate their places of origin. Thus, the key insights that I have drawn about the mode of behaviour from all these distant efforts is that they are similar in terms of emphasising good action and thought. These thoughts may be good either because of our devotion to the Divine or our sensitivity towards others. Another point of similarity is the importance we must give to a positive mindset, in order to adopt appropriate positive action and thought.

'Thank you ladies and gentlemen. I think now we should go on to the discussion phase, based on your questions.'

References

1. Russell, Bertrand. *Mysticism and Logic*. UK and USA: Routledge, 1994.
2. Ibid, p 29.
3. Isherwood, Christopher. *Ramakrishna and His Disciples*. USA: Vedanta Press, 1965.
4. Ibid, p 39.

5. Guenther, Herbert V. *The Life and Teaching of Naropa*. UK: Oxford University Press, 1963.
6. http://www.kagyu-asia.com/l_nar_life1.html
7. Armstrong, Karen. *The Great Transformation: The World in the Times of Buddha, Socrates, Confucious and Jeremiah*. UK: Atlantic Books, 2007.

5

More Search for Benedict

As soon as David finished his lecture, Julian rose from his chair and addressed the small gathering, 'Let us give a round of applause for David, who has been most informative, lucid and thought-provoking. How many papers do you carry in your pocket David? You are a wealth of information, I must say.'

Everybody applauded. A few were already straining to ask questions. Julian came in again, 'As the host, I have to take care of all my guests, including David. Let us take a break for twenty minutes and then pose our queries.'

A lazy line instantly formed in front of the two large tables stacked with drinks. Most people took fruit juice. Benedict chose red wine and then looked around for Francis and found him deep in conversation with David. So he walked across to them with three glasses of wine, offering a glass each to David and Francis, while drinking from the third. Both accepted with gratitude as Benedict joined them. Francis introduced him to David, then continued with his conversation, 'And when did the Vajrayana Buddhist tradition start?' Francis asked David.

'One view is that Buddha himself taught people Vajrayana, but he was very careful in providing different levels of teaching, according to the ability of the people to follow that teaching. Interestingly, Vajrayana tradition went to Tibet from India through a great master called Padmasambhava, and later through others, including Marpa. The main spiritual teacher of Marpa was Naropa, as I mentioned earlier in my talk. It is interesting to note that when people think of Buddhism today, they generally think of Tibet, a place which preserved Vajrayana tradition,' answered David.

'So one could say that Buddha was not focusing only on daily action as such, but also on special methods of progressing to very high levels of spiritual achievement. However, he preached these intricate processes only to those who were highly advanced spiritually, so that they had the ability to handle these teachings effectively?' asked Francis.

David nodded, 'Yes, you are correct. For the majority, the best way to progress towards contentment is based on good action. This is an absolutely necessary part of any effective effort. Even if you are highly advanced spiritually, if you do not follow the basic path of good action, you will find it very difficult to move ahead to attain greater spirituality. It would be as if you are in a balloon that is rising above the earth through spiritual upliftment; but whenever your actions are not good, you are in effect binding that balloon by tying it with a rope to a tree rooted to the ground. The more you deviate from good action, the tougher it will be for you to have effective spiritual attainment.'

'So, good actions are essential in our progress towards contentment,' Francis commented.

'Absolutely,' agreed David as he gestured towards the circle of chairs, 'I think Julian is getting restless and wants to begin the question-and-answer session. Let us proceed towards others.' Looking at Benedict, he said softly, 'My friend, I know that you too are keen to ask follow-up questions. I am also eager to discuss the points you have in mind.'

Benedict was taken aback because he was not really paying attention since he did not fully understand the conversation between Francis and David. He wanted the discussion to turn more substantive and be pitched at a simpler level. So he just nodded and walked back towards the chairs with David.

When everyone gathered in a circle again, Julian said, 'Let us keep sitting while we speak. That includes you too, David. So let the questions begin.'

Looking at Benedict then, David nodded and said, 'I think you should start with the follow-up questions that you have for me and we can take it from there.'

Benedict almost blurted out, 'I feel uneasy with your message. I do not want to give up on material things. I want to keep enjoying my material comforts and be happy. Your talk seems to miss out on material aspects of life. It is based too much on asceticism.'

David shook his head in obvious disagreement, 'I want to clarify that my main emphasis was not on ascetic behaviour or on becoming non-material. I know the lifestyle emphasised, for example, by Mahavira, could give you that impression. However, my focus was not on that part of the discussion. Rather, I was trying to draw out a key lesson from the teachings of these two teachers, who emphasised upon the need for good action as the basis for happiness, for reducing our problems and sorrows. This is my main focus, seeking relevance, irrespective of the lifestyle you choose to follow.'

'What do you mean by "good actions"?' asked Benedict.

David started speaking even before Benedict had finished, as if he knew what the full sentence would be, 'The great teachers that I mentioned in my lecture and many others in their spiritual search have tried to specify simple codes of behaviour for actions that help you progress towards contentment. Let us go to the basic premise to clarify this idea.

'Normally, a person is considered to perform good actions, if those actions are good for others. However, the scope of good actions is wider than this. I think that good actions should be so towards all, including your own self. Benedict, I can see you shaking your head. Is it because you think there will be conflict in terms of one action being good towards some and not good towards some others and then how to decide in a situation of conflict?'

Benedict nodded, 'Yes, that is so. In addition, what good action should we take if someone is not being good towards us?'

David continued, 'Thank you, Benedict. There are a number of related steps to adequately consider what is meant by good action. I will discuss them one by one.

'First, let us see the scope of good action. One important reason why I focused on Mahavira and Buddha today was that both these great teachers considered a wide scope of action, including views, thoughts, intent, speech and conduct. Thus, the scope of good action is a collection of different explicit or implicit activities. In our context, we could, thus, use the terms "good activities" and "good actions" interchangeably.

'Another key aspect is to consider which of these activities is the most important part of our effort. Our effort should be to change ourselves rather than to show others that our actions are good ones.'

'What do you mean by this?' asked Benedict.

'Normally, we seek appreciation and approval of others and try to act in a manner which will get us such appreciation. Usually, our main concern is regarding what an external observer will notice about us—mainly our actions and, to some extent, our speech rather than what we may keep hidden, such as our thoughts and objectives. But all these are connected. In some sense, this is similar to the iceberg floating in an ocean, which has only one-seventh part outside the water visible to all, while six-seventh of it, that is a large part of it, is invisible because it is under water. Figuratively, the evident actions and speech are the parts that are visible; but views, thoughts, focus, intent, etc. are not visible in the same way. Yet, they are the base on which actions and speech float in the ocean of our interaction with others.'

Christina raised her hand, 'Is this something like the statement of Sigmund Freud, when he said that, "The mind is like an iceberg, it floats with one-seventh of its bulk above water"?'

David nodded in agreement, 'It is something like that but not the same. My point is that our actions are based on a whole sequence of underlying activities, and if we want to embody good actions in our behaviour, we should seriously address the foundation or the basis of our actions.'

Christina again raised her hand and asked, 'What is the use of all this? This is getting much too complicated for me.'

'I apologise,' said David. 'Perhaps we can make it simpler to understand if we combine them by an easy technique. My suggestion is to use the method of concentric circles—these are a series of circles, one within the other, something like the Russian nesting doll. Like this.' Saying this, David showed them a picture with four concentric circles.

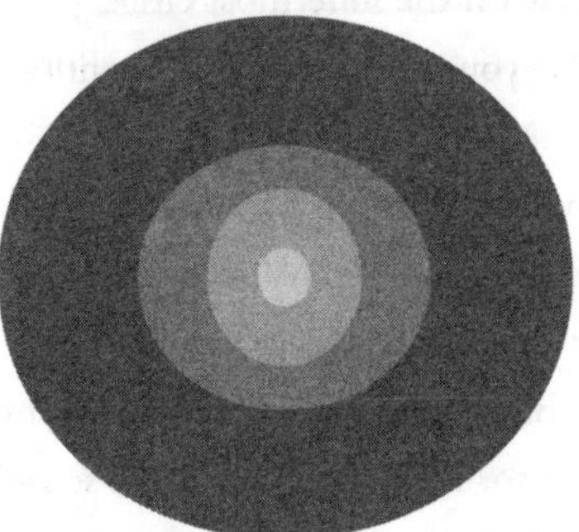

'These circles are all linked; it is a sequence of a larger circle around a smaller one. Within the circles, we could write the different concepts that I mentioned, one in each circle. In the innermost circle, we can write "views", then "perception" in the space within the next circle, followed by "conduct" in the space within the next circle, "speech" in the following circle and the outermost circle would have "actions",' David quickly wrote on the page that had concentric circles and raised it for all to see.

David continued, 'An interesting part of representing these concepts through such concentric circles is that we can very clearly see that the inner core of all that we do is our "views". Our objective should be to start working on the concept in the innermost circle, going outwards to cover all the others. In this way, we can systematically address the issues rather than in an arbitrary and temporary way.'

'Is this not extremely difficult?' asked Julian.

'Yes, true. Any fundamental change in behaviour is not easy, which is also true for this change. Therefore, we should move ahead with small steps across these concentric circles, aiming to become good in terms of the whole coverage of these circles. So start from inside and keep going outwards, taking small steps because it is impossible to manage large efforts that cover multiple components in the initial phase. This effort must continue irrespective of whatever we are doing. It will help to build our capacity to deal with all kinds of situations. You will also see that when you start acting on the innermost circle, you will affect the other circles also, including your actions that are mentioned in the outermost circle.

'There is yet another aspect in the scope of good actions, namely, the persons covered by these actions. Whenever we speak of good actions, we normally think of our actions in terms of how they affect others. We should extend this scope to include their effect on ourselves too.'

'And why is that so? How does this make sense?' asked Christina.

'The reason for focusing on good actions is that we want to have a good result for ourselves. Thus, through our actions we have to ensure that we are actually being good both to ourselves and others, once again using the method of progressing through small steps.'

'Do you mean that we should not expect success quickly and that we must keep progressing slowly and persistently to achieve progress, to whatever small extent we can?' Christina asked.

'You are absolutely right, Christina,' David responded and saw Christina sit up straighter, smiling. 'The concepts I am talking about are difficult and not quick as major progress cannot normally be made in a short while.

'Hence, an important point I want to make today is that it is our responsibility to be good towards ourselves, in the sense that we should lay the foundation for both good judgment and peace of mind for ourselves. Interestingly, the derived responsibility from this is that we should also be good towards others.'

'You mean I should be responsible towards another person because I have to be responsible towards myself?' Benedict was getting a bit agitated. It was obvious that he had some specific persons and incidents in mind. Julian also pitched in, saying, 'Yes, this seems strange. Can you please explain this to us?'

David could see that this was a sensitive issue. He spoke softly, looking at Benedict for some understanding, 'Yes, it seems illogical, but let me explain the basis for my statement. Part of being good to ourselves is that we should keep trying to improve and develop greater abilities to address various concerns. This is irrespective of what our focus may be—whether it is material achievement, spiritual progress, being a better citizen, father, mother, husband, son or daughter. If we have to focus on improving ourselves, then every interaction should be an opportunity for learning to improve ourselves. This implies that we have both an opportunity and a responsibility to improve ourselves when interacting with others.

'To do so, we need to understand the situation and the likely reactions of others to our actions. This will help our response be more logical, based on an analysis of options. Our effort should be to understand or even appreciate the actions of another person without any value judgment, hurt or indignation. It is also possible that if we react with understanding and a positive outlook, without agitation, the other person may similarly respond less negatively. Thus, an enlightened form of self-interest implies that we should try and not respond negatively whenever someone else is treating us in a negative way.'

'So you are saying that we should not react negatively to any bad behaviour towards us. You are asking us to be saints, like those two teachers you talked about. You expect us to become spiritual beings when we want to live in material society,' Benedict said with some indignation.

David was moving his head from side to side. Francis had an amusing thought: It is good that David is not an Indian. If he were an Indian, then he might be agreeing while Benedict might think it was disagreement.

His thoughts were interrupted by David's response, 'Benedict, I am not asking you to be passive about someone's bad behaviour towards you. Let us see my main points. The most important part is that our reaction must not be based on an agitated mind. For this, we should adopt whichever method we have of calming our mind, whatever technique works for us: Be it soft deep breathing, finding the square root of seven, or remembering that whenever we have sent a message or letter in anger, it would have been better keeping it with us overnight to have reviewed it again. Reducing mental agitation is the only way we will manage to look at the situation dispassionately, in a logical framework. It does not work immediately. Progress requires small steps together with the PPT that I talked about—Patience, Persistence and Timeliness. Though we can progress only with small steps, we will see that even with small steps, we would be able to cover a long distance.'

'Why do you say that I should have any responsibility towards someone who is bad to me? I do not feel comfortable with that,' intervened Benedict.

David saw that Benedict was feeling more relaxed than earlier, though he still looked a bit unhappy. David continued,'The responsibility starts with you attempting to be clear-headed. Take a situation of disagreement with your colleague, your spouse, or even with someone on the road. If you are able to look at the situation with a relatively cool mind, you may actually see what is the basis of the other person's action. You may realise that the point being made by the other person, even in a heated manner, may, in fact, be correct. Or the point may actually be different from what you initially thought it to be. In such a situation, a negative reaction would have spoilt matters.'

'Suppose the other person is being mean to me, or is actually wrong while I am doing things right?' asked Benedict.

'In such cases, it would be useful to pitch your argument not on a personal basis, but on the basis of the underlying logic of the situation or action. In that sense, the message from you should be that you would like to address the issue in a professional and thoughtful manner, without mixing it up with personalities. This is one way you could show "responsibility". Once you start adopting this method, you will see that over time, you can become more detached about the actions of others and even your own. That is the time when you will start being a practitioner of the important message that I mentioned to you, embedded in the Indian spiritual tradition—only our own effort is for us to make. The result of our effort is not within our control and we should not worry about it.'

Julian wanted him to elaborate further, 'How do you achieve this mindset, this behaviour pattern?'

David thought a bit before replying, 'I think we have to keep emphasising four points, which I have already mentioned. Firstly, always use a logical or analytical framework to understand any situation in order to assess the type of action to be taken by you. By definition, logical thoughts need to be free of bias, and in that sense, should be based on a clear and detached assessment of the situation. Secondly, always keep in mind your responsibility towards improving yourself and developing calmness of behaviour. Thirdly, following from this, remember that this objective will be met in a sustained manner only through good actions. And finally, build yourself with each experience, learning and taking further small steps across the concentric circles.

'The question Benedict asked was how to take good actions while protecting ourselves against those behaving badly with us. In such situations, good actions would be defined in terms of the "right thing to do". One way could be to reduce, to the maximum possible extent, the "not good" or "bad" effect of our actions. Thus, always keep in mind how "bad" the effects of your actions would be and try to minimise such adverse effects while protecting yourself. Judge your journey, your progress, in terms of these criteria, while ensuring that you are protected.'

David noticed that Ian was trying to catch his attention, so he nodded towards him. 'At the end of your talk, you mentioned that being calm would lead to being content. But I want to be happy, not just content. You have not mentioned happiness. Is there a difference between being happy and content?' Ian asked.

'Yes, there is,' replied David. 'In my opinion, happiness is an effusive or ebullient state of mind, while contentment is a peaceful state of mind. To be happy, you need to have some sense of achievement, even if it is a negative achievement. Thus, though I may be stretching this a bit, one could say that some may find happiness even in troubling others. Contentment, in my opinion, is a more long-term and less fickle emotion. It comes from a sense of balance, from being satisfied with a situation. Those who are content may have an underlying sense of happiness without it necessarily showing through in any effusive or ebullient behaviour. Thus, while there may be some overlap between happiness and contentment, the two are of fundamentally different nature. In my understanding, happiness is a short-term experience interspersed with periods without happiness. But contentment stays with us even when there may be no obvious reason for being happy.'

'Do you mean that it is not good to be happy? I would like to be happy,' reiterated John, the retiree who lived in the same village as Julian.

'No. That is not what I mean. I am focusing more on the reason for being happy or content. As long as the reason is in conformity with the objective of good actions, being happy and being content are both fine. I distinguish between them because I feel that a person could be happy even as a result of actions which are based on not-good feelings, such as jealousy, envy, lust, acquisitiveness, anger, arrogance and so on. Actions flowing from such thoughts may give you happiness, but they do not take you further on the path of contentment or peace of mind. In contrast, if the actions are based on good conduct, thought and actions, they will pave the way for contentment,' said David.

He saw that Benedict was whispering to Francis and from his body language it was clear that he was not comfortable with some viewpoint. David asked Benedict what was bothering him. Benedict got up quickly, feeling a bit sheepish that his concern had been noticed. 'In your talk, why did you mix up your discussion with spirituality and soul, rebirth etc? I feel very uncomfortable with that.'

David responded after some thought, 'You will recall that the first quotation I mentioned today was from Bertrand Russell. Bertrand Russell was a logical mind par excellence. As we know, together with a major mathematician, AN Whitehead, he co-authored the book, *Principia Mathematica*[1], a work that focused on grounding mathematics on logic. As I mentioned in my talk, even he acknowledged that an important contribution of mysticism or metaphysics was to improve us. I will quote the essential part again: "This emotion, as colouring and informing all other thoughts and feelings, is the inspirer of whatever is best in man."

'So we can see that spirituality contains within it a basis of "whatever is best in man". I would like to consider spirituality from this perspective, instead of rebirth, etc. There is a need for greater balance in our life. The fact that spirituality is important for us can be seen from the fact that everywhere there are many who seek solace through it. Likewise, look at societies, which tried to do away with or suppress spiritual practice. When these societies have opened up, there is still a presence and growth of spirituality. When we acknowledge the need for spirituality, it does not mean that materialistic achievements are not important for us. As in the case of spirituality, we see that people aspire deeply for material progress even in countries such as India, where spirituality is very strongly rooted in its culture. Therefore, my understanding is that both are important for our progress. What we need is a balance between materialistic and spiritual search, if we have to live in this world without becoming a monk.'

Julian attracted David's attention by raising his voice a little, 'I want to take you back to your main message, about good action being the basis of contentment. Often in life, people find that they can be better off by deviating from the path of good action. A sense of self is also important to people, and this may lead to them not behaving with compassion or understanding. Their "not good" behaviour is for being happy, and they often find themselves happy this way. What is your view on this?'

'The fundamental point is to sustain a positive state of mind. Actually, most of us are likely to be uncomfortable committing an action which harms others. Happiness or peace of mind arising from such actions is difficult to sustain because life is not a one-period game. The effects of your action come back to affect you. This is the basic idea that is captured in the views that get expressed in different ways such as, "you reap as you sow", "what goes around comes around", and so on. For these reasons, actions which are not good would normally cause tension and loss of peace of mind.'

'If people wish to live with tension, then of course it is their choice. But most of us want greater peace of mind. For this objective, we need a code of behaviour that helps us develop greater balance, self-assurance and peace of mind, which can be sustained over time. Like a self-correcting balanced doll, which many of you may have seen, the one whose heavy base helps the doll to always regain its balance after any disturbance. That kind of stability in our life will come only if we address the two points I just mentioned—the discomfort we feel after not doing good to someone and the fact that your actions will result in reactions from others. This requires a stable system of values and actions. An important part of such a system would be to avoid actions which are not good.

'These points are not based on any spiritual pursuit of a larger or different reality. However, it is interesting to note that this behaviour provides us with a basis to better achieve spiritual progress. It is a double benefit. It can have an even larger impact if you combine meditation with it.'

Julian entered the discussion, 'Do you have any specific indicators, which could be used to assess whether meditation is working? I think it will help us all who wish to meditate.'

'Thank you, Julian. I know from our earlier conversation today that you are practising meditation, so you might have already experienced what I am going to say now. I feel that we could use a number of useful indicators to assess our progress towards greater calmness and peace of mind. The first indicator is that after a few weeks, or within a month, you may notice that your breathing will become much softer, slower. The second indicator would be that the thoughts that take you away from meditation will lessen over time. This would take about six months or a bit more. If you will be regular with your meditation, then within the period of six months to a year, you will start feeling a sense of greater completeness after meditation. You will start feeling more stable throughout your day. This would be the third indication. In the next stage, the fourth indicator is that you will find it easier to focus or concentrate on whatever you want to do. The fifth indicator shows up after considerable time. Sometimes, if you have progressed well, then after a few years, you will have greater calm and peace of mind as part of your normal behaviour. It will help you to look at events from a distance, with less personal involvement and more objectivity. Another indicator would be a change in your attitude towards others, whereby, you will get more compassionate and caring about others.'

Julian raised his hand again. David smiled at him and asked him to speak, 'All this theoretical information is good, but it does not take us into a world with more solid evidence. Do we have any book or technical paper with scientific evidence of these ideas?'

'Yes, there are a number of such writings, but I think you would like to see a recent book by some scientist, based on specific investigations. It would be interesting for you to read *How God Changes Your Brain,* a recent book by neuroscientists Andrew Newberg and Mark Waldman.[2] This book gives evidence based on scientific method, including brain scan results. It shows that prayer and spiritual practices lead to stress-reducing changes, including beneficial physical changes in the brain. But all this would, however, be less meaningful, if we do not focus on good actions.'

David finished his answer and reached for the water jug to refill his glass. Julian took this opportunity to bring the session to a close, thanking everyone, in particular, David. Benedict and Francis thanked the host and the speaker, said goodbye to all and started walking towards their cars.

Even though he was far away for his voice to reach the others, Benedict whispered to Francis, 'Many thanks for this. I am still a bit uneasy, but this meeting has set me thinking. I would like to read some books to see how different authors have approached this issue. I need more food for thought. So can you recommend some authors? I will also check on the internet myself. Thanks again, Francis.'

Francis promised to send some initial references to Benedict and took leave. They would meet the next day in office.

References

1. Russell, Bertrand and Whitehead, AH. *Principia Mathematica*. Volumes 1-3. USA: Rough Draft Printing, 2011.
2. Newberg, Andrew and Waldman, Mark Robert. *How God Changes Your Brain*. USA: Ballantine Books Trade Paperbacks, 2009.

6

Ananda's Initial Insight

Ananda was in bed with his back resting on a couple of pillows propped against the wall. He saw himself in the mirror of his memories; he lay there thinking of all the great people who had walked the spiritual path. They were giants and he was a mere speck of dust in comparison. Nonetheless, he felt that he should develop a framework relevant for the common man. He felt himself suitable for the task, as he had seen the aspirations and desires of the common people, while having glimpsed the larger picture.

Ananda smiled with some satisfaction at how his friends used to praise his ability to keep cool under difficult situations. They all sought his advice on a range of personal matters, perhaps because of his spiritual experiences.

Suddenly, he heard his wife calling him from the adjacent room. She always referred to him by his initials—AC. Sometimes she joked that when naming him AC, she was influenced not by his initials, but her perception of Ananda's behaviour pattern. By AC, she meant alternating current because sometimes she found her husband fully focused on matters of substance and dealing with family concerns, while at other times, he was just unconcerned, thinking about everything except what he needed to do.

Vadya was busy in the children's room getting their daughters ready. She seemed to be impatient as she asked, 'AC, are you ready as yet? Please remember that you had promised to take the children shopping. Even more important is your promise to Dad that you will drive him to the dentist. Please get ready quickly because your father is very fastidious about punctuality.' He smiled, thinking how his wife had become the favourite of his father, and how they shared every secret, perhaps even jokes about him. Ananda got up to get ready. However, he decided to finish his cup of tea first.

'AC, please do not waste time. Remember your promise to the children and Dad,' Vadya was saying again. Ananda's reverie was broken. It was as if Vadya had seen through the wall that he had sat down again, instead of getting ready. 'I will be ready before everyone is,' Ananda said. 'Why don't you go and see if Dad is ready?'

'I am ready, AC,' his Dad had replied with a chuckle. Strangely, his father, Maha Chauhan, had also started calling him AC. Sometimes Ananda would catch his father and Vadya look at each other with much amusement when they referred to him as AC.

'Well, son, are you ready yet?' The tone now indicated danger, a signal that Ananda was highly trained to notice. So he got up immediately, leaving the half-empty cup of tea. 'Ready in a minute, Pa,' Ananda called out, quickly changing his clothes.

Within an hour, they were at the dentist's chamber. Maha Chauhan looked immensely happy as he looked down at his granddaughters, Juhi and Joy, who were hugging him. He turned towards Ananda and said, almost commanded, 'You should take the girls shopping while I wait at the dentist. Please do not rush back for me. Give the girls all the time that they need. I can wait at the dentist's waiting room for you.'

Ananda smiled at his father, aware of the fact that the disciplinarian and somewhat fastidious father that he had known most of his life was very different when dealing with the granddaughters. It was amazing how much care and affection Maha Chauhan showed towards the two girls.

'Yes, dad. But do give me a call when you finish with the dentist. We will not be very far away and the girls would like to do some of their shopping with you too, especially shopping for the new ice-cream flavours that the three of you have started enjoying together. Also, maybe you could buy something for Ma for her birthday next week.'

'Good. I would like the girls to help me with that,' said Maha Chauhan. Ananda had, over time, learned to enjoy the imperial tone used by his father whenever he was being the patriarch. It showed that his father was feeling very comfortable and relaxed, fully in his elements, with the authority and affection that is often seen simultaneously present in senior members of an Indian joint family.

He also noted that his father gave much more importance to the help in shopping he would get from the little girls than from him. 'Amazing, how greater affection makes a person suppress the ego and give more of unquestioning love,' thought Ananda as he turned to leave with his daughters. He suddenly stopped in his tracks. It was as if a window of perception had just opened to give him a glimpse of the answers he was seeking. And it started closing as suddenly as it seemed to have opened. Ananda felt that his father had again taught him an important lesson, this time unwittingly. He realised that his father's special behaviour towards the grandchildren carried an important general message for him.

'Daddy, can I buy shoes with wheels at the back? All my friends have those shoes,' asked Juhi, his elder daughter. 'I want shoes with light bulbs in them,' said the younger one, Joy, who always had to get a word in whenever Juhi expressed any view.

'Yes, of course. We will look for both those types of shoes. Please tell me if you would like anything else too. What about some nice pullovers that your mother wants you to buy? We will wait for grandpa to join us before we buy some really good ice-cream. Meanwhile, start thinking about what you will suggest grandpa to buy as a birthday present for grandma. Maybe you should think up two or three options for that,' said Ananda.

The two girls started walking with a bounce in their steps. Ananda marvelled at how much these two loved each other and yet there was this strong sibling rivalry, a need to assert oneself and demand equal or greater attention. An assertion of the ego coexisting with love and goodwill towards each other, thought Ananda. What an interesting dichotomy and balance of conflicting emotions! How will this struggle evolve and I wonder what will help resolve it over time?

Ananda was aware that the conflict between ego and love was not evident in the behaviour of his father or his wife Vadya towards the children. He realised with some embarrassment that he was not without ego towards his own children. Perhaps, this was the result of his cultural background where the father had to be the disciplinarian. Or maybe, it was his deep desire that children should respect the father figure.

Respect has to be earned, not imposed. How do I ensure that they continue to love me always? Ananda wondered. Lost in his reverie, his mind moved to a simple spiritual statement that he had heard so often: Only our own effort is for us to make. The result of our effort is not within our control, and we should not worry about it.

'This is not easy at all,' Ananda said aloud. Surprised, the two girls looked up at him with some concern, wondering whether their demands had put some undue pressure on their father. Ananda felt guilty and quickly said, 'Don't worry. I was thinking about a difficult technical problem that needs to be solved. Nothing to do with us. Have you thought of what you will suggest to grandpa?' The girls did not answer, but the bounce came back into their steps. They moved ahead, talking to each other.

Ananda felt he had perhaps taken another step towards understanding the overall framework he sought to simplify. He made a mental note of the key concepts that needed greater thought when he would be alone: Ego is a driving force, unquestioning love suppresses ego, balance between love and ego, and that we can only make the effort or action and not guarantee the result. With a flash he saw another, deeper meaning to the spiritual statement about only our effort is for us to make. It also implied that our effort is necessary even though it may not lead to what we seek. Without our effort, we would definitely not get what we seek irrespective of whether the objectives we seek are in the spiritual, social, material or a narrow family-oriented context.

He did not yet know that this search would progress much faster in the days to come when he would start sharing his ideas with a complete stranger from California—a young girl called Marie.

7

Marie of California

'Marie, you should live your life.' Two very different people, her mother, Anita and Professor Webb from her college, had the same message for Marie, with a major emphasis on 'live'. In her mind, she saw the message as: 'Marie, you should LIVE life.'

Was there really any difference in the two messages? If so, were they inconsistent with each other, wondered Marie. She was in her favourite corner of her bedroom, comfortable as she felt the soft touch of the big pillow she had placed there. She heard someone coming down the steps. Her mother was up early that day.

'Marie, it would be good for you to get some exercise. Would you like to join me for a walk in the garden, dear?' Anita shouted out to her daughter from the next room as she changed her shoes for the walk.

'No, mom. I have some work to finish and I want to start early.' Marie felt uneasy with her restless childhood and recalled her persistent attempts to be more peaceful. She thought of her mother, Anita, who had often felt strangely unhappy with her and would show her impatience with questions like, 'Marie, why can you not pay attention? Which world are you living in?'

Marie always found it very difficult to explain. She invariably got lost in her thoughts trying to seek some answer that made sense: Is the explanation—perhaps my extended adolescent years, somewhat beyond the norm? Or is it that my world is actually larger than the world my mother lives in? Am I being arrogant in thinking this way? I am not even sure whether the world I live in is really larger, or a result of my imagination, Marie smiled as she thought. My mother would never understand what I am trying to glimpse. Well, my mother is not the only one perplexed by this behaviour. I, myself, often feel that I am wasting my time and effort and I should listen more seriously to my mom.

Marie snuggled deeper into the soft large cushion. She liked doing that, especially when she felt unsure about her decisions. She thought aloud, 'How do I describe this larger world that I glimpse from time to time? It is like describing the colour "red" or "green" or even "black" to a blind person. I wonder how that would be possible, especially as I myself do not have a complete understanding.'

Often, she felt that she should not spend so much time or effort in her search. Sometimes, she was convinced she should give up on it, but soon she slipped back into her own special world. The desire to convert the hazy outline she saw into a larger and clearer picture was just too strong.

She was only twenty-three years old. There was so much time to settle down later into her mother's world, she thought. She could afford to follow her fancy, but she needed someone who knew more than her. A guide—someone who could see much more fully the picture or the framework she sought to understand.

It was not that she had not tried to find a guide. How much she had knocked on various doors, read many books, but she was still left with a sense of anxiety. She had tried different methods—prayers, chants, mantras, past-life regression and, of course, meditation. She had practised various forms of meditation—with a candle, focusing on a spot of light, eyes closed, eyes open, lying down, standing up, sitting cross-legged, dancing with gay abandon, concentrating intensely, not concentrating at all, trying to see inner light, colours and so on.

Marie had even read some simplified explanations of scientific concepts in an effort to get a better perspective, hoping that perhaps some scientific insight could enigmatically show her the window to a spiritual one. Am I still continuing with the games I played as a child? Are these glimpses merely a result of my imagination? Is this the spiritual reality I am after? Or is my mind playing tricks on me? Marie questioned herself, but had no answers, only a sense of inadequacy.

She had read somewhere that Gautama the Buddha had also felt the same way when he was trying different paths, before he found his middle path and achieved spiritual awakening. This made her feel better. She felt that she too was treading towards her middle path. In her optimistic moments, with the arrogance of youth, she felt that success was just a matter of time.

Marie recalled a spiritual insight: Only our own effort is for us to make. The result of our effort is not within our control, and we should not worry about it. Adjusting her cushion, she whispered to herself, 'I do not like this idea at all. Would such a mindset not be like accepting failure in a situation where my efforts do not give me the results I seek?'

'Marie, darling, are you day-dreaming again? Why do you not join some interesting school and follow your talent, my dear? Why don't you find a good teacher or join some classes to learn something new which interests you?' Anita said.

Anita suppressed a strong urge to say what had worried her for almost two decades now: Marie, why can you not be like other girls—interested in clothes, boys and all the pleasures the world has to offer?

Anita did not voice these thoughts. She knew that any expression of such views would distance Marie further. She knew that both she and Marie absolutely loved each other, but they were obviously from two different worlds. Was this some type of a generation gap, perhaps? Or some form of rebellion that an only child felt honour-bound to make? Anita hoped so because then after some time, Marie could change and become more focused, more normal.

A startled Marie looked around. She did not know for how long her mother had been watching her. There was truth in her mother's statement, but not the one which her mother saw. Marie smiled, 'You are right mom. I should find a good teacher. Give me two years to follow this special interest of mine. After that I will do something that may seem more meaningful to you. I know of someone who is a good guide. Guru Purna, that is his name. I believe his name means a "complete teacher", and I think he may be able to help me in my search to have a fuller idea to see the larger picture in life.'

8

Benedict Gets More Involved

Francis had been true to his word. He had sent an email to Benedict suggesting some books, together with his proposed sequence for reading them. They had decided to meet for lunch after a fortnight, once Benedict had read a few of these books.

Francis was waiting as usual in the restaurant where he and Benedict normally met for lunch. The tablecloth was the same red and white checks as always and on this occasion, it was Francis who was feeling a little nervous. He had arrived earlier than usual, a bit anxious about Benedict's progress. After waiting for some time, he started feeling more composed, helped by the fact that he was able to view his state of mind like an external observer. He realised he needed to work more on this and took a deep breath to steady himself.

Francis recalled discussing with Ananda the need to develop a mindset which took every task seriously, with professionalism, without getting too personally involved in the result. The important part was to not see the consequence of one's efforts as an extension of oneself. They had termed this state of mind as 'Personal Professionalism', where a person was able to be both the performer and evaluator of his own actions. Thereafter, a part of him tried to be an objective observer of his actions, while another strived to seek ways of improving his performance. He straightened himself with a resolve to focus more on personal professionalism, as he saw Benedict heading towards their table with a serious expression on his face.

Benedict sat down and Francis gestured to the waiter. A couple of glasses of red wine were brought to them, together with two menus. As usual, Benedict ordered pizza. Francis took some time and ordered pasta. They raised their wine glasses and clinked, wishing each other good health. Francis was relieved to note that Benedict was not as morose as he was fearing he would be.

'So, how have you been Benedict? Did you manage to read any of the books?' asked Francis.

'I have read most of them. I am still not satisfied,' said Benedict and Francis understood the reason for Benedict's expression when he had entered the restaurant.

'What is your concern?'

'The books seem to be focusing on similar points, the ones which David kept introducing during his interaction. They all talk about a larger understanding, a spiritual underpinning of our existence. I find the writers focusing on abstract concepts, meditation, soul and imaginary metaphysical worlds. One of the books even talked about past-life regressions and rebirth. I am not a religious person. I do not feel comfortable with religion. Why should I take these ideas seriously?' asked Benedict.

Francis nodded. 'Benedict, I see your statements as a very positive development. The beginning has to be in terms of an objective assessment, queries and seeking solutions based on a logical framework. You are now already way beyond the initial stage. Combined with your desire to get a better insight for improving yourself, this is a very positive development.

Essentially, you are at a training camp in which you can have guides, but ultimately you run it yourself, for yourself.

'Now regarding the points you have just made, I think we should be clear that the books I mentioned to you are not about religion. They cover various aspects, but not religion. Broadly, one could say that they cover spiritual and metaphysical issues. I have given you a whole spectrum to read about. The first part of the exercise is to see what would make some sense to you. But this process would be meaningless if you approach these books with a closed mind. You must try and see whether any of the ideas you read about is of use to you. All these books are bestsellers with reprints. People have bought them in large numbers because they have found them to be useful. So the first step in your search should be to approach them with an open mind. Only if you find that nothing in them is of use to you, should you reject them.'

Benedict was staring at Francis and wanted to respond strongly. However, he checked himself, recalling that this was a process aimed at helping him. Francis was doing him a favour. He said, 'I agree with you Francis, but I really cannot relate to them.'

Francis responded, 'Okay, let us see all the things that you did not like in them. Maybe, we can start by focusing on the issues that could take you forward on your journey.'

'Thanks, Francis. To begin with, I do not like the various terms used in the books, such as Zen or yoga, which relate to structured ways of looking at spirituality.'

'Okay. You find the use of terms describing a structured form of spiritual pursuit unpalatable,' Francis replied. 'Let us go back to our previous lunch when all this started. You said that you wanted to be more like me, more peaceful, successful at work and able to deal with tension. Irrespective of whether or not I fit this picture, the important point to realise is that you usually require a structured and disciplined way of dealing with issues. Whether it is to write your memo, to bring order to a paper you may be writing, advising people, making your investments or trying to improve your management capacity—all of them require a structured way of dealing with the relevant issues. So, a structured framework is not what should put you off.

'Similarly, it is not the foreign or alien name such as "Zen" or "yoga" which is your real concern. Suppose I was not called Francis, but had some other name from an African, Asian or Latin American culture. Would you not be having this discussion with me? Would you have focused on my name or rather the qualities to seek some friendly assistance? So, it is obviously not the name, which is bothering you. We need to identify what it is that makes you uncomfortable,' said Francis.

Benedict took another sip of his wine, and asked the waiter for a refill. He waited while the waiter was pouring wine. Francis politely waived the waiter away when he was approached for a refill because he normally did not drink more than one glass of wine at lunch. Neither did Benedict in general, but he probably required it today to broaden his perspective.

Benedict looked up from his wine and said, 'Francis, you are absolutely right. Neither the structure nor the terms really bother me. Rather, they signify something to me that generates a negative reaction whenever I come across them. You are right. What I feel uneasy about is the content of the framework. I do not feel comfortable even with the thought that I should rely on spiritual concepts to go ahead in the material world. I do not find concepts such as past life and soul to be of much use. I do not think that for me the answer to my happiness lies in developing love towards all. To me, using a spiritual road to go towards my material goal seems a wrong method. A spiritual road is obviously going to a different destination, not the one I want to reach. Spirituality is an other-worldly concept and I want to be happy in this world, not spiritually-oriented.'

Francis nodded, 'Now I think we are approaching the issue in a more substantive manner. I am so happy that we can see things clearly to decide what needs to be dropped or taken forward. For the moment, let us leave the concept of soul or rebirth and look only at the issue of spiritual pursuits. I think you are looking at the term "spiritual" in a very narrow way; that it is something which is not material. This seems to be the basis of your aversion. You do not consider spiritual methods as being meaningful for taking you ahead towards your goal. But in doing so, you are actually overlooking what your objective is. You told me that your objective is to be happy by removing tension and achieving material progress.'

'You are right. These are my main objectives,' said Benedict.

Francis continued, 'So let us see them one by one. Take being happy first. What is happiness, if not a state of mind, a non-material thing? You are linking it with the material results because in your assessment happiness comes from achievements in the material world—owning a house, car, status, job, eating well, holidays and so on. In each material situation, a person could be happy or unhappy, depending on the state of mind linked to the specific experience with events or personal relationships, at any point of time. How you react to any experience depends on your state of mind, your perspective and the balance with which you respond. Therefore, it is evident that our behaviour is fundamentally affected by what all of us consider non-material or even spiritual. Likewise, tension or lack of it depends on peace of mind. This, too, is a consequence of the same kind of factors and they are spiritual in nature.

'Let us now consider achieving material progress. For this you would need to work hard, with adequate preparation and develop the relevant interpersonal skills. In addition, you need to be alert and aware about possible options to deal with any issues, and be sensitive or responsive to people. How efficiently you are able to use your talents depends on your state of mind, your mental strength, clarity and balance. Once again you will see an obvious important contribution of the non-material part of our life to the objective of achieving material success. A spiritual perspective helps us strengthen these non-material attributes within us. Thus, to consider that spiritual matters are irrelevant for your material objectives is inappropriate.'

Benedict intervened, 'These are not the only issues which are covered by spiritual writings. What about soul, rebirth and such matters?'

Francis agreed, 'Of course, once we go into the issue of soul, rebirth, etc., that is a different realm of spiritual pursuit. I would like to discuss these after considering one more important point about material success, a point you had raised when we had lunch last time. You said that you want material success but no tension associated with the effort. Not only will you need spiritual resources to achieve this combined objective, spiritual progress also helps you to decide when to keep pressing for some objective and when to give up on it. It helps you see the value of your efforts in relation to the value of the results of those efforts more clearly. In a way, it helps you realise your capabilities more clearly. As you know, in economics, this is a process of maximisation of our benefits, subject to our constraints or limitations. Long ago, I read an interesting quotation in *Readers' Digest* which said, "Happiness is making a bouquet of flowers within reach." Spiritual insights help you determine more clearly the limits of your reach and the possibility of extending it to additional flowers for the bouquet. It also lets you enjoy the flowers in the bouquet rather than focusing mainly on those beyond your reach. This is fundamentally linked to the possibility of determining the appropriate balance between material success and peace of mind, especially when these two cannot be increased together for you.'

Benedict nodded, 'I know this saying. It is a simpler version of a quotation ascribed to Robert Goddard.' He then betrayed a hint of impatience, almost speaking sharply, 'Yes, but what about soul and rebirth? Are they also linked with material things?'

'You have a valid point. These are mainly spiritual or non-material aspects.'

'Non-material? What is that?'

'If you see the readings I have recommended, you will realise that they include two books on past-life regression. Both are written by psychologists. They are practising psychologists, who provide therapy through past-life regression techniques. It is, therefore, not just a purely spiritual issue. Working with souls and past-life experiences may give rise to a deeper understanding of a larger reality, which definitely is spiritual. It may, however, also provide a basis for better dealing with the material world. So while some parts of these issues span the world of spirit, they are also part of scientific enquiry and affect our actions and participation in the material world.'

'I am still not comfortable with these. Is there no way of achieving more focus and calm without relying on such diffused and unreal concepts?' asked Benedict with some concern.

Francis was quiet for some time before speaking again, 'I think it is all a matter of how far you want to travel on this road. You can try some exercises for calming yourself and collecting your energy. Do you pray at all?'

Benedict shook his head vigorously, 'No. I prayed enough as a child. My mother forced me to go to church every Sunday and I had to pray twice a day. But why do you ask?'

'I wanted to frame my suggestions to you based on whether or not you pray. Since you do not pray, I will suggest three small exercises for you. They are alternatives and you could choose which one to perform. It would be good if you could do the exercise for about fifteen minutes before you sleep or before you begin your day. I suppose you have a table lamp near your bed?'

Benedict nodded, somewhat perplexed.

Francis continued, 'Switch on your bed lamp and switch off all other lights in your bedroom. Sit comfortably on your bed, use some pillows to support your back, if you wish. Close your eyes and feel the light from the lamp all around you, within you, a soft glow of the light. For about ten to fifteen minutes, with your eyes closed, experience the soft light around, and imagine it also coursing through your body, within you. Think of a very nice scene, say a sunset or sunrise, or a beautiful object such as a flower, in your heart and let that also be suffused with the light in your heart. Your mind will wander and you will keep thinking of something else frequently and repeatedly. Do not worry. Just softly go back to the light and the picture and enjoy it in peace. You will see that you are able to do this more easily over time. See the result after about a month. You will notice that this exercise will help you to compose yourself and become calmer. It will provide you with a basis to collect your thoughts and apply them with greater clarity.'

Benedict seemed relieved and then a bit concerned. 'Will I need to do this every day? Who has taught you this exercise? Why is it important for me?' he asked.

'It helps if you do this regularly. Try it for some time and then decide. This was taught to me by a very good friend from India, Ananda, who used to be in Geneva some years ago. I have myself found this exercise very useful, which is the reason I suggest it to you,' responded Francis.

He continued, 'Let me now suggest another exercise to enhance energy levels and promote calmness. This is the same exercise with only one additional aspect. So keep the same position, sitting on the bed as for the exercise I just explained, but with your hands folded in front of your chest, touching them to your chest. Again, close your eyes and imagine the energy in the light around you, softly surging around you and within you. You are folding your hands to develop a feeling of humility within yourself. With this feeling, focus on the light energy around you and how it is a part of you, within your heart and body. Do it as many times a day as you wish, but at least once each day for ten or fifteen minutes. Feel one with the energy and try and be collected within yourself. Experience also the strength and peace given to you by this energy in the form of light.'

Benedict became concerned, 'Are you asking me to pray, folding my hands in front of my chest?'

'No, I am not telling you to pray. This is just to keep you collected and connected, to feel the energy in and around your body and develop a sense of humility. I hope it works the way it has worked for me. Trying it is the only way to get a clearer idea about the relevance of such exercises for oneself. If you do not feel comfortable with this, just do the one I mentioned first. Each such exercise is an effort to develop greater peace and composure within you, with the second or third ones adding something more.'

'Oh, yes. You said that there is a third one. What is that?' asked Benedict.

'Now, take the second exercise I have mentioned and add another feeling within your heart. Try and feel love for the energy within and around you, and in general towards your surroundings,' said Francis.

Benedict nodded, 'Thanks, Francis. I will give it a try by beginning with the first one, and then I will consider how and whether to move to the other two. I will also try and read the books with a more open mind. We could meet again after a fortnight for another discussion. I have found this lunch to be very useful. Thanks very much.'

'My pleasure. I look forward to our next meeting.'

9

Marie and Ananda

The guests that day were not unusual. They were a combination of Ananda's compatriots and foreigners. He was always a bit unsure of how the foreigners felt in India. Having lived abroad for many years, he thought he knew how to try and make them comfortable, but was also sensitive to the fact that sometimes, there was too much of an Indian in him. A mixed blessing, he thought.

Today, his guests included an old friend who had become a monk and had transformed into a completely different person. He was peaceful and quiet most of the time and seemed to require little to make himself happy. His new, adopted name was Guru Purna. Ananda hoped this was not a name his friend had chosen himself. That would reflect certain arrogance because the name meant 'a complete teacher', or 'a teacher complete in every way'. It was a matter of some satisfaction to Ananda that Guru Purna's behaviour was not at all arrogant.

Guru Purna had come to stay for three days with Ananda in Delhi before returning to the United States of America. This was his third visit this year. Every time he had different persons accompanying him, each of them radiating innocence and inquisitiveness.

How do they deal with the disorder and bustle of India, I wonder. What are the questions they have managed to answer, thought Ananda, as he smiled to welcome them when they joined him for a buffet lunch. The Indian dishes were spiced lightly for the foreign guests. Food was first served to Guru Purna. 'Thank you. Please start your lunch. I will not eat unless all of you also serve yourselves and begin your lunch,' said Guru Purna.

It was a winter afternoon in New Delhi and they were sitting outdoors, in the warmth of the sun, which was always welcome. The same sun would become unbearably hot in summer but in winter, it gave special pleasure. Ananda remembered several Indians abroad recalling this experience with nostalgia.

Ananda joined the circle of chairs, which had formed spontaneously. Perhaps, everyone wanted to be a part of the group around Guru Purna. The guests carefully balanced their plates in their laps. Vadya kept fussing over them to eat more and explained some of the dishes. It was a genial environment with a major lacuna. No one except Vadya was talking at all. Ananda felt he had to begin the conversation.

'So what are some of the key concerns that have brought you to India with Guru Purna? Was your experience different from what you expected?' asked Ananda in general. No one answered. Ananda noticed a beautiful young woman seated two chairs away from him. She was a picture of diffidence and hesitation. Clear blue eyes took in Ananda quickly, then she looked down and began speaking. Ananda almost missed her words, so he strained to pay more attention to what she was saying.

'I see diverse books in your collection. What interests me particularly is that you have kept books on simple explanations of physics and evolution of scientific ideas together with books on spiritual topics. Is there any specific reason for this?' asked Marie.

Ananda was evidently happy with this question and smiled at Marie. 'I thank you for ascribing some order to my books. Vadya keeps chiding me for being haphazard. On a more serious note, yes, I have kept books on these two different topics together because I feel they cover the same broad subject. The insights that one gets from spiritual texts are sometimes clarified by the books on science and vice versa. I feel that science is trying to unravel the thoughts which some of the spiritual masters have presented long ago in their own special ways. The problem is that scientific methods cannot be applied easily to obtain better spiritual insights. So, search for spiritual insight at a general level largely remains at the level of theories. Nonetheless, those who have themselves had spiritual experiences sometimes look at these two topics together.'

'You know, I keep getting glimpses of what seems to be a larger reality, but I am just not sure whether I am hallucinating or there is some meaning in that,' Marie said. 'It is as if there is a larger picture that keeps emerging in small parts to me. I feel so unsure and want to know how to get a better understanding, a fuller picture.'

Ananda was taken aback. He wondered whether Marie was playing a trick on him, whether Guru Purna had put her up to raise an issue which was so personal to him. Then he recalled that except for Vadya, he had not shared this aspect of his life with anyone, his repeated glimpses of parts of a larger picture. He looked at Vadya and wondered whether she had mentioned to Marie the concept of a larger picture of reality. It was obviously not the case. He found that Vadya, who had also heard Marie, was looking at her with confusion and even alarm.

Ananda looked around to see the reaction of others. They were all busy eating, unconcerned about Marie's statement. Some of the guests had started talking to Guru Purna, asking him questions about meditation and some social work projects that they had begun in India. Ananda smiled at this new role of an old friend. He felt very comfortable and happy with Guru Purna's presence at his house. He suddenly realised that Marie was waiting for his response.

Ananda could see his polite conversation transcending into a serious discussion. He did not feel ready for such serious conversation yet. 'Perhaps we should discuss this on some other occasion.'

'Is there anyone who has written about deep spiritual experiences and also has an interest in science to take forward the spiritual pursuit?' asked Marie.

'Yes, there is,' answered Ananda. 'You should see the writings of Pandit Gopi Krishna. He was a deeply spiritual person with immense spiritual experience and an interest in the scientific knowledge that links with it.[1] However, he was not a scientist. There are a number of scientists who are interested in these matters. Some look at this through a study of the brain's response to different types of activities, including spiritual activities; in fact, they have come up with a new area of investigation which they refer to as neurotheology[2]. I will give you some references later.'

'How do you see the presence of the Divine in creation? Is that what my visions show me?' asked Marie.

Just then, Guru Purna looked at them and said, 'Perhaps we could ask this question to one of the most well-known spiritual teachers of the day, whom we should go and meet. Ananda, would you like to come with us?'

Ananda had spent a lot of time visiting such teachers and had decided not to go to anyone except his spiritual master who had effortlessly given him special insights and experiences. Ananda felt very privileged to be in touch with this great master who was truly exceptional and had decided to focus on his personal practices rather than spending time listening to discourses. Sometimes, he even wondered whether the teachers themselves were experienced enough. On such occasions, he recalled Pandit Gopi Krishna's book, *Kundalini: The Evolutionary Energy in Man*[3].

Gopi Krishna has written that he did not find any spiritual master or guru equipped to address the adverse physical effects of an increase in awareness through a rise in his *Kundalini*. Gopi Krishna's experience showed the importance of having a knowledgeable guide. Ananda had found only one such great spiritual master for himself. His good fortune was that the master had treated him with great affection like one treats a grandchild. He had experienced with his great master the affection that he saw in his father, Maha Chauhan, for his grandchildren.

'Well Ananda, would you like to come with us to have this very interesting experience?' Guru Purna asked again, breaking Ananda's reverie.

Resigning to his lot that day, Ananda was ready for déjà vu, once again. After lunch, they sat in two cars—one driven by Ananda and the other by Maha Chauhan—and started for this special experience promised by Guru Purna. Ananda thought that he should consider this journey as a part of the various new enriching experiences he had received through the influence of his master. He became much more positive about the trip.

References

1. See for example, Krishna, Gopi. *The Biological Basis of Religion and Genius*. USA: The Institute for Consciousness Research and The Kundalini Research Foundation, Ltd, 2006.
2. Newberg, Andrew B. *Principles of Neurotheology*. UK and USA: Ashgate, 2010.
3. Krishna, Gopi. *Kundalini: The Evolutionary Energy in Man*. USA: Shambhala Publications, 1970 (revised edition).

10

How Close is Thy Neighbour

Guru Purna and his group were received with a warm welcome at the large house in a posh locality, which was the residence of the spiritual teacher they were visiting. They entered the main living room of the house, which was huge, decorated with fragrant flowers, with people sitting in groups, waiting respectfully for the teacher to arrive and begin his discourse.

Guru Purna was well known to these people and they bowed to show their respect. Guru Purna greeted them with folded hands and a warm smile. He whispered to Ananda, 'We will go now for a special meeting exclusively for us. This is why I wanted you to join us. I would like you to meet this great man and keep in touch with him later.'

Ananda was pleased to hear this. He suddenly heard a gentle voice inside his mind, Oh! How we love our own ego and feed it with special indulgence. Why not extend this same indulgence towards others. It was the voice of his great spiritual master. Ananda had known the master for twenty-seven years now, but it felt as if he had known him forever. Smiling at how his presence was almost eternal for him, he wondered whether his spiritual master meant that we should extend our ego to encompass all as if they are a part of ourselves.

He entered a small room where the teacher was sitting with four others. Exuding comfortable confidence, the teacher looked at them with a very soft expression and a wide, welcoming smile. Ananda had grown up in the Indian tradition and despite his previous misgivings, he felt no hesitation in bending low to touch the teacher's feet after offering him a small bouquet of flowers. The teacher asked all of them to be comfortable and smiled at Guru Purna, 'You have brought some very special people to me today. I am very happy to meet them all. How are you?' he asked, his query showing a common Indian tendency to leave the question somewhat incomplete while providing clarity through an extended interrogatory tone.

'Thank you,' said Guru Purna. 'You are right. I am fortunate to have these good people with me. I was keen that they meet you too and hopefully start a long-term connection. In addition to my American friends, I have brought two Indian friends from this city, my hosts during this trip. They are Ananda, a very dear childhood friend and his father, Maha Chauhan, who has been like a parent to me too.'

'We are already connected for a long time and we will continue to be connected. I am happy to meet you all today. Would you like tea, coffee or something cold?' asked the teacher. Everyone declined politely and the teacher continued to smile. 'What can I do for you?' he asked Guru Purna, who replied, 'We are looking forward to your discourse today. Which topic will you speak on?'

'I have not decided as yet. I am waiting for the right inspiration. Hopefully, I will get it by the time I have to speak,' he said, smiling mischievously as he started smelling a white rose. Guru Purna put his hands together as a sign of respect, or perhaps to avoid any misunderstanding that his next statement may imply. He said, 'Would you consider speaking on the presence of the Divine in creation and how spiritual evolution is an attempt to become more aware of this presence? I believe this would be a useful topic today and for us it would mean an elaboration of some of the points we have already discussed.'

'It is evident that you are the inspiration I was waiting for. This is precisely what I will speak on today. I am sure that all of us will find it useful to take forward the discussions you have already had. Thank you once again. Please do stay for a meal with us after the discourse,' said the teacher, rising to leave for the living room. All those with him followed and seated themselves on the carpet, using the various large cushions to make themselves as comfortable as possible.

The teacher looked at the people scattered around the living room and asked them to come closer to him. He said, 'I want to begin by introducing Guru Purna, who is visiting from the United States with some of his friends. We also have with us two new Indian friends from this city itself, whom we will get to know better over time. Guru Purna wants me to discuss the presence of the Divine in creation. I will talk to you today on this topic.

'You may have heard or read that the balance in the universe, or in the world around us, has abundant evidence of the Divine in creation. In this stream of thought, the beauty, order and balance between so many different events, orderly phenomena or systems are taken to be the evidence of the Divine. I feel we should not rely on these aspects as evidence of the Divine in this world. They become more relevant once you have actually experienced the Divine to some extent. Otherwise, very quickly you would face difficulties in progressing further when you come across contrary arguments encompassed, for example, in the theory of chaos, in the difficulties that people face in life, or even the unexpected and seemingly arbitrary physical responses of different patients to medicines when tackling acute infection or life-threatening situations. These do not apparently show order and you may then say that the world actually does not have any order.

'However, even chaos does not necessarily mean that there is no order. It only means that we are not in a position to understand and accurately predict events where even small and seemingly irrelevant perturbations in the system can have large overall unanticipated effects that cannot be captured within our existing structures of analysis. Our inability to predict or to understand these links does not mean that there is no order as such. However, this can be a subject of a long and fruitless discussion. And that is something we should definitely avoid.

'Today, I want to talk about the presence of the Divine based on our own efforts to find peace within ourselves and in our individual worlds. All of you who are part of this gathering are definitely among those who are seeking such mental peace and stability. Some of you are perhaps even practising certain ways of achieving this, such as meditation. When you meditate, for instance, you will find that you breathe more evenly and slowly, as if the body is more at peace with itself. However, when you are disturbed, the process of meditation becomes very difficult. Very few can meditate effectively in that situation.

'When we meditate, not all of us do so thinking that we are seeking a link with or attempting to get some evidence of the Divine. For us, the evidence of the Divine in creation has to come in terms of some extremely powerful event or experience. We are looking for some form of miracle, something which defies the laws of nature. To have an evidence of the Divine, we require going beyond the natural order as we know it, or we wish such evidence to come through experiencing positive and good results in life. Thus, only when we have good times, do we say, "God is kind, or we are blessed". We start doubting the presence of the Divine whenever we have problems or face difficulties, or even when we see negative developments like war, natural disasters and tragic events. We, thus, doubt or find it difficult to comprehend the Divine, unless the evidence is positive, huge or unusual.

'Is this because we want to impose a specific form of predictability on the Divine without necessarily knowing the details of the entire system? Do we not ask for a much higher standard of evidence or understanding when we want to know about the Divine, in comparison to our efforts to deal with various developments in our own life? We forget that whenever we try to learn something new or get a new insight, we always do so in small steps. When a baby walks, or even a grown-up person who has been unwell for long, learns to walk again, it always involves small steps. Likewise, you do not become a nuclear physicist, a surgeon, or even an economist, a dancer or a good cook within a short period of time. Moreover, not everyone has the capability to achieve such goals. We have lots of evidence that with time, babies do start walking rapidly; that after physiotherapy, patients are usually able to lead normal lives again and people do manage to acquire special expertise if they show dedication and give time. In these situations, we have patience with the small beginnings and slow progress. But in our search for insight into the Divine, we are always in a hurry and want rapid results. This, I feel, we should avoid. Let us try to be consistent with respect to all the different ways in which we seek to achieve progress for ourselves, with new knowledge or capabilities.

'Consider now what we do when we seek more peace of mind or insights through meditation. You would already be familiar with the concept that in meditation we are trying to go deeper within ourselves to seek our objective. What does this mean? Many of you would have seen X-ray pictures or scan results of yourselves. Do you see something which makes it meaningful for you to go deep within yourselves? To me, meditation means withdrawing away from the world around you, in order to try and go to another dimension of existence. With meditation, we are trying to be with ourselves without external influences. Some would even call it trying to be with the Divine.

'I treat this process as an attempt to experience some key attributes of the Divine, something we are unable to do well in the course of our normal lifestyle. When we are disturbed and unable to meditate properly, we are not able to experience the Divine world, but end up mostly staying within a narrow dimension. When I meditate, I experience a strong thrust of my mind surging inside me, folding in my external attention so that I am detached from other thoughts. But if I am disturbed or my thoughts are occupied by various concerns, this usually does not happen. Nonetheless, even when I am not fully collected and detached, during meditation I am more peaceful.

'In this process of experiencing the Divine or the attributes of the Divine through meditation, we are, in effect, trying to be more and more like the Divine. What we feel through this process is a glimpse of the Divine seen through these attributes. The important part is to recognise that these are attempts to become more and more like the Divine. This can be useful for what we are discussing today, the presence of the Divine around us. The serenity that you may feel, or your love for those around you, and a clearer thought process with a broader perspective—these are all developments within you. At those moments, these experiences take you towards becoming more like the Divine. This is the type of evidence that we all should seek. With time, as our small steps cover a much longer distance, we will get more and better evidence of the Divine. I wish you success in your endeavour. Let us now take some questions.'

The teacher was smiling as he looked around the room. 'Do you have any questions? Should we first allow our visitors from the United States to ask their questions? Please come forward without hesitation. It helps me better understand what I have just said to you.'

Ananda noticed that one of the persons with Guru Purna raised his hand to ask a question and the teacher nodded at him.

'When describing the attributes of the Divine that we may experience during meditation, you mentioned feeling love for those around us. I am interested in knowing more about this. I have read about the importance of loving God with all your heart, soul and mind and also of loving your neighbour as yourself. Would your statement be something along these lines?'

The teacher had started speaking even before the question ended. It was an amusing sight because the teacher had his eyes closed as if he was fully immersed in the world of his answer. He said softly, 'You are correct. The coverage of "neighbour" or even of "loving God" here, however, would be much wider than you may consider under ordinary circumstances. For instance, would the concept "love your neighbour as yourself" that you have just mentioned imply that when you are living in one place, you love the neighbour there as yourself and if you move to another locality you stop loving the original neighbour and start loving the new neighbour as yourself? No, that is not the teaching according to my understanding. The coverage of "neighbour" is, thus, much wider than its meaning in ordinary usage. The term "neighbour" covers all those affected by your actions, including those you may not know. Likewise, the coverage of "God" should not be seen in a limited sense. God covers and includes all of us. Loving God means loving the creatures of God, the creation of God. It is an all-encompassing love. Not easy to understand because our normal mindset is different. Do try to think about this and see the limits of your love in terms of your own behaviour. Then you have to keep working on those limits to extend the frontier of your achievement.'

Ananda was lost in thought. The teacher's answer had triggered a very pleasant memory of a visit few years ago to his spiritual master. After spending some time with the master, all those present had moved to a large meeting hall for some quiet reflection and rest. Ananda had decided to sit with his back against a pillar in the hall and meditate for some time. He wanted to be by himself and closed his eyes. Suddenly, he had lost the sense of his physical body. He saw himself only as light, white soothing light. He saw the surroundings, the whole scene even beyond the hall, as if he was not just a participant or an observer, but also one who encompassed it all. Even in the form of light, he saw himself smiling with immense happiness, which far exceeded any joy he had felt earlier in his life. Another interesting sensation was that he saw all others in the hall as his children, whom he was snugly holding close to himself, enfolded in his form of light. They, too, were white light, sleeping with great confidence and comfort on what would be akin to his chest. He felt such deep affection for them at that moment that he was overjoyed beyond description. He was not aware how long he was in that state. When he woke up from his trance, things appeared as they were earlier. The glow of happiness that he had felt stayed with him for a few days, before disappearing slowly.

One feeling, however, remained forever. It was the realisation that the depth of affection he felt for his 'children' in the hall at that moment far exceeded the intensity of love he had ever felt for anyone in his life. Perhaps, it was something like the love a mother feels for her child. For him, there was no way to make such a comparison. He did remember though that at the moment of his special experience, he thought of himself as the 'mother' of all those around him and them as his 'children'. In his state of supra-consciousness, he was their mother and not father. After this strange but exhilarating experience, he had begun looking at all mothers with a new respect.

He also had a new understanding of Vadya's personality, and his admiration for her had gone up manifold. Ananda knew that he would never be able to love as intensely as Vadya did. She made efforts for others with devotion to their cause and happiness. He recalled how Vadya had looked after everybody during lunch that day. Ananda resolved to learn more from Vadya as he switched back to the ongoing discussions. He realised that acquiring that higher intensity of love for his family was a process to be completed over time. A process with small steps covering greater distances to enable progress towards his objective.

He saw the analogy with the teacher's answer today and a geometrical pattern with concentric circles emerged before his eyes, each circle containing one part of the higher-level aspiration of the total objective that we aim for.

The teacher was finishing his last response. 'Any other questions?' he asked and Ananda raised his hand. 'Yes, Ananda. Let us hear what you would like to discuss.'

Ananda thanked him and said, 'In your answer to the first question, you mentioned that the coverage of "neighbour" or the "Divine" was much larger than what we normally consider. To help us understand the scope of this coverage, suppose we draw a picture with concentric circles. The innermost circle would be just us, individually. Our ego and self-gratification would imply that we love ourselves very much. The next circle would contain our nuclear family, including our parents. These too we love a lot, but perhaps less than ourselves. The next two concentric circles would contain our extended family and our friends. The order of placement for these two groups within the third and fourth concentric circles could differ for various people. In this framework, the fifth concentric circle would have those whom we do not know. The last one could contain those we do not like or those who wish to do us harm. As shown by your answer, the coverage of neighbour is an extended one. For "love thy neighbour as thyself", where would this coverage end? Is there any of these circles which we would not include in the coverage of our "neighbour" in this context?'

'I think the clue to my answer is in the coverage that I defined for God,' said the teacher. 'Ideally, all these concentric circles would be covered. However, that is never the case in our lives. You have provided me with a very interesting picture. If we draw the concentric circles which you have just described on a piece of paper, we get a picture in two dimensions. But each of these circles is actually a different dimension of relationships. We need to work through each dimension of the relationship and within each of these dimensions, we may not be able to treat each person the same way.'

Ananda had a technical mind, the mind of someone who liked to solve puzzles. He got more involved in the conversation than he had expected. He raised his hand and interrupted the teacher, 'What you are describing seems like a simultaneous and independent effort to be made by us in each of these circles. This also means that at any point of time, we may have different levels of success with each of these different circles. We could even try to measure our success in terms of each of these as if we have separate measurement meters for each circle.'

The teacher asked Ananda to draw a picture to explain his concept. The group around the teacher stirred and people got up to look at the picture. The teacher asked Ananda to bring the paper to him, saying that his old eyes wanted to understand it from a closer distance. He looked at the picture and nodded. He turned to Ananda and said with a smile, 'Ananda, this is very good indeed.'

Ananda was looking at the teacher with deep concentration, as if he was able to see beyond the two-dimensional picture. 'If we consider this picture in three dimensions with each circle rising up, we could have something like the different levels of the Pyramid of the Sun in Teotihuacan, Mexico,' he said softly.

The teacher looked appreciatively at Ananda, 'Yes, the Pyramid of the Sun in Teotihuacan, Mexico. That is an interesting idea. We could have our own toy which coverts concentric circles into a pyramid—a toy to measure spiritual progress. What an interesting idea!'

'Are there any other questions? If not, let us now have dinner. We have all earned it well,' said the teacher.

Ananda looked towards his father and Guru Purna to take their lead and followed them to a room where a simple meal had been served. He ate silently, lost in thought. He saw Guru Purna and Maha Chauhan looking at him, both with paternal affection. How much Guru Purna has changed. My friend is becoming paternal towards me! He has really taken his shepherd of the flock role very seriously, he thought. As soon as this thought crossed his mind, Ananda started chastising himself. Why do I get such contrary feelings? I actually like Guru Purna very much and am strongly of the view that he is a good person. Why do I suddenly get such thoughts, which are so contrary to my abiding feelings? Is there some part of me, which keeps raising its head to show that I need to consistently work on improving myself? Are these the demons that I must face before becoming a better person? Guru Purna is a good man. He has moved so far away from his previous life that it is bound to bring about major changes in personality. I must not judge him hastily, with such harsh cynicism. He may after all be feeling very affectionate towards all of us, like a mother, as I did in the large prayer hall at my master's place. It would be good to talk to Vadya about this tomorrow morning.

11

Benedict, the Diligent Reader

Francis was waiting in his apartment for Benedict, lying down in a corner of his living room, listening to some soothing music. This was his favourite spot when he wanted to relax. It had a couple of single mattresses, one on top of the other, covered with a beautiful soft cotton sheet and several pillows of different shapes. On these mattresses, with lights dimmed in the room and soothing music switched on, Francis always felt transported into a different world. The experience was almost therapeutic and over time he had many interesting experiences while lying down in this corner. He particularly remembered one occasion when he felt that a huge block of light was falling upon him from above, almost like a part of a bright glacier or a star. It was a scary moment and instinctively, he had raised his arms to cover his head. The light had vanished, and he felt distraught as soon as he recovered from his surprise, as if by raising his hands, he had prevented himself from being engulfed by that special light, a light that seemed so special and other-worldly. It was strange. Had he committed a grave error in doing so?

He got some comfort later upon discussing it with Ananda. He recalled Ananda's comments. 'Francis, this is a very special experience. I see no reason to worry about the fact that you raised your hands to protect yourself. Since when has light been blocked by holding up one's hands? That light was meant to be part of you, of your body. So please enjoy the gift without any concern.'

Francis had felt relieved after the conversation, though doubts did emerge whenever he thought about his reaction. Sometimes he re-enacted the scene to get greater clarity. Today again, he raised both his arms, enveloping his head with them, cowering with simulated fright in his corner. That is when the doorbell rang, announcing the arrival of Benedict.

Francis slowly got up, still lost somewhat in the experience of several years ago. He had recovered by the time he reached the door and welcomed Benedict. They both decided to drink beer and settled down on a sofa in the corner facing the mattresses. Benedict had a cloth bag with books and a few papers in his hands, including the detailed email that Francis had sent to him with titles of books to read. He had obviously done much more work than when they had met earlier.

Francis offered Benedict a beer and took shandy for himself. It was a legacy from his days at the university in England. He had preferred this drink which combined beer and lemonade since his youth, despite being a butt of many jokes amongst his friends.

'So, Benedict, I can see that you have read the books and even made some notes to organise the discussion. How would you like to start?'

'Francis, to begin with, I want to thank you for making this effort to prepare such an interesting list of books and even sending several of these books to me. It was an interesting combination of different topics. I was amused to see that you had mixed books on spiritual concepts with self-help books and even scientific books that would be of interest to the layman.'

Francis smiled as he noted that while working with the international diplomatic community, Benedict had naturally acquired the habit of beginning his conversation by appreciating the efforts of the other person. This was consistent with his own view that sensitivity towards others and appreciating their efforts is a very important part of improving oneself. It is a necessary step to develop compassion and consideration, provided it does not remain a perfunctory starting point for any statement thinly camouflaging an underlying narrow self-interest. Francis had seen on several occasions that with effort, a natural transition could be made beyond self-interest to encompass a wider interconnected interest.

He thought of an interesting recent presentation where the speaker had discussed a related point noting that normally people started their statement with, 'Yes, but...' This was to agree with others and then immediately disagree. The speaker was of the view that if we change only one word in this sentence and combine it with a constructive attitude, we could bring about a very useful and fulfilling change in ourselves and achieve a far better result.

He recalled the speaker's words: 'Instead of "Yes, but...", we should start saying, "Yes, and...". In this way, we keep the views and concerns of others within our framework of reference and add our own to supplement them, rather than maintain only our views and concerns. This is also a method to connect people rather than separate them in a discussion.'

Benedict saw Francis lost in thought and said with some concern, 'I apologise, Francis. Is something worrying you that you are so quiet? Should I come some other day?'

'No, not at all. Your statement reminded me of some interesting experiences. I promise I will be all attention now. Yes, I had mixed various types of books, including a few on simple scientific discussions. That is because in my view, all these perspectives are linked to the efforts that both of us are making. Each offers us insights for self-improvement.

We need to be sensitive enough to glean the relevant parts from them and expand our mental horizons. In fact, we can learn from all of nature around us, as shown by some of the deepest forms of special knowledge, including advances in science. And judging by the papers with you, you have obviously done a lot of intensive reading and thinking.'

'Many of these books had a lot of spiritual content,' pointed out Benedict, 'that did make it unattractive for me, but I read them nonetheless. However, I was more interested in reading some of them because I could see an overlap with many of my specific areas of interest.'

'Which ones would you like to begin with?' Francis asked.

'I want to start by discussing four of them and then we could take some others. First, the book by a physicist who invented a special form of laser[1]. Then, I want to discuss the book by a neuroscientist that David had mentioned towards the end of his lecture. I want to follow that with two self-help books, which have been major bestsellers.'

'Fine, let us begin. I had suggested each book to you with some specific objectives in mind. I will share those with you as we discuss them.'

'Francis, I really enjoyed the book written by the physicist who invented the special laser that is now used for corneal surgery. He is an exceptional man, who overcame deep deprivation and poverty to earn immense fame and wealth. The book explains some very complex ideas in a simple way, making a bridge between science and spirituality. Once again, my instinct was not to delve too deep because of the spiritual content, but I found that the book had a useful focus. My simple objective was far more limited than the scope of the book. For my purpose, I did nonetheless pick up some important points.'

'I like that book a lot too. It talks about scientific ideas while taking you towards a larger spiritual reality. You are right that its scope is far wider than your current focus, but sometimes people need a larger, consistent framework to adequately understand and deal with a smaller part. I am very interested to know what you found relevant for yourself,' said Francis.

Benedict hesitated a bit and then started explaining, 'I learned a number of things from the book like using scientific insights from the world at a very small, subatomic level up to the largest level covered by cosmology, which studies the universe as a whole.'

'That is very interesting, Benedict. I am all ears.'

'There are many interesting points. One, everything is interconnected. Two, we never have full information, but whatever happens around us is a combination of external factors and our own actions. We change the existing situation with our efforts, though the final result depends on a combination of factors that are both uncertain and beyond us. Three, reality is far deeper than what appears on the surface. There is an underlying field of energy, or reasons, which gives rise to any situation. It is useful to bear this in mind and thus, make an attempt to understand the underlying factors in any situation to enhance our efficiency and effectiveness in addressing that situation. I found one particular sentence very interesting in this context.'

'Which one do you have in mind?'

Benedict picked up the papers he had with him and started reading the relevant part: 'Both elementary force particles and elementary matter particles are merely excitations of their corresponding underlying fields, which makes the quantum fields, in a sense, the breeding ground of material creation.'[2]

'Why do you find this so interesting?' asked Francis.

'This statement shows me that since all that happens in any situation is due to underlying perturbations, we should try and maintain our calm with a sense of distance or detachment to better understand the underlying reasons for what we are facing. That way, we could try and address the fundamental cause rather than the superficial effect.'

'Great, Benedict! This is a wonderful projection of a scientific idea to help us handle personal situations,' exclaimed Francis. 'Which other relevant points have you gleaned from this book?'

Benedict brightened up, sat a bit straighter and spoke with greater confidence, 'Yet another insight from the scientific work which is relevant for our daily behaviour is that "an excited state tends to be unstable". I think that indicates the importance of addressing issues with a stable mind.'

Francis was nodding slightly. 'I agree with you. However, do you remember another book in the list that explains how we can have structured results even in states of disequilibrium or instability?[3] Let us keep this in mind when we discuss insights from that other book later.'

'You are right. Let us continue with this book. The overlap between scientific analysis and our material experience is also depicted by the fact that the actual situation keeps changing; it is never still. This implies that we need to identify whether and when it would be appropriate to make an effort to change the situation. Another very interesting point is that all of creation, the entire universe, started with a very small beginning. It is not only that the beginning of the big bang was extremely small, but also that it was the light and small elements of hydrogen and helium that generated the universe from basic energy. All that we see today is based on these small elements combining together to give us more complex elements.'

'Are you by any chance saying that we should start our efforts with small steps and use them consistently to achieve larger goals over time? Do you think that is the natural way even when we have large objectives?'

"That is exactly what I have in mind,' Benedict answered.

'Benedict, how will you bring about such a change if the underlying basis of quantum physics is that events are uncertain and we can't clearly anticipate them?' asked Francis.

'The book has helped me understand this aspect too. The author has combined advances in scientific thought very well, I think I can best answer your question by reading another interesting sentence from the book.' Saying this, Benedict picked up his papers again and started reading:

> In quantum physical experiments, an observer's consciousness is capable of bringing about a particular outcome from the coexisting possibilities inherent in any quantum system. Thus, quantum physicists have achieved a victory of sorts...by demonstrating beyond any reasonable doubt that observer and observed are fundamentally connected; their relationship is interactive and participative.[4]

'Francis, this shows me that I can affect events around myself and the manner in which I behave will affect the reactions of others and bring changes in the prevailing situation,' explained Benedict.

'This is very impressive, Benedict. You have got a lot from this book. Just to supplement these points, I want to mention how this book illustrates some other perspectives also,' Francis encouraged.

Benedict smiled mischievously. With a glint in his eyes, he started speaking quickly, 'You wanted me to change my attitude towards spiritual efforts. This book gives a very interesting account of the underlying scientific insights, which take us towards a spiritual way of looking at the universe. In fact, some of the text goes quite far in that direction. For example, the author has cited from a biography of the famous quantum physicist, Erwin Schrodinger, saying that Schrodinger was intuitively influenced by the ancient Indian school of spiritualism known as Vedanta, when he formulated quantum mechanics. Similarly, he quotes the argument of another quantum physicist, David Bohm, that even an electron has a rudimentary "mental" aspect. Based on these insights, the author provides an interesting conclusion about consciousness when he says that "consciousness is not simply in our heads. It is everywhere we are, and it is everywhere we are not. As we move in space–time, we move through the potentiality of consciousness." The author also briefly mentions the string theory and the six or seven hidden dimensions in addition to the four we know.'

'Benedict, there is another recent book of collected articles[5] which contains an explanation of our evolution and interaction in terms of a cell-centric view. According to this, each cell is an individual entity, preserving itself and living in a community of other cells. This way of looking at evolution moves it away from being a highly self-oriented process to one that is more involved with its surroundings. This assessment shows that a cell-centric view is not necessarily a self-centric view, but also exhibits altruism and concern for others. Would you like to read about these ideas?'

'No, thanks, Francis. I am really up to my gills with the information and knowledge that your books have provided me. It is important I assimilate this before I embark on any other such readings.'

'That is fine. You can read other books later. For me, an important part of the effort was to make you see that there isn't such a dichotomy between science and spirituality. Without talking about God or the Divine in any form, science has shown more and more of the same kind of insights, which spiritual masters have talked about for ages. In addition to the views of the leading scientists, which you have just mentioned, it is worth noting that some other great scientists, whose works define the framework of extensions in scientific knowledge, also see such overlaps. These include, Heisenberg, who is well-known for the Heisenberg Uncertainty Principle, which provided a major advancement in quantum theory. He was not only aware of such parallel insights, but according to him, his own scientific work had been influenced, at least at the subconscious level, by Indian philosophy.[6] Likewise, Geoffrey Chew, a pioneer of the "bootstrap theory" that extended perspectives in physics, though not influenced by spirituality, was astonished to see the overlap of his work with Mahayana Buddhism.[7] You could read the book with these references later, when you have the time.'

'Thanks, Francis. You have perhaps forgotten that this was one of the books you lent to me. I have read it with interest and enjoyed it very much.'

'Apologies, I had forgotten that, Francis said sheepishly. Let us again go back to the book we were discussing, the book by the laser physicist. The author has also emphasised the importance of meditation and mentions some of the simple meditation techniques, especially at the end of the book. Did you read the two books I had given you on meditation techniques?' asked Francis.

'No, I did not. I do not want to go there yet. If I am able to do the meditation exercise you explained to me earlier, that itself would be an achievement.'

'Did you note that in addition to deep meditation, the author also mentions a very simple way, one he used initially to calm himself—by counting backwards from hundred to zero? That does not have any spiritual content, but it helped the author feel more calm and energised. Perhaps, when you are agitated, you could do something like that, starting from twenty, maybe?'

'I can try. Should I do anything else with this technique?'

'Yes. While you are counting backwards, try and see positively whether there is any possible justification or basis for whatever it is that is upsetting you. And try to do so with humility,' Francis instructed.

'I will try. Does not seem easy, but I will try,' Benedict promised.

'It gets easier with time. Benedict, since you have quoted some sentences from the book to explain your points, I want to bring one more sentence to your notice. Could you please pass the book to me? I have marked that passage,' Francis requested.

Benedict passed the book to Francis, who opened it at a page almost near the end and nodded as he found the part he wanted to read.

'Based on his interesting analysis, the author says that "there is compelling evidence, in the sciences of both matter and mind, of an abiding calm behind the storm, a coherence beneath the chaos." This idea is very important for us because it is possible for us to reach that calm beyond the chaos. His suggestion for meditation is precisely to achieve this calm. I am happy that you will try at least some form of meditation, which I discussed with you earlier. Let us now see which other books you would like to discuss.'

'Thank you, Francis. I am already feeling a bit better because I can see the potential for a positive change in me. I can see this because of the books and the light-based small exercise you taught me the other day.'

'Interesting! Please tell me more, based on the second book which you want to discuss.'

'This second book is the one written by two neuroscientists.[8] The book is very good for me because it shows how certain activities, which are not spiritual in nature can help our brain to grow. These include learning music, doing aerobics or even deeply thinking about work-related issues. It mentions evidence collected through scientific experiments and I feel better about accepting such evidence. The main points are that with spiritual exercises we can become calmer and develop additional capabilities, and that certain benefits which we get from meditation or prayers and other spiritual practices are not available through other activities. With spiritual meditation, our brain activity and capacity changes to enable us to be more peaceful and capable of more positive thoughts. My problem is that deep inside, I do not feel comfortable giving in to an idea which I have disparaged my entire adult life'

'Why do you say that, Benedict? The evidence on the effect of spiritual practices on development of the brain is also scientific evidence reported by the authors of this book. Why do you negate the value of that evidence, while comfortably accepting large extent of the evidence on non-spiritual activities?'

'I just cannot bring myself to accept it as easily. Doubts start coming into my mind and I feel I would be giving up a long-standing promise to myself,' Benedict admitted.

'Do you realise that such a view is unscientific, the opposite of the very standard which you want to apply for accepting something in your search?' Francis enquired.

'Yes, I do. And that makes me very uncomfortable. But I am only searching for consistency. I did not say that I have become consistent. This bothers me deeply but it also makes me realise that I am on a journey, moving towards a desired objective. I must recognise this gap and continue my efforts to move closer to my goals. That brings me to the other point emphasised by you—the exercise you taught me. I find that I am benefiting from it. I can already see my breathing becoming much slower when I do it, more relaxed. But my daily behaviour has not changed yet. Is this exercise something that can change the behaviour and sense of comfort in my daily interactions?'

'I am very impressed, Benedict. I can see you have made very rapid progress. You have realised that there is a desirable goal towards which you have to move, a goal that is sensible and logical. You have realised that at present you have some shortcomings that keep you away from the goal, but you want to work on them to achieve it. You have noticed the beneficial effects of a simple meditation exercise as well as the limited progress that you have made in addressing some fundamental concerns. You are curious to know whether this exercise by itself is enough to address these fundamental concerns or whether you would need some other supplementary actions. All these show that you have an open mind and a willingness to identify and achieve desirable targets. These are the necessary conditions for moving ahead towards your goals. This is very impressive,' Francis commented.

'Francis, please. You are not really addressing my question. I am grateful for your praise and also your guidance. Please help me move forward now with respect to the question I asked about the exercise you taught me.'

'Good. I think that you are asking me two questions, not one, about the meditation exercise. I will explain. Your evident question is whether the exercise would be enough to help you address your daily behavioural patterns and feelings. The other question, which I see hidden in our conversation, is whether this exercise can be the type of spiritual meditation which the book by the two neuroscientists talks about? Can this give you the spiritual results which they recommend without you actually conducting a spiritual exercise?'

'You are right. This is something I was hoping for, almost being surreptitiously Janus-faced,' Benedict agreed.

'I will address each question separately. First, whether this exercise would be sufficient on its own. A short answer is no, not in your time frame. What I mean is that if you continue this for some time, maybe several months, it can affect your capability to bring a fundamental change in your daily interactions. If you want to address your concerns more immediately, as you obviously would like to do, then you need to supplement this exercise with very specific efforts to control your emotions and see any event or action in an objective manner. The exercise will provide you with an improved capability to work with such supplementary effort every day. It is important to make continuous effort till it becomes second nature. As they say, life is a never-ending school. We have to keep learning and facing exams every day, irrespective of whether we are in a happy or sad situation. So, our effort should be to face every day with calmness and try and improve each day.'

'Easy to say but not so easy to do so when one is facing difficulties,' Benedict pointed out.

'Yes, it is always easy to say these things, but difficult to implement them. However, they are not impossible, not beyond our reach. You will see a number of persons who have made significant progress on this path. You yourself mentioned that I have managed to substantially achieve such a behaviour pattern. All of us, from time to time, have achieved an objective or detached state of mind and behaviour pattern. We have to make an effort to extend the period and frequency of such positive achievements. Today, you made a deep statement that you do clearly see a goal which you have not yet achieved but want to work towards. This is true with everything in life. So, walk the path. You have to progress, one step at a time. At the end of each day, spend some time to analyse how you can improve your performance, move closer towards your goal. Try and apply your insights in your future interactions. Try again, if it does not work. As you said, these are not easy objectives. Your meditation with light will help you to move towards your objective.'

'Can you not give me an indication of what I should focus on to judge whether or not I am moving ahead? I find it difficult to judge progress in this task.'

'You are discounting your abilities, Benedict,' Francis said. 'The first point that I want to emphasise is to not think in this way. Be positive. You mentioned today that you can see your breathing becoming slower and more peaceful when you do the exercise I taught you. That is awareness and an indication of progress. Similarly, there are other indications which become relevant when you bring them about through effort and awareness. You will find that slowly, you become more participative and sympathetic to others. This will be reflected in your interactions, showing greater open-mindedness for considering the viewpoint of another person and in your willingness to show appreciation. Further, you may be able to find some justification for another person's behaviour, which you may have criticised otherwise. Other indications could include your willingness to give up on your own view and enable yourself to compromise or correct a possible error that you may have made. Likewise, you may become more willing to value the presence and contributions of others and you may feel more peaceful in all interactions. These are all indicators of progress. As I said, they need a combination of your enhanced awareness and sustained effort. Progress is not continuous; it is more like an undulating path, like a roller coaster, but with a final upward slope so that you keep reaching higher levels over time. Of course, there are times of major lows. Just remember, you possess the resources to address any situation through your own effort, mindset and the time you make available for developing the appropriate mindset.'

'Let me write it down. What about the second part of my question?' Benedict asked.

'Please do not worry about writing it down. I will send my thoughts on this in an email to you. Maybe refine them a bit. On whether the light-based exercise can give you the same result as a spiritual meditation exercise, my answer is that of a typical economist: It depends.'

'What do you mean? Now you are making it complex for me, Francis.'

'I hope not, Benedict,' Francis said. 'What I mean is that the exercise will have a spiritual effect on you, if you have spiritual intent in it. It is a question of your frame of mind, which, in turn, can affect the specific type of progress you achieve when building certain parts of your brain to gain greater peace, calm and positive thoughts.'

'Now I am lost. You have to do better than that to make me understand.'

'Okay, let us consider the way you do the exercise at present. You close your eyes and visualise a soothing light within and around yourself. Very softly, put your attention in your heart and see this light strongly present there. This does not hold spiritual content for you as yet. You can easily combine this exercise with a spiritual idea.'

'That is what I do not feel comfortable doing,' Benedict protested 'Can you not give me another way of extending myself? I do not want to think of God, religion or spirituality. No mantra or Divine presence for me, please!'

'I did not say that you have to think of God, mantra or religion. I said that you can combine your present exercise with a spiritual idea.

This is the idea of energy being present all around us and all that we see is actually composed of energy. Interestingly, as you have seen from the first book we discussed, this is also an accepted scientific view. At a fundamental level, all this energy is the same. So, when you do your exercise, think of yourself and the light within and around you as energy, not just as extensions or parts of each other, but the same as each other. Think of the heart as the seat of this energy in your body and focus there. Visualise the soothing energy emanating from there within and around you. Continue to feel the peace and joy provided to you by this engulfing energy in the form of light. This is the spiritual idea you could add to your exercise.'

'How is this a spiritual idea? There is no God in it, or any other direct manifestation of some spiritual act.'

'That everything within and around us is the same energy is not just a scientific idea, it is a spiritual one as well. Spirituality does not end at this thought, but this view is an important part of spiritual insight,' Francis said.

Benedict was laughing, 'So, you mean to say that $E = mc^2$ is a spiritual concept?'

'Yes, it is. Of course, spiritual insight tends to go beyond this idea. Basically, I am emphasising that we do not need to see the Divine in any specific form. Whichever form we feel comfortable and positive with, we could see the Divine in that form. In this case, you would be effectively visualising an all-pervasive and soothing energy, which is one of the ways in which people visualise the Divine. But you need not think of it as the Divine, if you feel uncomfortable with that thought.'

'So, when I do this exercise, I should not think of a well-known picture of Einstein sticking his tongue out?' joked Benedict.

'No. Both the concept and the embodiment of the concept in your mind should remain at the level that I have mentioned to you. No pictures, no words, no formulae—just light. This exercise should give you an additional sense of energy and peace. Be relaxed while doing this. Please do not focus hard to be in your heart. Do not feel disappointment if your mind wavers because that is normal. Just softly go back to the light in your heart and enjoy that sensation. Do not hold yourself back, have your pleasure, as you feel the seamlessness of the light within and around you.'

'This does not seem difficult. I think I can do this,' Benedict said.

'Should we discuss the other books now?' Francis enquired.

'I do not want to discuss many of these books in detail. I need more time to absorb them. I also would not like to discuss the books written by psychologists on past-life regression. I find even my present concerns difficult to handle.'

'Benedict, these past-life regressions which you mention are actually a form of therapy. It is possible that this method may make it easier to forget, forgive or adopt a more positive attitude.'

'Have you had any such sessions?'

'Not with a psychologist, but with a friend who did past-life regression. I have experienced it only once, during a holiday in the South of France. I did not feel like doing it again. But I am not closed to the idea.'

'How was your experience?'

'It was surreal, yet, very satisfying to me. I saw myself in very interesting circumstances, living most unexpected life.'

Benedict was shaking his head vigorously; in fact, most of his body followed the movement of his head, indicating deep disagreement. His words, however, were much softer. 'At present, I think I am not ready for it. Maybe later. Perhaps we could go together to some good regression therapist. But I want to keep my efforts simple right now.'

'That is reasonable,' Francis commented, 'and you should follow your heart in this. Now, tell me some points from the books you do want to discuss today.'

'I want to take up a couple of books which help achieve progress through a wider perspective than we normally have in our material life. I will share with you some key points from a book[9] that was extremely interesting. I still have some doubts and concerns, but I have also benefited from the book. I have tried to organise different points under certain broad categories.'

Saying this, Benedict picked up a paper and started reading from it, 'The important points from this book include:

- Have self-discipline, self-responsibility; use your untapped willpower to wage war on weaker thoughts to eliminate them; have a deep sense of faith in your abilities and an indomitable spirit; reduce your needs; do not seek ever-higher and elusive goals.
- Value time, focus on current tasks, direct your life to live in the present time period and you will have boundless energy; prioritise your activities, concentrate on your life's main aims, focus on high-impact activities.
- Focus on yourself because we can love others only after mastering the art of loving ourselves; aim to improve yourself; small victories lead to larger victories; visualise whatever you want and you will achieve it; meditate on "I am more than I appear to be, all the world's strength and power rest inside me"; identify things that hold you back and address them.
- Devote yourself to the service of others and your own life would be improved; practice acts of kindness daily.
- Be positive, concentrate on being cheerful, energetic and happy; notice beauty in the most ordinary things in life; do not think negative thoughts; concentrate on positive things in your life and learn from failure or negative experiences.
- Enjoy the process of self-expansion; experience events instead of judging them; do not focus only on the result; happiness is

a journey and not a destination; each day is the first day of the rest of your life; start on any objective in a small way; even a long journey begins with a single step.

- Practice the art of gratitude.
- Keep working on the never-ending enrichment of mind, body and soul; embody principles of industry, compassion, humility, patience, honesty and courage; do the things you fear; the only limits in your life are those that you set yourself; participate actively in family activities and give them love; make and maintain good friendships.
- Have daily important rituals: A mandatory period of peace, vigorous exercise and deep and effective breathing—belly moving up and down; eat vegetarian food; read regularly for good and substantive knowledge and apply that knowledge to life; reflect on how to improve your actions and thoughts; wake up at sunrise; get energy from the sun and nature; ten minutes after waking up and ten minutes before sleeping, think only the most invigorating thoughts; plan your day every morning; laugh frequently; treat every day as if it is your last; listen to soft music; talk to yourself with positive and encouraging messages—they are like mantras, which energise and free your mind.
- Techniques to use:
    - Meditate: Focus on and examine the rose from its heart outwards. Do not get perturbed with extraneous thoughts. Just go back to your meditation without any concern for these disturbances.
    - Visualise your goals and take the time to write them down in a journal you should create for yourself; review that journal daily; put positive pressure on yourself to achieve the objectives within a specific time-period.

- Associate pleasure with good habits and punishment with bad ones.
- Practice your desired action for at least twenty-one days to inculcate it as a habit.

'Benedict, this is quite a list, a very rich one to work on! I am not surprised because this is a book with many substantive and deep thoughts,' said Francis, as he extended his hand to take the list from Benedict.

'You are right,' said Benedict. 'And this list has only those points which I am emphasising. Someone else may consider other points. My concern is that this is a very long list. Too many things to do. I do not know how to make this manageable, how to organise it better for my purpose.'

'Benedict, you are unduly worried about this aspect. I think you have already done a good job of organising the various points in certain broad categories, which can be your starting point and your initial focus. Within each of these categories, you have other points which provide further direction. In a sense, you have already classified them within a conceptual framework we have come across earlier,' Francis said.

'Which one do you mean?'

'Small steps and concentric circles. Your broad categories are like the concentric circles and within these circles, the detailed points are similar to concentrically arranged issues within different sub-circles. You could organise the different points or objectives according to their relative levels of difficulty, with the easiest one in the innermost circle.'

'But what about the fact that we may wish to focus on them simultaneously?' Benedict asked.

'Organising the objectives in terms of levels of difficulty does not mean that you address objectives sequentially according to the levels of difficulty. Your efforts could span across all the circles at the same time. However, you may be able to achieve the easier objectives earlier than others, and for that reason it may be worthwhile to give it some priority.'

'Will I be able to have such a wide focus for my efforts? Will my efforts not get diffused?'

'The important point is to make an effort. Even your summary says that you should begin with a step in a small way. So you could begin with some small steps for each major category of objectives. You may achieve them with different levels of success.'

'But all these objectives appear to be major ones, like being able to control one's mind and be positive all the time. That is a very tall order for an ordinary person like me.'

'Yes, but if you consider your list in some detail, you will see that the detailed items under any broad category in your list are like sub-objectives within an individual concentric circle covering a primary objective. So keep taking small steps to cover your journey across any collection of such sub-objectives.'

'But is controlling the mind not something of a fable, like a fairy tale, something unreal? Is it possible to achieve this in our material world?'

Francis thought for a few minutes on how best to address this point because the answer he had in mind could irk Benedict, sensitive as he was about adopting any spiritual practice.

'Benedict, this may appear to be an impossible task because you are not recognising the innumerable examples of people being able to better control their mind. You are a highly trained economist who has studied at an elite university. You had to train your mind a lot to reach the levels of competence that you possess. Look at our boss. He is a superb technocrat, very focused, well-organised and solution-oriented. He is clear about his objectives and does not waste any time with issues that do not make a meaningful contribution to his objectives. That is a training of the mind to a very high degree, a control over the way the mind functions. These are all examples of the possibility of controlling the mind. Many items in your list provide you with some directions on how you could control the mind. Just choose what you feel most comfortable with and begin your efforts.'

'This does not convince me. I feel I cannot do it,' Benedict declared.

Francis paused, as if reaching some inner agreement with himself. 'Benedict. I just gave you instances of how we commonly train the mind to build capabilities. In the context of our conversation, the content and orientation of our trained minds are more relevant than merely developing skills, discipline or training the mind. That is where positive thinking comes in.'

'But positive thinking is not the same as control of the mind, is it?'

'It is an important part of it, to the extent we use it to orient the mind in a particular direction. Benedict, this is a basic thrust of spiritual endeavour.'

'Are you saying that in a spiritual context, controlling the mind is easy and straightforward?'

'No, it is not easy, but it is possible and has been done by a large number of people. The important point is not to give up on your efforts, and over time you will see the results.'

'Why do we keep talking about consistent efforts?'

'Because that is what we need for progress. I will give you an interesting example from an Indian book on the need and efficacy of consistent efforts to control the mind. It may help make this concept more tangible. The mind is like an unbridled wild horse and the process of controlling the mind is similar to taming this horse. Initially, when you try to control this horse, you are thrown off. If you give up, the horse remains wild and you do not have any control over it. Every time the horse throws you off, you should try to get back on it. If you are consistent with your efforts, then this process would continue till you are able to tame and control the horse. That is when you are able to ride the horse with full control and the horse moves according to your desires. In the same way, one has to keep trying, again and again, to tame and control the mind, getting rid of the "wild" characteristics.'

'So you are telling me that with effort and time, I will be able to control my mind better and orient it in any direction that I focus on.'

'Absolutely correct. These changes need time and commitment.' Francis nodded.

'So if I manage to control my mind, is it possible over time for me to always stay positive and not think any negative thoughts? Will I be able to be happy all the time after this achievement?' Benedict asked eagerly.

'If we are able to control our mind, we will be able to achieve several of the objectives in the list prepared by you. However, the kind of control required to stay positive and happy and not to have negative thoughts is not really linked to the mind. Its cause is much deeper, linked to our ego and our desire. Till we manage to distance ourselves from our pride and the sense of seeking greater achievement in comparison to others, we will not be able to limit negative thoughts or be positive.

'You can see examples of this in exceptionally successful persons, who have achieved a high level of control over their minds, but are still not content or happy. A narrow self-oriented focus keeps us within a constricted circle of ego. This limits the growth of a multidimensional positive attitude, which is so essential to remain happy in any situation. Two necessary conditions for finding sustained happiness are not being arrogant and being good to others. Staying peacefully within your heart, in touch with your energies, will help.'

'How do I be good to others when I am focused most of the time on my own work?' Benedict enquired.

'It is in the way you interact with others. Be open-minded about their views and considerate to their concerns. In any interaction, listen carefully to what others are saying and try to see whether you could get some useful points from their views. If there is a difference of opinion, consider the extent to which a reasonable solution may be possible that takes account of different concerns. Wherever possible, make efforts to meet the objectives of others rather than emphasising your own importance. In essence, this requires building an expanded sense of civic responsibilities and developing at least a weak form of philanthropy.'

'So how should I take the components of the list that I have prepared? How do I combine them? I am not clear on how to work with these different elements, Francis.'

'Benedict, actually I think you know it very well. The list you have prepared already shows that you are highly competent in meeting these objectives. Whatever you think is relevant, based on our discussions, books and your own analysis can be considered in terms of three categories of focus.

'First is the overall approach, that is, to consider issues at the most aggregated level, identifying their essential broad thrust. For instance, in your list, this would include being positive and taking small steps towards your objectives. This helps to orient your efforts and helps give them better focus.

'At the second level, consider the main categories of objectives within the approach, such as the categories and subcategories in your list.

'These two aspects—the approach and objectives in terms of conceptual issues—provide us with the elements of different concentric circles. Traversing across these concentric circles with small steps is aided by techniques which help you achieve your objectives. I have explained a form of simple meditation as one such technique. This is the third part of our conceptualisation. Once you address the various points in this way, the path ahead will appear less complicated.'

Benedict was nodding slightly, lost in thought, 'Thank you, Francis. I had prepared a list of queries and points for clarification, writing them down for easy reference. You have already covered some of them, but a few remain.' Saying this, Benedict handed a piece of paper to Francis to read.

'This is quite a list, Benedict. Should we have our lunch and then address your queries? I have made some soup and sandwiches with some green salad.'

'Thanks, Francis. We could do that. I am sorry that I got carried away and did not realise how much time had passed.'

'No problem. I am enjoying it, but it will be good to have some nourishment. Timely food is very important for remaining focused. I will put on some soothing music and lay the table. What will you drink with the food? I am having some red wine.'

'I will have the same,' said Benedict getting up. 'I will help you lay the table.'

References

1. Bhaumik, Mani. *Code Name God*. India: Penguin Books, 2005.
2. Ibid, p 136.
3. Gleiser, Marcelo. *A Tear At The Edge Of Creation: A Radical New Vision For Life In An Imperfect Universe*. USA: Free Press, 2010.
4. Ibid, p 171.
5. Davies, Paul and Gregersen, Niels Henrik (eds.). *Information and the Nature of Reality: From Physics to Metaphysics*. UK: Cambridge University Press, 2010.
6. Capra, Fritjof. *Uncommon Wisdom: Conversations with Remarkable People*. UK: Flamingo, 1989, p 43.
7. Ibid, p 55.
8. Newberg, Andrew and Waldman, Mark Robert. *How God Changes Your Brain*. USA: Ballantine Books Trade Paperbacks, 2009.
9. Sharma, Robin S. *The Monk Who Sold His Ferrari*. India: Jaico Publishing House, 2003.

12

Addressing Benedict's Queries

After finishing lunch, Benedict and Francis cleared the dishes and Francis made some strong coffee. Carrying two cups of coffee, Francis came back to the living room, followed by Benedict. They made themselves comfortable and Francis picked up the list of queries prepared by Benedict and read them out slowly:

- These tasks are very time consuming.
- How do I focus on myself and at the same time strive to improve the lives of others?
- What is the importance of physical exercises and of breathing strongly in a manner that the belly moves out every time we inhale? How is this important for my happiness?
- How feasible is it to visualise what I want and then be able to get it because I have visualised it? How useful is the concept of mantra that is mentioned in this book?
- If we emphasise on the objective of fulfilling all our dreams, is that not inconsistent with the objective of reducing our needs and not running after ever-higher and elusive goals?

- If I focus on an objective and a dream, how do I enjoy the process and not worry about the final objective?
- How should we address failure in the process of meditation or combat the negative thoughts entering our mind? Is punishing ourselves the correct way of dealing with negative thoughts? What about the statement of the mystic Krishnamurthy, who said, 'Therefore, to free oneself from desire cannot be achieved by suppressing or avoiding sensory experience—the way of the ascetics. The only way to be free from desire is to be free from thought.'[1]

Francis nodded as he finished reading the list, 'We have already discussed that significant consistent effort will be needed to achieve our objectives. That is true of whatever we do in life. There is no reason why we should expect anything different for such a major endeavour, when one is attempting to fundamentally change oneself and become a deeper and more effective person. The conflict you see in different instances would get resolved if you consider each situation within a spiritual frame of mind.'

'What do you mean by this? Do you want to bring God into this? Should we start being pious and reverential? This seems very strange to me.'

'Benedict, you are caricaturing spirituality. Perhaps I should explain spirituality further to you. I hope you will not mind and accept my views in the spirit of a friendly exchange of thoughts. I want you to know certain perspectives that have helped me.'

'Francis, I value the time and effort you are investing in me and feel grateful. I apologise if I was facetious. Please tell me what you have in mind.'

'Thanks. Spirituality is embodied in limiting the arrogant and self-obsessive effect of our ego. It is being open to others and sharing their concerns. This easily translates into being patient, being willing to listen to the views of another person, giving due consideration to it, having a balanced view based on these factors and being positive about different events in life. It is interesting that you do not question the importance of being positive. I see this as your implicit agreement; you realise how fundamental it is to your objectives.'

'You are correct,' Benedict said. 'I realise the importance of being positive for my peace of mind. Only problem is that I find it difficult to be consistently positive in every situation. Also, please explain how these spiritual concepts can help me resolve other conflicting points too.'

'Okay, first, there is the concern that all these changes take time. I have broadly responded to this point. To take that discussion forward, though we take time to reach our goals, we will see that with consistent efforts there will be small signs of progressive achievements. Take for example, the experience you have had with the meditation exercise that I taught you. You have already seen signs of progress, which you should relish. Be patient with the process and enjoy each sign of progress. Take any book on improving yourself and you will find this message there. It is an abiding message.'

'That is a good point. What else should I do to achieve these important objectives?' Benedict asked.

'At the cost of harping too much on a simple concept,' Francis said patiently, 'my answer to this again is small steps and concentric circles. Actually, I have been fascinated with this concept after a discussion with my friend Ananda and I have been interpreting it and working on it. Break down the larger objective in terms of these smaller milestones of sub-objectives. And till you achieve the next higher level of progress, enjoy the one you have already reached. In some time, maybe a month, maybe six months, you will start enjoying the process itself rather than hankering after whether or not you have achieved specific objectives. If you are able to adopt such a mentality with all your tasks, then you will be able to enjoy the process and relish each point of personal growth. In this way, you will also resolve another concern that is encompassed in "if I focus on an objective and a dream, how do I enjoy the process and not worry about the final objective?"

'Now consider a situation where we are able to develop by being considerate towards others. Incorporate it as an important part of your objectives. This is a spiritual mindset in which our own objectives do not remain limited to a narrow focus that excludes others. Instead, we focus on ourselves, and at the same time, strive to improve the lives of others. In this process, our joy, our happiness would depend on an augmented objective with a combined and balanced consideration of the desires of people important to us. This expanded perspective helps us deal with another concern of yours that the focus seems to be only on oneself, without accounting for other persons in our lives. In life, one has to make compromises based on the concerns of family members and the work environment.

'In fact, such an act of balancing one's own and others' objectives helps us make progressive changes in our emphasis. Our self-worth will, thus, increasingly be defined in terms of what we can contribute to others, rather than in terms of how we compete with others. This is a spiritual transformation of our focus. Try it and you will see for yourself that our basis of self-evaluation changes as we become more spiritually oriented and balanced. With these changes, we will start comparing our own progress in terms of these criteria rather than whether we are better than others in performing our tasks. In fact, by definition, if we start comparing ourselves with others, it would be an indication of moving away from a spiritual mindset.'

'Please explain this a bit more, Francis,' Benedict said. 'I am still not able to get a hold on these concepts. I find it difficult to visualise this change.'

'Okay,' Francis said encouragingly. 'Let us take these ideas in their sequential substantive stages. As we enhance our spiritual attributes, we develop concern and sensitivity for others, and hence, incorporate and balance them within our own concerns. This alters our perspective on life, making it more widely grounded. It also develops within us a tendency to more easily make efforts to benefit others. As we are fulfilled by these acts, we will generate within our heart greater stability, sense of peace and satisfaction. Our connectivity with others will make our presence larger than ourselves. All this helps develop a greater sense of security, substance and self-worth within us.

'Moreover, as we are less self-indulgent, we are in a position to see situations with greater objectivity. If we take all these into account, the apparent conflict within some of your other concerns will get resolved, such as in "if we emphasise the objective of fulfilling our dreams, is that not inconsistent with reducing our needs and not running after ever-higher and elusive goals?"'

'Francis, you are asking for a fundamental change in an individual perspective, aren't you?' Benedict enquired.

'A change in perspective, yes,' Francis agreed, 'but in a sense that it is not as fundamental a change as you think because the basis or the seed of such behaviour is already within us. Even now, we normally live our lives taking into account the desires and sensitivities of our near and dear ones and of those who work closely with us. This is because we live within systems, within a framework of emotions and relationships. By adopting a spiritual attitude, we are only going to develop such symbiotic and considerate interactions to a much higher level and be able to assess the trade-offs among conflicting positions in a more balanced way. The spiritual attitude makes us give greater weightage to the aspirations of others, but also helps us become more objective and clear in terms of making a choice among our key objectives. This would ensure greater peace of mind with our decisions. In rudimentary terms, a spiritual attitude gives us a highly mature way of looking at issues and an ability to develop sensitivities about interdependent and interconnected relationships. It builds our willingness to work for the benefit of others.'

'I think I will have to take your word for it, Francis. There seems to be some basis for what you are saying and I guess there is also empirical evidence. Even with the meditation exercise you have taught me, I can see some difference in myself, albeit small and sporadic. However, another thought I have is: Should we pitch our objectives to a low level? And if we do so, then what is the importance of the view that if we visualise whatever we want, we can obtain it with the power of our mind?'

'The main purpose of all these efforts and discussions is to assist you to increase your effectiveness in life, living life more fully. The spiritual part is essential for that. The concern you have just raised could be resolved if our efforts have a specific directed focus that involves going beyond the preconceived limits that we set on our abilities. Approaching this with a positive attitude actually encourages us to have no fear of failure and to reach out for greater achievements in our chosen objective, by extending our normal reach. Thus, we must view our ability and reality to be larger than we may otherwise think, so that we can reach increasingly higher levels of objectives through a series of steps, small steps covering concentric circles.'

'So the aim should be to constantly try and excel, extend our capacities to achieve ever more of an effective lifestyle and balanced objectives, while being practical and realistic. That is quite a package,' Benedict commented.

'That is very well put, Benedict. Very succinct, substantive and to the point. With effort, it can be done. We keep doing this in several ways, every day, when we learn something new. Only when we try, will we know what is needed to achieve specific objectives,' Francis said.

'Thanks Francis, I will keep this in mind. What about my other queries?'

'Which one should I address first?'

'How about the importance of physical exercise and strong breathing, such that the belly moves out every time we inhale?'

'Physical exercise is important to keep you healthy, vibrant and more focused. Physical exercise could range from walking to swimming to martial arts to aerobics. If you remember the main results in the book by the neuroscientists which we discussed earlier, you will recall that aerobics is the third best way to exercise your brain.[2] So, exercise is required not only for keeping our body fit for achieving other objectives, including spiritual ones, it also improves the functioning of our brain.

'Benedict, do you recall what is the best technique for expanding our brain capacity according to these neuroscientists? It is faith. Yes, faith.[3] That is interesting, isn't it? Well, faith develops when you start seeing incremental results of spiritual and other effectiveness exercises. This brings me to my other point. You would have heard about yoga as a form of physical exercise. Do you know that the system of yoga has at least three components? One is breathing exercises. Second, certain physical exercises, the ones we normally identify with yoga in the West. Third, the deeply spiritual exercises which include meditation but go way beyond that into deeper practices to achieve physical, mental and metaphysical goals. Thus, in this scheme of achieving higher goals, both breathing and physical exercise have an important role, showing their importance as an integral part of the activities which help us to go beyond our perceived capabilities.'

'Is there some yoga physical exercise you could recommend, any single one which would be very useful?' Benedict asked.

'Benedict, this is precisely the question I had asked Ananda and he suggested a yoga exercise which I find very useful,' Francis said. 'It is called "*Surya Namaskar*" or "salutation to the sun". It is best to do it as soon as you wake up. Since it is a salutation to the sun, the best time would be early morning, which means you should adopt the practice of waking up early. You can easily find its description on the web, but it is always good to do it with someone who knows it or alternatively by following some good illustrations of the exercise. It has twelve different steps, which exercise most parts of the body. An interesting aspect of yoga exercises is that there is a specific pattern of breathing, inhaling and exhaling, corresponding with each step of the yoga exercise. You can get this pattern easily, if you speak to some yoga instructor or even look up the web.'

'Thanks, Francis. I will really appreciate the web link. I will also look it up at other sites, but getting a link with animated guidance would be very useful.'

'Okay, give me a minute,' saying this, Francis went to his desk, opened an old diary and brought it to Benedict. 'I will give you the web link with animation.[4] I really like the animations because they bring out the child in me. Of course, the important thing in any exercise is that you should not strain yourself while doing it, so whatever may be the instructions, please make sure you do not cross the point beyond which you feel discomfort. Further, if you have any special medical condition, then please check with your doctor before starting the exercise.'

'Thanks, this seems useful, Benedict commented. 'I do not have any special medical condition, so I will be able to do the exercise easily. Can you now explain to me the importance of breathing with the belly moving out every time we inhale?'

'Yes, Benedict. I am a little amused by this question. You have picked up a peculiar and interesting point in the book. Expanding the belly when you inhale is a form of yogic breathing. It results in deep breathing, which helps to fill the lungs more fully than normal breathing. This type of breathing also helps relieve tension.'

'You said that breathing exercises are a separate part of yoga. Any suggestions on that?'

'In yoga, breathing exercises are collectively called *pranayam*, which means control of breath or control of our essential energy. *Prana* is a term for the life within us. It also means the smallest unit of energy. Seen this way, *pranayam* implies control of the smallest unit of energy of life within us. Instead of going into details, I will mention some simple principles which aim at increasing the flexibility and capacity of our breathing system.'

'Please do that. I like simple principles,' Benedict requested sheepishly.

'Benedict, do you know that at any given time we breathe from only one nostril,' Francis asked. 'An important part of *pranayam* exercises is to activate both nostrils by alternatively breathing through each of them in a structured way. This practice is called *anulom-vilom*. The idea is that you inhale from one nostril, keeping the other closed while you do so. Exhale from the other nostril, keeping the first one closed. An additional intermediate step can be to retain the breath for some time within yourself, keeping both nostrils closed, before you exhale. You can use your thumb and a finger of either hand for closing the nostrils while you perform these different steps of *anulom-vilom*. This exercise could help with several medical problems, including improving blood circulation, relieving stress, controlling blood pressure and some others.'

'You said that there is a pattern for doing this exercise. What do you mean by that?'

'The three steps of inhalation, retention and exhalation can be done by timing them in different ratios. Take any unit of time for which you inhale. You could retain the air within yourself for the same time or a multiple of that time, say double or triple of that time. When you exhale, it could again be over the same time period as for inhalation, or a multiple of that time period. This is what I mean by structured breathing. It helps to calm you down and gives you a sense of stability and greater focus. You need not do it for long, and you could do it several times during the day, even when you are working.'

'Fantastic. I will definitely do so. I will also look up *anulom-vilom* on the net. Thank you, Francis,' Benedict said.

Francis was smiling to see Benedict happy. 'It is a pleasure, Benedict. Let us now consider your concern about visualisation and the use of specific words or mantras to motivate yourself. Visualisation and sounds are both very powerful techniques, which we can use to spur ourselves and link up with our other energies. Visualisation is a useful mechanism which gives form to our aspirations. It is a technique used in multiple areas including science, archaeology, history, architecture, psychology and spiritual pursuits. Visualisation is a part of certain simple meditation techniques as well as the deep, metaphysical meditative exercises practised in different parts of the world. Even the light-based meditation that I have taught you involves visualisation. Examples of visualisation in meditation being practised in different parts of the world can be seen in a number of books.[5]

'What do you mean by deep metaphysical meditative exercises? Do you mean when we have deep self-immersion during meditation?'

'No. That is deep meditation. I am talking about deep metaphysical meditation which sometimes involves very formal or even secret meditation practices.'

'Francis, that is way beyond my understanding or scope. You did not provide any books on these, did you?'

'No, I did not because you are averse to most spiritual activities. So I introduced you very gently to this world. I can, however, give you some references if you want.'

'I might like to read some books to see how outlandish these activities could be. Okay, jokes aside, can you give me some references in case I do want to know more about this at a later date?' Benedict asked sceptically.

Francis was smiling. He could see that Benedict was moving from his initial position of being allergic to spiritual matters. The books and discussion had obviously some impact on him. 'Let me write down the names of some authors for you,' he said. 'I would be happy to lend you these books whenever you want them. There is, for instance, a book which talks about a whole range of deep meditative practices.[6] If you want to read about any specific deep metaphysical meditation practice, you have a choice among various examples.'

'Just give me two such examples, Francis.'

'Okay. You could see a book by an exponent of an Indian school of yoga[7] and another book on the specific practices of a special school of Buddhism, the practice of Vajrayana.'[8]

'In case I change my mind on these matters and want to get into deeper practices, can I read these books and start practising whichever deep meditation practice appeals to me?'

'No. Please do not do so, Benedict. These practices should be done only under the expert guidance of an elevated spiritual guide. If ever you do feel like walking this path, I could introduce you to a very powerful presence not far from us. But not before you want to practice this meditation on a regular basis.'

'But I can use the technique of visualisation without such guidance?'

'Yes. Visualisation is a useful technique to be used with a positive mindset. Of course, it does not guarantee progress because that depends on the various linked efforts which we have already discussed. All these efforts help one to walk the path step by step. You could continue to do the meditation exercises based on visualisation of light as energy that I told you about.'

'I intend to keep doing that meditation. What about mantras or repeating encouragement to ourselves? Is that going to be powerful enough method so as to remove all our obstacles? What about the self-encouraging statement mentioned in the book, which we should keep repeating to ourselves?' Benedict asked eagerly.

'Self-encouraging statements, such as those used by tennis players are good to stimulate and focus our minds. However, they are not mantras as such. Mantras are spiritual energies embodied in the form of sound or thought. Their vibrations are such that they link up with the larger and more substantive energy forms within ourselves. They may or may not have specific meaning because the essence of a mantra is its energy and not its meaning. In fact, several mantras cannot be deciphered at all. Examples include the seed mantras, called *beej* mantras, which are mostly monosyllabic sounds, though in some cases may have two syllables.'

'What do you mean by seed mantras, or that the mantras do not having any meaning? This seems strange.'

'Well. You can see some examples of mantras without any apparent meaning in the books on deep meditation, which I just mentioned to you.' Francis said.

'They may not have any meaning? Can I read about this? The important part is their sound energy, is it?'

'You could read various books, including the ones I mentioned. As far as the kind of energy in mantras is concerned, it is both sound and thought energy. Chanting or *japa* of mantras can be done in four different ways. One is the loud pronunciation, which you have read about. This is *vachik* or *vaikhari japa,* and here sound energy embodies the mantra. Second is soundless chanting, with only your lips moving. This is *upamsu japa,* where thought energy becomes the embodiment of the mantra, keeping this activity to ourselves. Third, and most private is when you chant it in your mind or your heart. This is *mansika japa,* where the mantra is embodied in deep thought energy. *Japa* of mantras can also be done by writing it down repeatedly. This is *Likhita japa,* which again involves concentration and mental energies.'

'So a mantra is very useful because of its special energy form? How do you know so much about these things, Francis?'

'I know about these topics because of long discussions with Ananda, who both explained them to me and referred me to some interesting books. And I have my mantra too, given to me by my spiritual guide.

An important point is that similar to deep meditation, mantras, too, should be obtained from a spiritual guide. It is good to rely on this process because the guide chooses the mantra appropriate for the person.'

'So I should wait for a spiritual guide to get a mantra?' Benedict enquired.

'Yes, that is correct, at least according to tradition and for a deeper understanding of these matters. So feel free to chant the messages encouraging yourself, but for mantras, please wait for a spiritual guide,' Francis replied.

'What about my last two questions, those pertaining to negative thoughts? The first one was about inconsistent approaches to dealing with failure and the second one was about the correct way of dealing with negative thoughts.'

'When negative thoughts come to us, we should not pay much attention to them and try to slowly go back to our positive way of doing things. If we dissuade ourselves through punishment, we will only suppress these thoughts within ourselves rather than traverse beyond them. Therefore, I agree with Krishnamurthy over the fact that suppression is not the answer to the problem. We have to face the problem but not be perturbed by it. We have to slowly, gently go back to our efforts to improve ourselves. This is the best way.'

'Will we be able to get rid of our negative thoughts this way?'

'Over time, they will become less and less, but they never fully go away till we reach most highly elevated spiritual state. In fact, even the process of evolution through meditation gives rise to negative thoughts.'

'I do not understand what you mean by that, Francis.'

'I think the best way to explain this is to read from the work of an expert. Benedict, you remember the book I gave you which contains a conversation between a father and son, where the father was a philosopher and the son who left a potentially brilliant scientific career to become a monk?'

'Yes, I remember the book and want to discuss it with you later.'

'The son, the monk, has written on meditation and explained nine methods for cultivating attention. Let me get the book for you and read from it.' Saying this, Francis went to his bookshelf and returned with a small book.

'Benedict, in the seventh such method for cultivating attention, he says, and I quote:

> Pacify your mind completely by using sustained and energetic attention to abandon all attachment to meditative experiences that may arise. These experiences can appear in a number of forms, such as bliss, clarity or absence of discursive thoughts. They can also take the form of spontaneous bursts of joy, of unshakable confidence, fear, exaltation, discouragement, certainty or doubt, renunciation of worldly concerns, passion, intense devotion or negative views. Any of the experiences can arise for no apparent reason. They are signs of profound changes going on in your mind. It is necessary to keep yourself from identifying with these experiences, and from attributing more importance to them than you would to the landscapes going by outside the train window. Perfectly pacified attention will cause these experiences to fade away without upsetting your mind. You will then know profound inner peace.[9]

'This sounds impressive, but what do you mean by it?'

'Negative thoughts keep coming to us. They do so for no apparent reason, even for those who have practised meditation for a long time, irrespective of whether or not we have progressed much in our meditative practices. These negative thoughts are diversions in our path. They are like efforts by some larger force of nature to hook us on to a thought process and put us on a path completely different from the one we seek. The more we give our attention to them, the more we deviate from the positive path. The more we focus on our main activity of meditation, the more we will find peace and inner strength to take objective decisions. Over time, you could become like a person who is observing your own actions dispassionately, evaluating their content and impact.'

'I can take the word of this monk, which you have just quoted to me. But do you have any other good examples of such a view?'

'Yes, I do. This has been the experience of Ananda too. Also, Benedict, I am saying this on the basis of my own experience. I read this passage to you because it beautifully expresses, in such wonderful prose, my own experience.'

Benedict looked completely taken aback. He knew that Francis was different and he had himself said it so many times. But somehow he had not realised the depth of progress achieved by Francis. Suddenly, as it became apparent to him, he was quiet as if he had suddenly found himself in the company of a stranger.

Francis guessed Benedict's thoughts and said lightly, 'Benedict, let us have some wine.' He got up to get two glasses of wine, patting Benedict on his back before leaving the room.

References

1. Capra, Fritjof. *Uncommon Wisdom: Conversations with Remarkable People*. UK: Flamingo, 1989, p 29.
2. Newberg, Andrew and Waldman, Mark Robert. *How God Changes Your Brain*. USA: Ballantine Books Trade Paperbacks, 2010, pp 160-162.
3. Ibid, pp163-165.
4. http://www.abc-of-yoga.com/yogapractice/sunsalutation.asp
5. For example, Crowley, Brian and Crowley, Esther. *Words of Power. Mantras and Chants from East & West*. UK: Jaico Publishing House, 2008.
6. Bodri, William and Shu-Mei, Lee. *Twenty-Five Doors to Meditation: A Handbook For Entering Samadhi*. USA: Samuel Weiser Inc., 1998.
7. Saraswati, Swami Satyananda. *Sure Ways to Self-Realization*. India: Yoga Publication Trust, 1980.
8. Gyatso, Geshe Kelsang. *Essence of Vajrayana*. UK: Tharpa Publications, 2003.
9. Ricard, Matthieu. *The Art of Meditation*. UK: Atlantic Books, 2010, pp 101-102.

13

Discussion with Vadya

Ananda woke up very early. Talking to Vadya always helped him clarify things he didn't understand, but she was sound asleep. The normal time for everyone to be awake was still at least an hour away. Ananda waited anxiously for Vadya to wake up.

He was surprised to hear a murmur and looked at Vadya who was whispering with her eyes closed, 'It is still not time to get up, is it? You will get very tired if you do not get enough sleep. It is not good for your health. No use taking blood pressure medicine and then not sleeping enough. Please get some sleep now.' However, she herself got up and sat against her pillows in the bed and said, 'You obviously have something important to discuss. I can feel your anxiety. What is it Ananda? Is everything okay?'

'Yes. Everything is okay. More than 'kay', as we say in our village,' said Ananda. 'The past few days have given me a number of different insights. I always find discussing with you most useful because it clarifies things in my mind and you raise pertinent questions, which help me focus on the key issues. So do you feel like listening to me now or should I wait till you are more rested? Would you like to sleep some more?'

'I am fine. After living with you for so long, I can manage to give you considered responses even in my sleep. So go on,' said Vadya as she rubbed her eyes a bit and sipped some water from the bedside table.

Ananda was visibly pleased with this indulgence, 'Thanks Vadya. You know my learning, my happiness, my existence itself derives from our great spiritual master. I see his hand everywhere, including in providing me my spiritual guide.'

'I know, Ananda. Please remember that he was my spiritual guide too. Tell me, what is making you so happy that you find it difficult to sleep?'

'I can see an emerging framework to help move forward in the material world while progressing on a spiritual path. It came to me in my discussion with Francis and I have been building upon it. My main point is that one should take small steps and move ahead in concentric circles of different objectives we need to achieve. Would you like to hear about it?'

Vadya was smiling at him and Ananda was already getting a bit concerned. 'Why do you smile, Vadya?' he asked with some foreboding that he would have to go back to his drawing board.

'Small steps and concentric circles. I just got a feeling that every homemaker is doing this every day. I find this amusing. I am not trying to belittle your effort, Ananda. Please tell me more. I would like to know the details.'

Ananda was relieved. 'I have tried to interpret the requirements for managing spiritual progress together with our daily routine. Let me first explain the main points and then we could discuss them further.

'We begin with the usual spiritual messages—that we should be less egotistical and more compassionate towards others. These include the ever-present important points about loving everyone, loving one's neighbour as oneself, that our ego is the dominant factor in our existence and that we need to control it in order to progress on the spiritual path.

'What are my thoughts about these, you may ask?' continued Ananda, looking expectantly at Vadya, who nodded. He then said, 'Though controlling your ego and loving others are distinct acts, they are both linked. Success in either one can lead to achieving success in the other. The causality can work both ways. To understand this two-way link, I think what is relevant is not controlling your ego, but extending your ego. By extending your ego, you include others and treat them in the same way as you would yourself. That is what is meant by compassion, or by concepts such as loving others the same as oneself. Similarly, when you love others, you basically extend your ego, for you include them in your self-centred attitude. Every relationship is, thus, a combination of different parts of love and ego. For example, my dad's relationship with his granddaughters, Juhi and Joy, does not involve him controlling his ego. Rather, he extends his ego to include the two girls as a part of him. That is how he can easily be more loving and caring about them than even for himself.'

'Your dad loves you very much too, but his behaviour is not the same with you,' intervened Vadya.

'This is what I like about our discussions, Vadya. You are right. Dad loves me very much too and, in that sense, he has extended his ego to include me within that. In fact, I am an expression of his expanded ego since the time of my birth itself, perhaps even before I was born, when I was just a twinkle in his eye. But this expanded ego has been combined with two important feelings. One is his aspiration about my achievements. He is anxious that I achieve success, which he would consider a reflection of his own capabilities. Second is his view that his son should show traditional respect to the father. Thus, he has always approached the relationship from a pedestal, which has resulted in a very interesting combination. There is both an extension and a confirmation of the ego in this relationship. It is, therefore, quite different from the relationship he has with Juhi and Joy, where there is only an extension of the ego.'

'It is interesting you put it that way because as a parent, there is always a necessity to teach appropriate discipline to the children. Would you have done your homework or eaten spinach or shared your toys with others if your father had not adopted a paterfamilias attitude with you, instilling respect and discipline?' asked Vadya.

'I agree there is a need for discipline and that discipline is important for all activities in life. Without discipline, we would be either overindulgent towards ourselves or make inadequate use of our own abilities and potential. Nonetheless, the discipline applied by my father contained assertion of the ego. I could see that sense of authority whenever the rules were laid down.'

Vadya was looking at Ananda with a smile, 'What about other relationships? Father and child is not the only relationship one has in this world, you know.'

'Thanks, Vadya. This brings me to the bridge between the first main point in my framework and the second one, which enables our consideration for different types of relationships. I think the most important analogy that I can draw for seamless extension of the ego is the relationship between a mother and child, particularly when the child is young. You remember my spiritual experience when I felt that my body was only light and I had deep love for all around me, like a mother would have for a child. I think that is also the essence of spiritual love, which in our physical world is manifested most closely in the feeling which a mother has for her child.'

'I see what you mean by this, but what about the other relationships?' asked Vadya.

'The framework I am talking about covers all relationships, including people with whom we have no obvious or conventional links. We interact with everyone through the filter of our own behaviour and our own views. Through our thoughts and behaviour, we extend ourselves to cover others. Alternately, we could consider a larger perspective, considering ourselves as an expanded self, covering the whole world. As a paradoxical spiritual message says, we have to lose ourselves in order to find ourselves. When we think of the expansion of our ego, we are actually dealing with an expansion of ourselves, giving substance to our larger self. How do we manage to provide this substance to our world view? We find this easier in some cases than others, but we could slowly work on the issue. This brings me to the next key point in my explanation.

'We should recognise that most objectives such as extending the ego, loving others like yourself, being disciplined with understanding towards others are all large objectives which are not easily met if we start pitching ourselves to achieve any of them fully. In fact, for most of us, it is impossible to achieve them in a comprehensive way. We have to keep working towards them with small steps.

'Any large or complex objective can be achieved by addressing it in terms of a sequence of more manageable concepts. We need to take small steps to achieve these smaller level concepts sequentially. Over time, by covering more and more of the smaller objectives, we would achieve the larger overall objective. This is the sequence of small steps. We need to consider these steps to cover two conceptually distinct parts of our journey. One is the nature of actions that we should focus on and the other is the persons whom we wish to cover with the extension of ego. The various persons we interact with could be considered in different categories and we could try to address each category separately. We can describe this effort pictorially, through the concept of concentric circles, with each circle containing a specific category or group of persons. We need to cover each circle in small steps to go ahead in our spiritual journey.'

Saying this, Ananda took a piece of paper and drew some concentric circles and started explaining, 'Take a look at this diagram, starting with the smallest one. We should place ourselves in the innermost circle and label it as "me". The next one has our immediate family. For me, it would be you and the girls. The concentric circle after that is with our parents, yours and mine. The next circle would have my extended larger family and friends. Then we have a circle with acquaintances, followed by a circle with those we do not know. The last circle will have our enemies, or those who wish us harm.' Saying this, Ananda showed her the diagram.

Vadya was getting a bit more involved now, 'Is there any method or pattern in the sequence of the circles that you have drawn here? Can I draw them in any different sequence and then examine the issues?'

Ananda raised his hand as if to stop Vadya from redrawing his circles, 'The circles I have drawn can be seen as expanding from the smallest to the largest, based on the increasing levels of difficulty in extending our ego across them. It is easiest for me to care deeply for myself. Apart from myself, it is easiest for me to extend the ego or deep care and affection to my immediate family and so on. As we move out from the innermost circle towards the outermost one, this act becomes more and more difficult. We should start working from the inner circle which denotes the least difficult target and move with small steps to cover more and more of any particular circle. Thus, even within a circle, small steps would be needed to cover it fully. These small steps can then move us ahead to cover the adjacent concentric circle and so on.'

'You were saying that we do not love different persons the same way. Is that significant in your framework?' asked Vadya. 'What do you mean by moving with small steps to cover more and more of any particular circle and then moving with small steps to cover the adjacent circle, Ananda?'

'Each task and objective should be manageable and limited in nature. We could have more than one objective at the same time, say loving myself, loving my family members and some close friends. Keep moving towards minimal results. Since loving others has to do with our feelings, the objective should be considered at two different levels:

One, the superficial level of our interactions; second, at the level of our deeper feeling. When we extend our focus to those beyond our close relationships, we should identify and focus on the specific problems that may be arising in our interaction and not on a whole range of potential issues. Also, we should not extend the scope of any single issue or problem to cover the whole relationship itself.'

'My, my! This is quite a long list. How does one manage this?' asked Vadya.

'Actually, the list may seem long, but in effect, this is a set of a very small number of actions. I have just separated some linked steps so that they can be clearly understood. Take another look,' said Ananda, passing the paper back to Vadya.

Vadya was nodding in comprehension. Ananda felt encouraged to continue with his explanation. Vadya intervened, 'Please explain again concepts such as "extend your ego" or "love others the same as yourself". I love you very much and have even married you. This is not an emotion that can arise whenever a person wants to develop it. How can one extend selfless love to so many others? I think we would all perish in this effort, facing repeated failures.'

The question Vadya asked was one that had bothered Ananda for a long time. But the words of the teacher, when he had described the Divine in his lecture had given Ananda an interesting insight. The teacher's suggestion had been to look at any large and incomprehensible concept or entity, in terms of its various attributes, as a way of better understanding the Divine. Ananda wanted to make this a general technique for addressing large concepts or issues. He felt that this would also be a good test for him, testing for flaws in his own understanding.

'Vadya, you are now touching upon the first of my two ways for going ahead with small steps. You are absolutely right when you say that love, or the extension of one's ego, is not an emotion that can simply be generated at will. I think that there are two ways to achieve this. One is the expression of a spiritual state of mind, which easily brings love or deep affection towards others. The second is to look at the components of love in terms of small tangible steps that help us move towards the objective in our daily behaviour.'

Vadya was listening carefully, but was not satisfied, 'Please explain this second part to me. I find it difficult to understand,' she said.

'When a concept becomes too difficult to comprehend or implement properly, one way of understanding it is to consider the attributes of that concept, which would help define it. In the case of "love", for instance, though we generally know about love and have experienced it in different ways, we normally do not analyse what it involves. One approach would be through the relevant attributes which describe it.'

Vadya had an enigmatic smile, which Ananda could not read. He only hoped that he was making sense because in his own mind the idea was crystal clear, but that was after considerable effort and thought.

Vadya asked, 'Which attributes do you have in mind when you try to describe the emotion of love or extension of your ego?'

There was an emphasis on 'you' and Ananda understood that Vadya had seen this as an opportunity to gain a deeper insight into his mind. He was amused. So many years of marriage and still this need to know each other better! He warned himself that his answer should be objective and faithful to his understanding, rather than an attempt to project himself as a deeply caring and understanding husband. It suddenly dawned on him that actually Vadya herself was very clear on this matter. She was only trying to enhance his understanding of his own emotions.

'We need to consider the concept in terms of how we behave with a person whom we love. We should be considerate towards the person, using this attitude to develop increasingly deeper caring for the views and feelings of the other person. If there is something they wish for and we do not agree with that, we should at least try and understand the basis for their desire and examine whether there is any way in which we may be wrong. If we conclude that this is not the case, we then need to see whether we can still indulge their desire. These are all examples of different attributes of "love". We can try and make a list of these and emphasise them in our interaction with the person we are focusing on. It is not easy to do so, which is why we need to move ahead with small steps,' explained Ananda.

Vadya asked, 'Is there a difference between the attributes of love and those of extending our own ego to others?'

'Unlike love, when I talk of extension of the ego, I am focusing on the way we behave with ourselves. If I am deeply considerate towards myself, I would indulge myself in a manner similar to that in which I would behave with someone I love. So, the term "extension of the ego" is paradoxically the extension of our self-oriented and self-indulgent behaviour towards other persons,' said Ananda.

Vadya was relentless with her questions, 'That is fine. You have explained the ideas without giving me any indication of how this concept of moving with small steps over concentric circles applies in real life. Your diagram is still not a living picture to me. Can you give me some examples?'

Ananda knew that Vadya was a practical person and would like real-world examples. In this case, he felt, he had them readily available.

'In our everyday life, we easily accept the structure of making progress with small steps towards increasingly higher levels of achievement. So, a child does not start walking or running immediately. It takes time, patience and persistence. A dancer or a cook does not become adept very quickly. It is a process requiring discipline and persistence. It is important that we keep taking our small steps because by the very nature of our task, progress can only be made that way. There is no big leap, no possibility of even running fast towards the objective. Rather, as in the case of other objectives, here too, we need to take small steps moving across different levels of our major objectives in concentric circles.'

'What if we fail in our efforts? What should we do in that situation, Ananda?' It was evident that Vadya would not stop pushing the limits of Ananda's understanding of the issues.

'Signs of failure do not mean that we should give up. It only means that we need to keep working on the objective we seek. This process is not like a game of baseball, where if you have three strikes, you are out. It is not even like a school exam, where if you fail, you do not progress further. Here, we are trying to achieve the goal of self-improvement or of spiritual progress. We have to face our failure and still move ahead. It is important to keep in mind that no failure can take away the progress that we have made till the point when we fail. In fact, even trying once again after failure is an evidence of progress. With each small step, we build some personal spiritual capital to help prop our work further. Failure gives us an opportunity to assess and improve ourselves. Every failure is like a pit stop for a racing car, to make necessary changes and move ahead towards the goal.'

'What do you mean by making the necessary changes?' asked Vadya.

'When we fail to progress further towards our objective, it is because we have not done something which could have sustained our progress. There is always a set of options to choose from, with patience and a positive or constructive attitude. We need to examine whether there is any possibility of our response being different, which could avoid failure. If there is such a possibility, then that is the change we need to bring about in our response. The important point to realise is that usually there is such an alternative and we need to try and consider it with a calm and objective mind.'

Ananda was feeling more relaxed and he continued, 'In personal interactions, when we fail to extend our ego in the way that I have explained, say due to loss of our temper or patience, then it may be necessary to address the consequent problem in the interpersonal situation. This may require an acknowledgement of being wrong, both to ourselves and others. It is through our actions that we affect both the conditions under which we operate and the path we take under those conditions towards our objectives. Acknowledging to ourselves that we took an appropriate or inappropriate action is an important way of affecting our own frame of mind and through that we can change our potential future actions and opportunities. It also helps us progress on the spiritual path, recognising and addressing any shortcomings in our journey across the notional concentric circles.'

'Are you not being too far removed from many situations in this world? There may be a manager who may have to control and be distinct from others whom he or she has to control and manage. Similarly, there may be persons who are not your well-wishers and you may have to protect yourself from them rather than extend your ego or love them as yourself? How does your framework apply to these conditions? And what do you mean by the process of addressing failure itself helping us on the spiritual path?' asked Vadya.

Ananda nodded, clearly enjoying himself now, and wrote down her questions so that he could take them up in sequence, 'Okay, one by one. First, the manager's task. The extension of the ego, in this case, takes another form. It is based on having a system that accords fair treatment to all concerned. In this case, the extension of the ego can be achieved by putting yourself in the shoes of the person you are managing and understanding that fair treatment of that person involves treating him in the manner in which you yourself would have liked to be treated. This requires reasoned and objective response within a specified system. Both these aspects are, in effect, an extension of your ego to place yourself in the situation of the other person and treatment of that person in a fair, objective and transparent system.

'This brings me to another objective of the spiritual journey.

Along with loving others, we should also aim to be detached with respect to our actions,' continued Ananda, almost as an afterthought.

Vadya was quick to express a concern, 'Detachment? What do you mean by detachment when you are talking about connection, with deep care and even love for others?'

'I think you are interpreting "detachment" as the way in which self-oriented people are detached from what happens to others. Such detachment is basically a lack of concern and it is appropriate to question its consistency with a seamless expansion of the ego. My use of "detachment" is not "indifference". What I understand by detachment in the spiritual context is that we need to maintain our sensitivity and balance in any situation. We should not become so emotionally affected by any situation that we lose our objectivity or the ability to logically assess both the situation and the relevant options required to adequately address it. That is precisely what a good manager has to do in the process of extending the ego while managing others.'

Vadya was not satisfied, 'Ananda, you are talking of a need to maintain sensitivity and balance, which is as abstract as you can get for someone who is actually facing a difficult situation. Do you have any suggestions for an easier way which is more tangible?'

'What do you mean? Do you have any specific concern that is bothering you?' asked Ananda.

'I find that I get irritated more often nowadays, with so many different tasks to manage. I even lose my temper at times. How do you think I could control my anger?' asked Vadya.

'This is another example of a key objective, which can be broken up into either smaller sub-objectives or smaller steps comprising different and distinct actions that could be taken to achieve the main objective. The sub-objectives could be in terms of addressing anger with respect to yourself, your husband, children, other family, friends and so on,' explained Ananda.

Vadya was giving the issue serious thought and interrupted as Ananda spoke, 'And what about the smaller steps?'

'Yes. The main, larger objective is to control anger. This objective should be approached in small steps. For instance, an important first step could be to try and always keep your voice calm. Then build upon this and detach yourself from the source of the anger by examining what is causing the anger. Do not identify the cause with the person, but link it to the event or action that caused it. Take each cause separately and work on it. Keep an open mind because you may eventually realise that your understanding about the cause might have been wrong. Thus, there is a need to carefully assess the cause of your anger and also the steps that you need to take to address that cause. By being calm you would be able to better evaluate alternative options. All these are steps towards detachment, towards objectivity. After some time, these small steps have the potential to help you travel a relatively long distance in controlling your anger,' said Ananda.

'That is clearer. But does this new factor—detachment—affect the operational effectiveness of your concentric circles?' Vadya seemed to be getting deeper into the discussion. It was evident she was feeling comfortable with concentric circles but wanted to test the limits of the concept.

'The concentric circles do not get affected at all. Similar to the concentric circles which I had drawn earlier with people, you could also have consecutive steps, with parts of any larger objective—sub-objectives arranged in a different set of concentric circles organised according to the levels of difficulty. That is because the use of concentric circles should be seen as a tool to assist us, rather than limited to describing or achieving any specific objective. It is like any mathematical method, formula or technique, which may be applied to clearly specify issues and get solutions to different problems. Think of this as a method to address issues and concerns.'

Vadya started imagining diverse possibilities of using the method of concentric circles and sought confirmation of her understanding. 'Ananda, what you are saying is that in the same way as you had earlier drawn a set of concentric circles to explain the objective of expanding the ego, you can have another separate set of concentric circles for looking at diverse objectives such as detachment or controlling anger. In each case, this technique can be used to consider them in greater detail and then address them with small, manageable steps,' Vadya summarised.

'Absolutely correct. For example, in the case of "detachment", we could draw a separate set of concentric circles with one sub-component in each concentric circle. These circles will be specific only to the sub-objectives of detachment and not linked to any other objective, sub-objective or set of concentric circles. As I explained, we start with the relatively easiest of the sub-objectives in the innermost circle and go outwards in the concentric circles towards more and more difficult sub-objectives. We address them taking small steps. In the concentric circles linked to detachment, for example, the innermost circle will contain my enemies or those I do not know because I would find it easiest to be detached with respect to whatever happens to them. The outermost circle will have me or my immediate family, because I am most concerned about myself, and my immediate family, as it is most difficult to be detached from anything which affects any of us. The other sub-objectives for detachment would be organised in the circles in between, with the outer concentric circles containing relatively more difficult sub-objectives compared to the circles closer to the centre. We address this issue with small steps too, starting from the central innermost circle, covering more and more of the sub-objectives mentioned in adjacent concentric circles. So, the scheme of concentric circles remains relevant, as does the use of small steps,' said Ananda excitedly.

Ananda's excitement was now affecting Vadya too. She grew more involved with Ananda's efforts and wanted to add her own words of encouragement, 'Ananda, I think this is a very useful technique. We could apply it in many different situations.'

On being praised, Ananda felt very happy and satisfied. He thanked Vadya and continued, 'Thanks, Vadya. I also want to address two other questions in your list. First, whether it would be appropriate to extend our love to those who wish to harm us. We are after all ordinary persons, not like Gandhi or Buddha who would treat even their enemies with love. Till we become extremely spiritually evolved, I do not think it is possible for us to cover the outermost of the concentric circles. In general, we would not be able to extend our ego to those who wish us harm. When I talk about the extension of the ego, it does not mean submerging all aspects of the ego, including self-preservation. It is our duty to protect ourselves, using non-violent methods. Even as you extend your ego to the outermost circle, if efforts to diffuse a situation with positive steps do not work, there may be cases that require you to take precautions—seek legal redress or perhaps, withdrawal from the scene. When we face really difficult situations, the appropriate spiritual advance has to be in terms of recognising the negative or even dangerous situation.'

'What about the spiritual basis for the various concepts which you have mentioned?' asked Vadya. Then she heard the girls, Juhi and Joy, chattering and laughing, coming towards their room, 'The girls are here, Ananda. Get ready for some really interesting questions now.'

Ananda looked at Vadya and whispered, 'I will discuss the last question later. Right now, even in terms of priority, there is nothing more important than meeting the children and learning from them, is there?'

Just then Juhi and Joy entered the room and ran straight to Vadya and hugged her. Vadya whispered something into their ears. They nodded and ran to Ananda, one on each side. Ananda hugged them close and they kissed his cheeks, Joy on the right and Juhi on the left. All three sat hugging each other and smiling with great happiness. Ananda looked up and saw Vadya smiling broadly at the three of them. It was one happy moment engulfing all four of them. Ananda felt that his two inner circles in the diagram—covering 'me' and 'my family'—had just merged into one.

14

Vadya is Interested

It was late afternoon and Ananda was trying to do his daily quota of five Sudoku puzzles. Someone had told him that this was a good way of postponing Alzheimer's disease. Vadya entered the room with a cup of tea for him and he relaxed, keeping the book of Sudoku aside.

'Ananda, our new friends Marie and Nancy have stayed behind to see more of Delhi. They will be here for another week or so. I explained the gist of our recent conversation to Marie and now she is very keen to join us this evening. I hope that is fine with you?'

Ananda nodded, 'Yes, of course. Marie is a kindred spirit, far advanced in her understanding than she herself realises. Her lack of assurance is on account of growing up in an environment that was very distant and alien to the larger vision she has experienced.'

Vadya sounded slightly irritated and admonished Ananda, 'Do not be so supercilious, Ananda. Are you forgetting how many spiritually accomplished persons you have met in the West? Since when have you become so self-centred and chauvinistic?'

Ananda took a sip of his tea and responded, 'No. I was not making a general statement. My views are specific to the situation in which Marie has grown up.'

Vadya remained unhappy with this response, 'Why? Marie is from California, a place that has a wide variety of views and lots of people who are interested in spirituality. You seem to be treating her with arrogance, which is most unspiritual. I think because you have been lecturing to people on spiritual issues, you have developed undue self-importance. Is this the humility which you say should be the hallmark of a spiritual soul who has managed to extend the ego to cover several concentric circles?'

Ananda was taken aback by Vadya's words, more so because she was correct. He had started feeling a bit smug and even arrogant with his insights. His ego was taking him in a direction opposite to that normally travelled by a spiritual person. But Ananda also noticed in Vadya's response something more than a mere need to put him back on the spiritual path. He, thus, asked with some hesitation, 'Vadya, why are you reacting so sharply? Is everything fine with you?'

Vadya looked relieved. It was as if she wanted to share her thoughts quickly, 'I have spent some time talking to Marie who is a very sensitive person, even a bit vulnerable. You are right in saying that she herself does not realise her high level of spiritual attainment. Her vulnerability concerns me. She is too open to doubt and insecurity. I feel protective of her, as if she were my daughter. I do not want her to be hurt in this process. She will feel your arrogance and start withdrawing into her shell. I know you can help her, but I want you to approach her keeping both her potential and her sensitive nature in mind.'

Ananda got up and hugged Vadya. He was overwhelmed by such a clear demonstration of high spiritual behaviour. She was truly a motherly figure, blessed with deep affection, which was not limited only to her own small family. Vadya had already covered a number of concentric circles.

'Thank you, Vadya. Thank you for being my guardian angel. How often I have thought, sometimes even after very vocal disagreements with you, that the Divine has put you in my life as a great favour. For me, you are a major instrument of the Divine.' No sooner did he say this that Ananda felt another window of perception opening in his mind, and he wanted to make a special effort to keep that window open. He realised that it may not be possible, so he scribbled down the last part of his statement—a major instrument of the Divine. This would help rekindle his memory later.

Just then, Marie and Nancy walked in. Marie seemed hesitant and apologised, 'I am sorry for disturbing you. Vadya had invited us to be with both of you so that we could take our discussion forward and I was very interested. However, I feel we should also give both of you time to be with each other.'

Vadya went to Marie and hugged her. 'You are always welcome Marie. In our society, and especially in this household, we feel happier when we are with our friends. And you have become our special friend in such a short time. You are a part of our family. You know, we Indians have extended families. This includes our friends too. That is why my daughters Juhi and Joy refer to you as aunty. So please be assured that you are always welcome to be with us, both of you.'

Marie seemed relieved. She sat down on a cane chair. Close by stood a table on which some tea and snacks had already been placed for them. Vadya looked at Ananda and asked him to initiate the discussion, 'Ananda, you wanted to explain some concepts to me. It would be a good idea to start with a general part of the discussion, the spiritual basis of what you have been explaining to me these days.'

Nancy intervened, 'In our everyday life, we do not often have the time to consider events from a simple perspective. Do you have something practical and simple?'

Vadya was looking at Nancy with a new interest. She turned towards Ananda and reminded him, 'Ananda, you have always sought insights which would help us progress in our daily lives, both materially and spiritually. Nancy's question is basically one for which you have been trying to seek an answer for so long. Are you in a position to address this today?'

Ananda was deep in thought and nodded enthusiastically, 'Vadya would have mentioned to you the concept of extending the ego to encompass others within our ego, meaning that we should love others as ourselves. Think of this as giving effect to the idea that we have much wider links than are normally perceived by us. Our existence is larger than what we normally perceive.'

'How can you be certain of this?' asked Marie.

'For one, I have my experiences and insights. Our social relationships show this as well. Even otherwise, our connections and links exist in several ways that go beyond normal channels or understanding. For instance, some scientists use the term "Quantum Entanglement" or "Quantum Coherence" to describe a situation for two entities or systems that are located at great distances and appear to us to be separate but they act as if they are a single system, one entity linked to the other without any known obvious connection. Similarly, the phenomenon of holographic object, where one can see an object to be larger and complete under laser, while normally we see it as a smaller piece. Likewise, the view in science that there are more than four dimensions of existence. Only the mystics have experienced these multiple dimensions of existence.[1] There is so much which shows that the reality is much larger than we perceive. This implies that even our existence is much larger than we normally realise. There are different descriptions of this, including, for instance, the concept of an extended mind.'[2]

'Can you read me something from one of your books that tries to simplify such an insight?' asked Marie.

Ananda got up and returned a few minutes later with a book.[3] He went to almost the end of the book and said, 'This text shows that we are actually a part of a larger reality, and in effect, function on the boundary of a larger reality. I will read this out to you:'

> The species of quantum field theory Maldacena identified as living on the boundary is among the mathematically best understood of those particle physicists have studied since the middle of the twentieth century. ...Operating way out on the boundary of the universe this quantum field theory embodies all physical features, processes and interactions of strings that move within the interior, a link made explicit through the dictionary translating phenomena between the two. And since we have a sure-footed mathematical definition of the boundary quantum field theory, we can use it as a mathematical definition of string theory, at least for strings moving within this space–time shape. The holographic parallel universes may thus be more than a potential outgrowth of fundamental laws; they may part of the very definition of the fundamental laws.

'This says that we operate only at the surface of a much larger reality, whereas the total operational area is larger and deeper. But this is highly esoteric. How do we apply this type of insight?' asked Vadya.

Ananda sipped his tea and continued, 'In life, each situation arises from the interaction of our efforts and the conditions we face when making those efforts. The focus should be on understanding these conditions. That would help us to decide the appropriate efforts that we should make to improve them.'

'How do we achieve this?' asked Nancy, who had been quiet all this while.

'There are basically two techniques; both involve distancing ourselves from our situation. The first one is basically to remove ourselves from any situation with the help of three factors that I will mention. I would like to term this technique as the "compassionate detachment" technique, a "top-down" or "outside-in" way of developing the desired attributes. In this process, we end up developing spiritual attributes without necessarily being aware of it. The journey has setbacks and we need persistence to go onwards with the perspective that each situation we face offers us at least one option which takes us in the appropriate direction.'

Marie, who had been silent for long, asked, 'From your description of the first technique, can I presume that the second technique is a "bottom-up" or "inside-out" way of achieving the objective?'

Ananda confirmed with a nod, 'Yes, that is true. This "outside-in" technique is to try and apply logic as if we were an external observer of the situation and have to advise the person concerned on the best course of action. The important point is that the person we are advising is our own self. This requires calmness of mind, an ability to apply knowledge in a coherent way and assess the implications of different courses of action. The more difficult a situation, the more difficult it is to achieve such a distance from our own self.'

'Is this it? We try and distance ourselves from the situation, apply logic and analyse the implications of different options that we could pursue to address the situation?' asked Nancy. She was talking to Ananda in a tone which showed that she did not consider this insight very exceptional. In fact, so strong was this feeling in her that she blurted out, 'These suggestions are very obvious indeed. There is no special insight here.'

'The important point is that even after identifying the relevant insight, such insights are usually not straightforward to implement. We require certain important supporting efforts to successfully translate such insights into practice,' explained Ananda.

'What are the accompanying factors in this case?' asked Marie. Nancy nodded vigorously to show that she had the same question in her mind.

'To begin with, for the first technique or insight we need to keep three relevant factors in mind to promote greater balance,' Ananda answered, enjoying the fact that he had an interested audience, even if it was only three people, 'One, is the nature of the objective that we wish to achieve. It is important to be aware of two things here: Whether the objective is within our reach and the extent of effort that we have to make in order to achieve that objective. If the objective is extremely difficult, then part of the logical assessment should be to recognise the fact that the objective is extremely difficult. If we still wish to make an attempt to achieve it then it should be with this knowledge.

'Second, we should be clear about the nature and extent of the effect on us, if for some reason, we are not able to achieve the objective being pursued.'

'Why is this relevant?' asked Vadya.

'It helps us see things in a proper perspective,' Ananda began. 'We should ensure we do not feel disturbed, nor lose our balance if we are unable to achieve certain objectives. For that, the objectives should either not be very significant for us, or we should be in a position to move ahead in our life without our situation being fundamentally worse than before.

'The third factor is the effect we have on others when achieving our objective. By this, I do not mean the reaction of others to our success in achieving the desired objective, but whether we bring harm to others through our actions. Our effort should be not to have such negative effects on others.'

Vadya enquired, 'There are very few major tasks which do not result in a combination of good and harmful effects. Do you mean to say that such tasks should not be performed if we have to develop greater balance and peace of mind?'

'My view is that in every situation, we should act in the interests of the "larger good". In addition to achieving a positive result, we should try to limit or tone down the negative effects to the best possible extent. If you think in terms of the extension of the ego, a simple rule could be to assess how you would address the consequences of your actions if they were directly affecting you.'

'What is the spiritual basis of this mode of behaviour? To me this seems only to be a logical way of dealing with the situation,' interjected Vadya again.

'Logic is not inconsistent with spiritual behaviour. It is what you emphasise in your logical framework that provides a spiritual content to your actions. In my previous discussions, I have explained the importance of extending your ego—treating each situation as if it were directly affecting you, where every other person is also yourself. This is the spiritual foundation of these ideas.'

'Based on what you are saying, every action—good or bad—has a spiritual basis,' questioned Marie.

Vadya now intervened, saying, 'Your point is that the spiritual framework within which we exist, is just that—a framework of our existence, giving us the flexibility to use the resources within this framework. Whether we do something good or bad depends on what we ourselves decide to do. It is an expression of our own energy through our actions. So, we have a spiritual basis and framework for actions, but the steps we take with this framework are based on our thoughts and our actions.'

'Yes, Vadya. That is so. Thank you. Let us take this forward. Our own attitude when taking certain actions is an important part of the spiritual basis. If we think in very narrow and selfish terms, focusing on our ego whose coverage is limited to just ourselves, our thought energy is much more constricted than its actual wider spiritual base.

'Within the spiritual framework, expanding our links with our larger existence requires spiritual content. Hence, the main elements to bear in mind would include: First, a thought process which helps us consider the concerns of others as if they were our own concerns. Second, even if we are not able to have such a mindset, it would be good to emphasise that our actions do not bring harm to others. Third, to the extent that achieving certain objectives does involve harm to others, we should see how to limit that harm through any adjustments or assistance. The idea is to minimise harm and maximise overall benefits, taking account of all affected. Finally, once we have taken our action and seen the result, we should focus on what we continue to have and what is required for moving ahead, rather than what we might have not achieved.

'These points are not always evident when we consider alternate options for action. We often forget emphasising them in the process of trying to progress towards our objectives. Though simple in conceptual terms, these points are an essential manifestation of the basic content of our spiritual basis. The spiritual basis of our actions shows us how we can make our "best efforts",' explained Ananda.

Nancy nodded slowly and raised one hand as if she were in a class and wanted to attract the teacher's attention, 'Ananda, I am not clear about the importance of the first two of these four factors.'

'They help develop the requisite detachment that is needed for maintaining greater balance and peace of mind. Our happiness depends crucially on what we wish to achieve and how we perceive our success. Very often, we aim too high without a proper appreciation of the difficulty of achieving that aim, given our own capabilities and resources. Assessing incorrectly, we then lose our peace of mind if we are unable to be successful. The point is that we should be aware of the nature of the difficulty in achieving any objective, having clearly analysed all that is involved, including the relevant steps to take. This also helps us plan the best possible way to move towards our objective, as well as to be aware of the gaps or difficulties which may remain.'

'So, should we not address difficult objectives?' asked Nancy.

'No. This does not imply that you should not work at achieving difficult objectives, but only that your efforts should be based on clarity about the specific steps required and how to best address them. Part of this process is to also recognise that we may have made our best efforts, but perhaps the objective was beyond the normal reach.'

'Despite following this course of action, I may still be deeply disturbed, disappointed or even angry if I do not succeed. How do we address that?' asked Nancy.

'You are absolutely correct. That is where the second factor becomes important. If you succeed, then you would be happy, satisfied. If you do not succeed, it is natural to feel disappointed, sometimes deeply disappointed. The second factor I mentioned provides a method to address this situation. To reduce disappointment and to have a quicker recovery and peace of mind, it is helpful to assess whether we are in a position to bear the loss of not achieving the objective. Often, the condition we are in is reasonably satisfactory, or the extent of damage to our interest is not significant or fundamental, and the emphasis should be on recognising this. Such an analysis would quickly tell us if we are actually overreacting. This assessment would help us deal better with our situation and make us ready for whatever has to follow in our life,' Ananda explained.

'Is this a way to combine the twin objectives of dealing with normal concerns and aspirations in life while attempting to progress on the spiritual path at the same time?' asked Vadya.

'Yes, Vadya. If we follow this method in our daily life, we could focus on achieving our material objectives while progressing on the spiritual path,' responded Ananda.

Vadya nodded in agreement and faced Marie, 'This reminds me of a saying I had read long ago in a magazine that "Happiness is making a bouquet with flowers within reach." The focus should be on finding happiness in whatever circumstances you face and to appreciate the present rather than lament about lost opportunities.'

Ananda continued, 'Yes. It is important to realise that any situation we face is not entirely of our making, though we contribute to it. Any attitude we adopt or any specific action we take, however, depends on us. It is our decision, our responsibility and our instrument of self-expression.

In order to take the appropriate action, we must be aware of the various possibilities and evaluate them with a clear mind. Greater clarity of mind is a manifestation of a larger awareness. This clarity and objectivity reflects a larger than normal awareness. It also prepares us by showing the path to further insights about ourselves. When we combine this with the view that our present situation is a reasonable one, we can better focus on our objective without being unduly perturbed by the results of our efforts. If we are able to adopt this attitude as our way of life, we may be connected with our "result" and yet not be a prisoner of that situation.

'When we combine this attitude with emphasis on not harming others, we adopt the fundamental attitude of a mother, one full of compassion. This takes us close to our basis, our origin, our source which in effect is our progenitor, our mother. In that sense, not harming others is a reflection of our larger self from which we have come into this dimension. If we consider these three aspects together, the spiritual basis or compassionate detachment becomes clear.'

Ananda continued, 'Now I want to talk about the other method.' Turning to Vadya, Ananda said, 'I am in the mood to have some more tea. Maybe, we should continue our discussion after more tea is prepared. Is that okay with you?'

Vadya also felt like having more tea and especially with those biscuits that Marie had got from the United States. With Ananda's help, she provided a second round of tea for all. All of them relaxed a bit during this break, after the serious discussion.

'Does this materialistic joy not take you away from your spiritual objective?' asked Marie.

'I do not think so. It does not in any way conflict with the methods we have just discussed. Moreover, it is special because it is gift from you, a very thoughtful new member of our family. If I enjoy it without getting self-engrossed or being caught up in the process of self-gratification, I think I would still be on the appropriate path. In fact, this can be an instrument to help me on the spiritual path,' answered Ananda.

'My, my! This is just a biscuit. You give it far too much importance,' responded Marie. 'I like it a lot too and am pleased that you are enjoying it. But it is only a biscuit, a material object.'

Ananda sipped the fresh cup of tea, which had been prepared the way he liked it—tea leaves boiled with water and a bit of milk mixed in it just before taking the tea off the stove. This was how tea was made in his village and he loved the taste and its indirect link with his roots in rural India. He was enjoying his simple pleasures and the conversation. He looked at Marie and then at the biscuit. He shook his head from side to side in the way that only Indians do, showing his determination not to take any more biscuits, and replied, 'True, it is only a biscuit, but see how much pleasure one can get even from the small things in life. As long as we are capable of getting such pleasure without being attached to it, we have the appropriate mindset. We live in the material world, and material objects and experiences are the instruments of the Divine to provide us with opportunities for progress towards our larger reality.'

Nancy suddenly spoke in a somewhat loud voice, 'Instrument of the Divine! That depends on belief, doesn't it? If I do not believe in the Divine, how can I consider some situation or experience as an instrument of the Divine?'

Ananda thought for a few seconds and replied, 'Belief makes it easier to go ahead. However, if our response is appropriate or correct, then its validity does not depend on our belief. You could think of my statement in another way, i.e. we can learn and improve ourselves from each situation and experience. What we learn depends on our own thoughts and efforts, our own mindset. This is the basic idea. Each situation we face provides us with a basis to react with our actions, which again are tools to improve ourselves and reach the larger state of being. In a spiritual context, we could consider each situation we face as being an instrument of the Divine, providing us with an opportunity to improve.'

'This is perhaps a good entry point for the second technique, the "inside-out method",' smiled Marie.

'Yes, that is so. The second approach is not one of building detachment; instead it is a direct effort to link up with our spiritual base. Detachment may arise as an indirect effect, but it is detachment of a type that shows less preoccupation with ourselves and greater affection or compassion for others. Thus, I will refer to this as the method of spiritual attachment, involving simple practices of meditation, focused prayers, breathing exercises or developing compassion by recognising the presence of the Divine in others.' Ananda was warming up to his explanation.

Nancy intervened to ask, 'I can understand practices such as prayers, meditation and breathing exercises. What do you mean by developing compassion by recognising the presence of the Divine?'

'This aspect is an important part of the second approach, which must grow from within rather than be imposed. It has to be the result of the seed which is sown in the heart once we prepare ourselves with the spiritual practices. This is because the result of spiritual exercises I am talking about develops such compassion only after recognising the pervasive presence of the Divine,' explained Ananda.

Marie kept down her cup of tea and asked, 'Ananda, what kind of steps does this approach include? Does it link up in any way with the glimpses or pictures which you and I have been seeing for so long?'

'To understand why I am calling it an "inside-out" approach, we should first distinguish it from the previous technique. There we externally imposed discipline and a way of thinking that helped develop compassion within us. The factors are to be applied from outside, to generate compassion and awareness within us. That is why I called it the "outside-in" or "top-down" approach. The second approach is "inside-out" or "bottom-up" because we focus on achieving our objectives from inside, linking ourselves to our energy force which emanates from within us. From that inner source, we reach the external manifestations of our perspectives, our way of thinking. This way, we link our outward existence with the attributes of our inner self, the life force we all possess. These inner attributes are the basis of peace and achieving the larger perspective.'

'Thank you, Ananda. This is useful. Could you please tell me what we need to do for giving effect to this "inside-out" approach?' asked Marie.

Ananda looked at Marie as he answered, 'We should do whatever links us inwards, towards a much larger and more peaceful world, towards an existence which provides us with a much wider perspective than one limited to only ourselves. It could be prayers, meditation or any other method that achieves this objective, as long as we do it with devotion, recognizing the presence of the Divine within us. If we feel this energy of the Divine within and all around us, then what we need to do is to anchor ourselves inside, in the glow of that omnipresent energy. Feel ourselves to be one with that energy, to be protected and suffused with that energy in our heart.'

Nancy followed up with the question next on Marie's list, 'Is this very difficult or complicated? How difficult is this?'

'The extent of difficulty depends on how easily we can visualise the presence of the Divine within and around us and be with that energy. This is not always easy, especially when we are in difficulty or face problems. If we persist with this, and even if we do so for ten or fifteen minutes each day, it gets easier with practice. This is the "inside-out" approach.'

Everyone was quiet, trying to absorb this approach. Suddenly, Ananda recalled Marie's question aloud, 'Does this link-up in any way with the glimpses or pictures which you and I have kept seeing for so long?' He thought for a little while before responding.

'A simple answer to your question is that what you see is a larger reality. You might have noticed that the timing of the glimpses is not within your control, though when you are in a spiritual frame of mind, they would be more frequent.'

Marie started thinking and responded after some time, 'I do not really know. I do not have enough data to answer this, one way or the other.'

'Well, you are lucky to already have some doors open for you. Further effort on your part will make that more sustainable. This does not mean that you should focus only on spiritual practice or meditation as such. Part of the spiritual practice is also to meet your worldly responsibilities in the best possible way—with understanding and compassion,' explained Ananda.

'These partial and temporary glimpses leave me very unsure and sometimes I am even a bit disturbed,' said Marie.

'Yes, that does happen when you are not able to see any consistent pattern or meaning in the partial pictures that you see. It is an unusual experience. However, one strong feature of these experiences is that they never generate negative feelings towards others and they build compassion within us, with an understanding that we are part of a larger reality. With time, they lead to a greater sense of peace and also an overwhelming awareness that we are beneficiaries of a special and privileged experience,' explained Ananda.

'That is true. I have managed to handle it better with time. But I am still not entirely at peace when it happens.'

'Marie, that is perhaps due to the fact that you question these experiences with a view to assess whether they are a reflection of some weakness or defect on your part. You are superimposing these feelings on the experience. Therefore, your difficulties arise not necessarily from these glimpses, but possibly from this additional and separate concern that you have about yourself. If you feel uncomfortable, you could get medical advice also,' suggested Ananda.

'I do not have negative feelings. I will assess these experiences more carefully in the future,' said Marie.

Ananda continued, 'Let me explain with an example that has always appealed to me. Once a wise person, a spiritual master told me that we are like an earthen pot filled with sand, hanging from the ceiling of a room. This earthen pot has a small hole at the bottom. Now imagine the place in the ceiling from where this pot is hanging. In the ceiling above the pot, there is a small hole through which sand falls into the pot from above, i.e. from outside the room. If this pot is moving to and fro, two things happen—one, the internal movement of sand in the pot results in that sand slowly flowing out from the hole at the bottom of pot; two, when the pot is moving, the sand falling from above does not fall into the pot. In contrast, if that pot is completely still, then all the external sand falls into the earthen pot and fills it up. Also, the pressure of all the sand falling from above blocks the hole in the pot and the sand does not flow out.

'This is an analogy with our own deeper self. We are the pot and our ego is the hole at the bottom of the pot. The sand is our essence, our energy, which links us with the wider spiritual world. The movement of the pot is akin to agitation, mental or spiritual. With agitation, our energy is slowly dissipated in the same way that the sand flows through the hole in the pot. Consequently, we would have that much less energy or internal resources to use for our objectives. With agitation, our experience only grates on us and our energy flows out beyond the scope of our influence or understanding. When we are peaceful and calm, the whole of the sand remains within the pot. In other words, we retain our energy for whatever we need. In addition, we also manage to obtain the energy—sand—which is coming towards us from our spiritual source.'

'This example shows us that agitation can be a dissipating influence, so it is important to try and be calm. But I still do not understand how this example links up with my glimpses of a larger reality,' Marie commented.

'Let us take the components of this example,' Ananda explained further. 'The pot is hanging from the roof in a building. This is similar to the idea that we do not independently exist in this world and there is an important link that helps to stabilise our existence. External pressures, such as those in the room where the pot is hanging, can dislodge us from our stable position. When that movement or agitation occurs, it makes us expend our energies, slowly weakening us. To stabilise our position, it helps if we take actions that conserve our energies—retain the volume of sand in the pot and allow for more to be filled in. Thus, with such actions we can also replenish our energies—allow refills of sand in the pot, which makes us substantively richer. To achieve this objective of preserving and increasing our substance and allowing the additional energy to flow in, we need to be mentally calm and still.

'We see that the additional energy, sand, is provided from a source that is linked to us, fills us with substance but is not always known to us. This energy is, in effect, from another dimension of our existence. The external energy, sand, is always within reach and we can get connected with it through our own actions—actions which help to stabilise us. When the link with this external energy is strong, we are in line with the additional energy. The stream of external sand into the pot helps us become more aware and connected with this external source, which keeps replenishing us. It is, in essence an extension of our own substance, expanding us effectively beyond our limited self. Marie, you have the glimpses more clearly when the link is strong. This link also provides you with substance to enhance your capacity and existence in a fundamental way. Keeping still and calm, you can reach the stage of connectivity where this flow of external energy will fill you up and then at one stage, it will start flowing from you to others.'

Marie was paying deep attention. This issue was so personal and intimate to her that she felt a bit exposed, uncertain and even vulnerable. However, this was the first time someone was seriously discussing the topic with her. She wanted to extract as much information as she could. 'Ananda, can you please tell me if there is any indication confirming that these experiences are of a spiritual nature and not hallucinations. What has your own experience been in this context?'

'Before I share my own experience with you, I just want to clarify that each one of us may have a different experience of the same phenomenon. Nonetheless, if my experiences can address your concerns, I will share them with great happiness. I have seen that without making any specific effort, sometimes I start feeling as if my thoughts have crystallised and I feel at peace. I even feel someone caress me within or on my head. That is when some silent and gentle force within is driving me to be with myself, away from external interaction. I even feel a tingling sensation at the top of my head, in the middle of my eyebrows, or in the centre of my forehead. It is as if the energy is collecting in these places and would like to go inwards. Sometimes, such a feeling of collected energy occurs in the region of the heart. When I am in this state, it puts me in the frame of mind to link up with a larger reality. This may happen during meditation or prayers, or even when performing normal chores like talking to people or driving. The common abiding sensation on all these occasions is a strong feeling of inner focus, somewhat separated from my surroundings and with a sense of raised energy content in the head or the heart. At the same time, while being collected, I also have a strong sense of affection for others around me. I have nothing else which can distinguish the situation from my normal daily experiences.'

Ananda was not looking at anyone when he was explaining this. It was as if he was talking to himself, or perhaps communing with, and there was some deeper connection, which seemed to be moving him intensely. He suddenly started crying softly, tears rolling down his cheeks. Marie and Nancy were embarrassed, but Vadya was silent, watching, caring. She had seen Ananda in this state several times, often crying with uncontrolled emotion, giving up any effort to stop his tears. He covered his eyes with both hands and stayed like that for some time. Marie and Nancy were looking at Vadya helplessly but she gestured to them to remain calm. After about five minutes of this intense emotional outburst, Ananda got up and went to wash his face. He returned to the room and apologised. Sitting down in his chair then, he resumed talking as if nothing had happened.

'You will notice that when I was talking about specific efforts in the two approaches, I described them in terms of distinct and disaggregated steps. This makes it possible to treat our progress in terms of small steps, going slowly across different issues or levels of difficulties. Conceptually, we could think of these as concentric circles to be covered through small steps. Let me provide some clarity on this aspect.'

Vadya came and lightly placed her hand on Ananda's back. She was aware of how detached and drained Ananda would be feeling at that moment. She wanted him to rest. 'Ananda, let me try and explain the framework of small steps and concentric circles to Marie and Nancy. This way, I would be able to test my own comprehension and you can take some rest. Is that okay with you? Also, would you like another cup of tea?'

'Yes. That would be very nice. Can you please give it to me in the bedroom? I think I will rest for some time and join you later.'

As Ananda got up, Marie and Nancy rose too, looking a bit awkward. Vadya asked them to sit down and feel comfortable, 'I will just join you again once I have organised some tea for Ananda. Please do not worry.'

Marie and Nancy sat down again and waited for Vadya who returned very quickly. She saw that both her guests were still looking very worried. Patting Marie softly on the shoulder, Vadya sat down near her and tried to reassure the two girls, 'There is nothing wrong with Ananda. This is not unusual because sometimes while talking about his special experiences, he feels deeply connected with another force, maybe another dimension. It is an experience which overwhelms him, moves him immensely and he starts crying.'

Marie and Nancy both looked at Vadya with concern. Vadya wanted to lighten the atmosphere and wondered what to say. She decided to be direct, 'I realise that this reaction of Ananda's can be very disconcerting for others. Initially, I used to get very disturbed, wondering whether in some way I was responsible. With time, I realised that the common feature in every such episode was Ananda feeling deeply connected to his spiritual world, which kept pulling him, even making him impractical at times.' Vadya smiled again and continued, 'Perhaps Ananda's own earthen pot needs to be more stable when the external energy is filling it up. This is not a sad or disturbing experience for him. It is an experience of joy, of being more complete. Right now, he must be in a state of deep mental comfort, all alone, yet with a much larger presence.'

References

1. See for example, Krishna, Gopi. *The Real Nature of Mystical Experience*. USA: Bethel Publishers, 1978.
2. Sheldrake, Rupert. *The Sense of Being Stared At: And Other Unexplained Powers of the Human Mind*. USA: Crown Publishers, 2003.
3. Greene, Brian. *The Hidden Reality: Parallel Universes and the Deep Laws of the Cosmos*. USA: Vintage Books, 2011.

15

Vadya Explains Some Concepts

Vadya was quiet as she organised her thoughts. She explained the diagram of small steps, concentric circles and extending the ego to both Marie and Nancy.

Nancy asked, 'How does one bring this into effect? I am clear about what I should be doing to control my ego. But how do I extend my ego?'

'We could do so through a technique of focusing on small manageable concepts reflected in our daily behaviour. Take any desirable concept, such as love or extending our ego, and examine how we would behave if we embodied that concept as a part of our daily life. And then, we should start by incorporating those attributes of behaviour in our interaction with others. For example, extending the ego would require that we treat others the way we treat ourselves, with care, consideration and love, show understanding and affection in our thoughts and actions towards others, in the same way as we do for ourselves, be aware when we deviate from the requisite behaviour and try then to make adjustments. This process helps give more substantive content to esoteric concepts and converts them into manageable steps, which we can address more practically. And if we do not succeed, then this method also provides us with a basis to evaluate the reasons for our lack of progress.'

Nancy responded, 'I am a mother. I think mothers are able to love their children above themselves.'

Vadya continued nodding and agreed, 'That is a very important point. I think that women are perhaps more able to extend their ego towards their children than others. Even with them, however, their own ego plays a major role. That is most apparent if we consider the classic mother-in-law kind of stories, where we may tend to give precedence to our own views rather than the feelings of our children for their spouses.'

Marie was thinking deeply. Vadya enquired whether there was any specific concern. She shook her head, 'No, not at all. I feel that if we work on this concept of expansion of the ego, it could also enhance our ability to control the ego. We would also develop a greater sense of humility, together with a desire to effectively participate in sharing other people's interests and joys.'

'You are absolutely right Marie. There is indeed a two-way relationship between controlling the ego and expanding the ego. However, the causal links are not straightforward,' explained Vadya.

'What do you mean by that?' both Marie and Nancy asked together.

Vadya explained, 'If we focus on combining humility with concern and consideration for others, then these two aspects develop together. Otherwise, one follows the other only if we give a deliberate focus on expansion of the ego. Curbing our ego will develop humility, but that alone is not adequate for us to care about the feelings and views of others.'

Nancy was nodding, 'Thanks for this. What does this mean for our daily life?'

Marie did not agree, 'I am certain that people would find it difficult to progress in terms of the specific objectives you have described, even if they form part of a much larger objective. It would take long to achieve these aims, they will probably keep failing and end up starting from scratch every time. Something like the game of snakes and ladders, where we keep getting bitten by the snake of failure and drop down almost to the initial starting point.'

Vadya started softly, 'Marie, my personal view is that whatever progress we achieve on this path is like an investment which stays within us, even if we err or fail repeatedly. This investment or spiritual capital is actually the experience we gain during our efforts; the diverse situations we face in life and our progress in learning to deal with issues in a calm, collected and analytical way. In effect, it is like a safety net, which does not let you fall too far. This helps us to both recover and travel faster towards new achievements. Paradoxically, this experience is, in fact, most important when we fail to make progress because if we maintain our objectivity and tranquillity in that situation, it makes us stronger and enables us to better apply our cumulative understanding to identify the appropriate path for our progress.'

When Marie asked whether Vadya could give some example to clarify the idea, she explained, 'We do not lose in this game because there is always progress, as well as potential progress. With renewed efforts, we could quickly regain the original level of progress; something like learning how to ride a cycle and then being able to do so at any stage in your life.'

'Are you actually saying that whenever we fail to be considerate or expand our ego with love, we should examine the reasons behind our failure and take corrective steps to keep moving forward? Will such sustained focus prepare us to deal better with failure? Will it make us experienced and capable enough to identify ways of moving ahead on this road?' asked Marie.

'Yes. Practice helps us hone our abilities, equipping us to deal with both material and spiritual concerns. In our journey, it is crucial to recognise that whenever difficulties tend to deviate us from our objective, it is both a test as well as an opportunity to improve ourselves. To succeed in this test, the relevant action always has to be our own. No extent of knowledge, understanding or experience can take us forward in a meaningful way, without specific action on our part to live the concept, to adapt our understanding in terms of our thoughts and actions,' explained Vadya.

'I completely agree with you on this point. In fact, in the place where I come from, there is no doubt at all that one's own efforts are the only basis for achieving anything in life. However, in a spiritual context and in cases where people believe that external conditions primarily determine the outcome for us, belief in the primacy of own effort starts getting eroded. Isn't it the spiritual view—all that happens is because of the Divine and that we are only a small, insignificant part of the events that take place, without any real control on the results of our actions?' asked Marie.

Vadya thought for some time before answering, 'Living in a deeply spiritual environment since childhood even while being educated in the Western system, I used to often struggle with this issue. This is a very deep question and could be addressed at various levels. However, for our purpose, it is important to consider that normally all spiritual progress is due to the efforts we ourselves make. Of course, even if we consider that everything happens by the dispensation of the Divine, it does not imply that our role is small in any way. Part of the Divine's dispensation is that with effort, it is possible for us to keep on improving ourselves in every area, including spiritual pursuits. Therefore, normally our own thoughts and actions will determine both the direction and extent of our movement on the spiritual path. If it was otherwise, great spiritual masters would not have had to work at spiritual progress, nor would each spiritual path specify code of behaviour or actions that helps people achieve spiritual progress. Therefore, we have to focus on progressing through our own thoughts and actions. This does not mean that our efforts should be devoid of the spiritual part. It is in this context that the Divine dispensation must be seen in a much larger perspective, along the lines of the spiritual advice that you would have often heard in India: Only our own effort is for us to make. The result of our effort is not within our control and we should not worry about it.'

Vadya saw Marie and Nancy nodding and smiled with obvious pleasure. 'In a spiritual frame of mind, we perform our action in two simultaneous states: Being the doer and the observer of action, with both participation and detachment, which will help us reach the pinnacle of clarity and objectivity.'

'This is getting very interesting, indeed,' smiled Nancy. Marie was smiling too. It seemed to make her happy that Vadya was enjoying this ambient exchange. It was a lighter moment that brought them all closer.

Vadya then asked them if they would like to eat something. Marie asked her to check on Ananda as well. Vadya soon returned with the snacks, looking happy. She felt the atmosphere was far more relaxed than when they had begun the discussion. Picking up a biscuit, she spoke with the obvious satisfaction of one who has foretold an event, 'Ananda is at his computer, completely engrossed, munching at the snacks from the plate on his table, without realising what and how much he is eating. He is miles away from the state of mind in which we saw him earlier today. No disturbance, only communion with the computer and email. So, let me take this discussion forward.'

'Thank you, Vadya. I was a bit concerned about Ananda. He is like a teacher to me now, as are you. I feel so privileged,' said Marie.

'I cannot tell you how pleased I am to have you both with us! In India, we have a very peculiar mindset. We do not think of our friends as friends in the usual sense. We think of them as part of our family.

You are now part of our family. There is no teacher or student, just family,' Vadya said.

'Thank you. We feel truly privileged,' Marie said, looking at Nancy who was solemnly nodding.

'Should we continue with our small steps and concentric circles, slowly travelling across these concepts?' asked Vadya. Marie and Nancy nodded.

'Is there some specific criteria or behavioural norm that we should keep in mind to help us succeed in fully extending our ego to others? We are clear about humility and sensitivity to others. What else could help us improve?' asked Nancy.

'Let us use the technique of converting certain concepts into more tractable or manageable ones. Consider the implications of being humble by specifying or identifying the main attributes of a person who shows humility. Such a person has no arrogance or self-obsession, nor easily is there a loss of temper. Therefore, it is very important that we should control our anger when dealing with others. To be fully effective, we need to supplement this with being sensitive to what others would like us to do for them,' explained Vadya.

Marie intervened, 'This is not always easy. In fact, it is seldom easy. Should we have some disincentive mechanism to punish ourselves if we do not succeed? Maybe, then we would be able to focus more on achieving our objective and avoiding failure.'

'I have often wondered whether a disincentive mechanism is really a useful technique. If we really want to make spiritual progress, achieve greater contentment, objectivity and a positive attitude towards events in our life, I do not think that a disincentive mechanism will help us achieve the desired result. If we punish ourselves whenever we do not succeed, we will perhaps not repeat an undesirable action again, but such punishments could generate within us additional distortions, which themselves would need to be addressed over time,' responded Vadya.

Nancy was not feeling comfortable, 'Negative thoughts or actions are normally part of our behaviour and we need to address them somehow. The disincentive method would seem to be one way of doing so, even if it creates additional complications. These additional aspects could be dealt with later, when we are able to control our negative thoughts or actions.'

'Nancy, you have touched on two very important points which are fundamental to address this concern. First, whether this method will help us control negative thoughts and actions. I think this method suppresses them, but does not eradicate them from our personality or mind. Second, whether negative thoughts or actions are a normal part of our behaviour. This is exactly how we should treat them—as normal parts of behaviour and then keep up our effort to go beyond them.'

'What do you mean by going beyond them, Vadya?' asked Nancy.

'Instead of trying to combat or overcome them, treat them as a normal part of growing up or making progress and continue the efforts to keep improving. It is like a child learning to walk. If the child falls down while learning to walk, you do not punish the child. Instead, the child is encouraged to continue making efforts. Take another example—in meditation, when we sit still, within a few seconds, all kinds of thoughts start coming to our mind. We persist with our meditation. With time and practice, our mind wavers less and less. The process is gentle, without any disincentives or punishment to control extraneous thoughts. Each time we have extraneous thoughts, we recognise their presence and go back to our meditation, without being perturbed. The same method would apply for encouraging positive thinking, including for the process of extending our ego. This would also be a useful way to approach Ananda's "inside-out" method.'

Nancy joined in with another question, 'Why do we get these extraneous thoughts? Why do we not succeed in being positive and caring all the time despite wanting to do so? It can be very frustrating. Though I said these are normal parts of our behaviour, I feel bad whenever I find myself in that situation. I do not want this to be a normal part of me.'

'Nancy, I think you should look at your situation from a positive perspective. Someone once said to us that the essence of spirituality can be described by two concepts—compassion and being positive. Take your present state of mind in which you feel a need to address negative thoughts and actions. This is a positive thought, a sign of progress. A small step and a step in the right direction. Many persons do not reach your state of mind. Once you are in this frame of mind, you should realise that each situation you face is an opportunity to test you, to help you grow. Instead of getting stuck in its details and seeking ways of changing yourself, just pick yourself up and continue with your efforts, with a peaceful mind. Think of it as a road going in a particular direction towards your goal. Each time you move in the opposite direction, the only appropriate way is to turn again in the right direction and move ahead.'

'But why do these failures arise? How can we go ahead without them?' asked Nancy.

'The simple answer to your last question is no, we cannot go ahead without problems. They are a normal part of our life. There is a very interesting mythological story, which is instructive in this context. In India, we have this story about churning of the ocean by the gods and the demons, all trying to get the ambrosia of life, or the equivalent of the Holy Grail from the ocean. In this story, a number of special jewels and divine beings emerged from the ocean, but the first thing to emerge was a very strong poison. No one could deal with this poison, so the gods requested Lord Shiva to help them. Lord Shiva drank the poison, holding it in his throat and the strong poison turned his throat blue. Thus, Shiva is known as the Blue Throated One.'

'What is the significance of this story?' asked Marie.

'The story can be seen in allegorical terms. The ocean being churned is our life itself. We possess within ourselves, both the good and the bad. When we desire to have special divine objects or the ambrosia of life in terms of peace of mind and happiness, they can only come through our efforts to churn the ocean of life. When we begin our efforts, the first thing which emerges is poison—obstacles which would be negative and even harmful. We have to deal with them and continue our efforts. Only then will we get all the jewels of success we desire. But the process is definitely one which disturbs our surroundings, churns them into waves and the poison does emerge. These failures or blockages on our path of progress are not only normal, they should be expected and have to be addressed when they arise. At each stage, as we reach a higher level of achievement, the churning has to begin again, the process being broadly similar till we reach a situation where we only have special divine gifts of peace and contentment, high energy states and objectivity, together with active participation in our daily life.'

'So much wisdom and so many difficulties. The mind boggles at how to deal with them,' said Nancy.

'With small steps and concentric circles, breaking each problem into manageable and tractable components and addressing them with practical and objective steps. And keep recognising the distance we have already covered with success. On the road towards the goal, we may tend to reverse for some time, or even rest, but after that we should again go forward in the right direction. We should choose a pace which we can manage,' said Vadya.

Marie started speaking in an excited voice, 'Vadya, a light just flashed in my mind. If being with our real self—the Life Force—paves the way for a strong spiritual state of mind, then whatever keeps us away from it will be an obstacle in making spiritual progress. Such obstacles then are our feelings and actions which disrupt the conditions necessary for being with our deeper entity. For example, anger, excitement, acquisitiveness, arrogance and bias. If we can control such feelings and the actions based on them, we would in effect be on a spiritual path with our true self, the Spiritual Force. So, if we are calm, objective, unbiased and compassionate, these attributes would show that we are in our spiritual realm, with our deeper self.'

Vadya too seemed excited, 'That is brilliantly put, Marie. This is indeed a very useful way of looking at it. One way of progressing in this is to treat yourself as if you are in a spiritual school. We are never thrown out of the spiritual school. If we make sustained efforts, positive results do take place. Even if we succeed in only one subject, that success is there for us. It is effectively a promotion from our starting position, the class where we began. Which other school is so generous?' asked Vadya.

Nancy was nodding, trying to digest Vadya's words. Vadya looked up and noticed that the other two were silently giving her space to think. Glancing at Marie and Nancy, she then gestured with the teapot to check whether they would like some tea. When they nodded, she poured out tea for them.

'Thank you, Vadya. We really enjoyed ourselves today. We have to thank you, Ananda and Guru Purna for making these interactions possible. It has been wonderful for us,' Marie was saying, as she looked up to see who else had entered the room.

It was Ananda, who now looked rested and rather happy. He sat down and smiled at everyone, 'Who wants to thank me? If it is Marie or Nancy, I would then like to thank you both too. You have done me a great favour, being such willing participants in our interaction. With you, I managed to clear several concepts in my own mind.'

Marie and Nancy did not respond, just smiled back and looked at Vadya to assess whether they should stay or go, leaving their hosts free to talk. Ananda noticed this and assured them that they should stay on.

'You would be very tired of the topics we covered in our discussion. Time to catch up with other serious aspects of life like what to have for dinner and also our travel plans. Talking of which, I have two developments to report.'

'Two developments? What do you mean by that Ananda?' asked Vadya, who by now was used to surprises that Ananda kept springing from time to time. A sense of trepidation, thus, overtook her whenever Ananda spoke in general terms about travel plans.

'Yes, Vadya. Both very positive. I have received two emails, one from Anil Baba in Varanasi and another from Francis in Geneva. I had told Anil Baba about Marie and Nancy and their interest in spiritual matters. He has invited all of us, kids included, to the Ashram in Varanasi. How about taking up his offer?'

All the three women brightened up on hearing this. For several months, Vadya had been planning to go to the ashram and work in the school and the hospital for the poor. Marie and Nancy too had heard about the ashram and were keen to visit the place of spiritual peace. Being a trustee, Ananda was very emotionally involved with the place. They, therefore, decided to leave for Varanasi on Friday and return after the weekend.

'What about the email from Francis? What does he say? Is he coming to Delhi? That would be wonderful Ananda. I have not met him for so long,' said Vadya.

'Actually, Francis has invited me to a conference in Geneva. He also wants to organise a special picnic over the weekend to a place nearby, Combloux in France. If it is fine with you, on my way to Geneva, I would also like to visit my spiritual guide near Milan,' Ananda explained hurriedly, hoping his plans would not cause any complications for Vadya, who would have to manage everything in Delhi while he was travelling.

Vadya knew that Ananda found the Geneva trip attractive because of the possibility of meeting his spiritual guide. Of course, the conference would be important to him professionally. But his heart would be focused on a small village, at half an hour's driving distance from Milan.

Marie was looking a bit puzzled, 'Ananda, it's interesting to learn you will be visiting your spiritual guide near Milan. Is he some Indian adept who is living there?'

'No, Marie,' explained Ananda. 'He is an Italian, a very highly evolved and deeply spiritual soul. He is a venerated part of an old Indian tradition, a guru to many of us. You know that in India we have the tradition of a guru who initiates a spiritual disciple through a specific mantra and takes responsibility for the disciple's spiritual progress. He is my guru and I am his initiated disciple. He guides me from time to time, having taken on this responsibility when my great spiritual master, who was also my father's guru suggested that I approach him for guidance. This great master is the one whose photograph you see on the wall in front of you.'

All of them turned to look at the large photo of a serene smiling face, the face which Ananda always saw in the depth of his heart. Ananda bowed his head slightly and smiled, happily looking forward to continuing a journey, which had begun long ago, longer than some in that room could imagine.

16

Discussion on Books Continues

'Should we move on to the next book on your list, Benedict?'

'Yes, Francis. I want to talk about another self-help book, but I also have a complaint. This book focuses very much on the spiritual plane. It is a popular book with important messages, but the bulk of the discussion is about spiritual practices. What did you have in mind when you suggested this book?' Benedict asked, holding up a book before Francis.

'Benedict, this book can be read at various levels, including lessons for our life at a very practical level.[1] Perhaps, we could start by discussing whatever you thought could be useful for you,' Francis replied.

'I noted that some of the points in the book are similar to those in the last one we discussed.[2] For example, do not judge any situation, make it a habit to monitor your mental and emotional state through self-observation, address what is bothering you and stop worrying and move ahead. Set goals and work towards them. Learn from the past so that mistakes are not repeated. Each situation that you face is just that, a situation to be addressed; it is not your life. Bring more consciousness into ordinary situations. By doing so, you enhance the power emanating from your inner presence at any specific moment.'

'This is very interesting. You will notice that you have seen similar thoughts in two different, substantive books. This suggests that these are very worthwhile points to focus on. What else have you seen in this book?' Francis enquired.

'I found some ideas especially interesting. Two of them seemed most important to me. One is that we should focus on the present moment, the "now", and be fully involved in addressing our objectives in the "now". The second one echoes the thoughts encompassed in the previous book that we should have control over our mind.'

'Can you please explain this to me?' asked Francis.

'My understanding of this idea is that we derive our presence from an entity within ourselves, our consciousness, which is separate from our mind. The mind projects itself over this deeper presence and makes us think about ourselves, in terms of our concerns and views, based on past experiences and future aspirations. It prevents us from looking at our essential presence, the consciousness.

'We can know our true self when the mind is still because only then is our presence and attention fully and intensively in the present moment, in our consciousness. I see three main points: First, we need to focus and operate in the present moment because that is the moment we have for taking any action that helps us to achieve our goals. Second, we have two entities within us. Our mind or ego is one and our consciousness or essential presence is the other. If we separate and distinguish ourselves from our minds and external preoccupations, and focus instead on our internal essential self, it helps us operate in the present, distance ourselves from failure, from pain or other shortcomings and find the strength to deal with our shortcomings. Third, such strength comes from our internal resources which are always available in abundance, when we are able to tap them without the constraints and aspirations of our mind.'

Benedict picked up a piece of paper and read out a few sentences from it, 'Some interesting statements that I have written down are: To the ego, only past and future are relevant. Present does not exist [to the mind]. Love, joy and peace cannot flourish until you have freed yourself from mind dominance. The pain-body is a shadow cast by the ego.'

'That is very impressive Benedict,' Francis remarked, but he saw that Benedict did not appear pleased with the compliment. Instead, he looked somewhat unsure and anxious. 'What is the matter, Benedict? Is there some problem?'

'Francis, I really do not understand what these points mean. I sense no ownership over these concepts, have no feeling about what they really mean. Can you help me understand them in a simpler and more practical way?'

'I can try,' answered Francis, as he thought for a moment. 'Let me get you this interesting article, it can illustrate some of my thoughts.' Francis then walked to the table in the middle of the room and picked up a recent copy of the magazine, *The New Yorker*. He opened it and looked pleased at having found the article quickly.

'First, let us begin with your point about separate entities—the mind and our deeper self. I came across this article only recently. Let me read to you from this magazine:

> Over the past few decades, geneticists, neuroscientists, psychologists, sociologists, economists and others have made great strides in understanding the inner working of the human mind. Far from being dryly materialistic, their work illuminates the rich underwater world where character is formed and wisdom grows. They are giving us a better grasp of emotions, intuitions, biases, longings, predispositions, character traits and social bonding, precisely those things about which our culture has least to say. Brain science helps fill the hole left by the atrophy of theology and philosophy. A core finding of this work is that we are not primarily the products of our

> conscious thinking. The conscious mind gives us one way of making sense of our environment. But the unconscious mind gives us other, more supple ways. The cognitive revolution of the past thirty years provides a different perspective on our lives, one that emphasises the relative importance of emotion over pure reason, social connections over individual choice, moral intuition over abstract logic, perceptiveness over IQ. It allows us to tell a different sort of success story, an inner story to go along with the conventional surface one.'[3]

Benedict took the magazine and read the text for himself. He looked up and asked, 'So what is the importance of this? It says, there is a conscious mind and an unconscious mind. How does this link up with what our book is saying?'

'Benedict, I think this text is relevant. It shows various studies spanning different disciplines recognising that the mind works at multiple levels. There is an explicit recognition of a conscious and an unconscious mind. We normally associate the objective process of thinking with the conscious mind, but from the text here we see that a major part of our cognitive thinking comes from another, deeper level. This shows that our entity, the entity with explicit awareness and thought, exists at least at two different levels.'

'Yes, but I still do not see a link with the concept in the book.'

'Think about it, Benedict,' Francis insisted. 'Now even the so-called rational thinkers acknowledge that there is a system, a superior system perhaps, of decision-making within us, which is at a level different from our mind. It has taken them quite long to reach this conclusion but they are still operating at the level of the mind, a conscious mind and a subconscious or unconscious mind. There are other levels of our existence, which they have yet to recognise or reach in a substantive, conclusive, more comprehensive way. To some extent, the psychologists that do past-life regression are uncovering a small part of these deeper levels of our existence.

'This still deeper level is also mentioned in the book. But is there some simple way for me to really feel that this deeper level is within me? And how can I be sure that when I focus on it, I will be clearer on how to address my problems?'

Francis thought for some time and then asked, 'Tell me, Benedict, do you advise your friends on how to address their problems? Can you analyse their problems clearly and give them balanced and considered advice?'

'Yes, I think I give them good advice. On several occasions, my friends have mentioned to me that they benefited from it,' Benedict admitted.

'Good. Now think about situations when you yourself face a problem. Are you as effective in analysing your own concerns and advising yourself as when you advise your friends? Give me your honest opinion,' said Francis.

Benedict shook his head, 'No, I do not see the situation as clearly when I am involved myself. But that is because I am affected more deeply, and obviously cannot be as objective as when analysing the problems faced by my friends.'

'Exactly. This illustrates one of the main points in the book. Ideally, we should be capable of addressing our concerns with the same efficiency and objectivity as those of others, without personal issues, emotional involvement and interference from our ego. The first step towards achieving such a state is to recognise that we actually operate at two different levels. One is the level of the mind, which contains our personal views on our place and position in society, our aspirations and our memories about events and persons. It is a repository of all the biases we possess. This is why when we use our mind to deal with situations in our life, we are basically utilising a mechanism deeply involved in and affected by the situation, reflecting all our self-oriented biases and emotions. To deal with the situation more effectively, it is necessary to look at issues from the vantage point of a level of our entity that is beyond these aspirations, memories and biases. This is the inner level of our entity, the deeper level of consciousness, which is the focus of this book.'

'How do I get there?'

'By making an attempt—an honest attempt.'

'Why is it beyond the biases which my mind contains? Is it something like intuition—pure intuition—which is not affected by any bias?'

'Benedict, your insights keep amazing me. I think you have hit the nail on the head. Do you know that the word "intuition" comes from the Latin word *intueri*, which means "to look inside" or "to contemplate"? Psychologists have linked intuition with certain parts of the brain, but we could also see it as having a deeper source: Our consciousness. This consciousness is the source of our abiding knowledge, objectivity and wisdom. It is at a distance from and unaffected by our own views and biases. At that deeper level, we are beyond the limited personal biases that arise from our ego, self-perception and aspirations. Benedict, from there you could access the same objectivity and wisdom that you show when advising your friends on addressing their problems. You could look at yourself as the external entity which deals with everyday events, as if this were some other person, like a friend of yours.'

'How do I make sure that I am actually at that level, Francis? How do I know that I am actually functioning away from the mind and present at the level of this consciousness?'

'Before I address your question, I want to clarify another important aspect. The fact that we function from the level of our consciousness does not mean that we should not be using our mind. It is just that when we are at this deeper level, we use all of our faculties with a greater sense of balance, clarity and effectiveness. Our intellect actually becomes sharper and more focused, better able to distinguish between different priorities.'

'Okay, Francis. I understand this at a conceptual level, but how do I reach there in a simple, practical way?'

'An important way is given in the book very clearly, that is to focus on the present and to do your tasks in the current moment itself, in the "Now". This is the first of the three points you wanted to discuss further.'

'That is correct. Can you please tell me why I should do so? Why is this important in a practical, everyday sense?'

'Benedict, when we start functioning in the present, we would become highly concentrated on our efforts. We must clearly determine our priorities amongst various tasks. This requires clarity of purpose and taking responsibility for our actions. A strong emphasis on the present also keeps our focus on our specific and immediate actions rather than the results likely to arise in the future. Hence, each moment becomes effective and purposeful.'

'I see the value of this, but how will I prevent my biases and self-oriented thoughts from intervening?'

'This process itself should enable you over time to do so. The litmus test is how you treat each issue, each concern and event.' Saying this, Francis picked up the book and flipped to a specific page, 'As the author says in his book, "Best indicator of your consciousness is how you deal with life's challenges when they come."'[4]

Francis smiled and thought for a moment before continuing, 'Benedict, let me suggest a mechanism based on what David had explained in his lecture. Do you recall David's description of some methods used by the great Shramanic masters? He had drawn two circles with arrows going from each circle towards the other, where one circle signified spiritual effort and the other referred to good thoughts and actions.'

Benedict nodded and Francis continued, 'That illustration tried to show that it may be easier to progress to a higher-level concept if your behaviour includes attributes which describe that concept. Conceptually, we could break it into a four-step process.

'First, visualise yourself in the state which you wish to achieve. Second, imagine the behavioural attributes you would have in that state. Third, incorporate those attributes into your behaviour. Fourth, keep repeating this process. It will help you reach the state you wish,' Francis concluded.

'Francis, the first step is clear to me. I wish to be in a balanced and clear-minded state of consciousness, where I am able to distance myself from bias and self-oriented thoughts. What is the second step? What behavioural attributes should I embody? This is the difficult part of this exercise, isn't it?'

'Yes, you are absolutely correct. The second part is the crux of the entire effort. Let us see which attributes are most suitable to progress towards our main objective. Try not to be emotional about any action, person or situation. This requires being calm, not being angry and not losing focus on the key action which one should take at any specific moment.'

'How do I do this, Francis? What should I really bear in mind to help me achieve this state?'

'You might realise that you are focusing on several objectives. Some may be primary objectives linked to your substantive achievement, while others may exist mainly to feed your ego when you react to a situation based on your sense of self in that situation. We normally act in any situation without distinguishing between these two types of objectives.'

'So, how do I distinguish between them?'

'First, by being aware of this distinction and then by being honest in our self-assessment by asking ourselves certain key questions, like, why I am emphasising a particular action, what the primary objective in this action is, which action will best achieve it, which action is not focused on my key objective but is an assertion of my ego or sense of self, what is the likely response to my action and will that make it easy or tough for me to achieve my main objective.'

'Is this it? Though I must say that even in this, you have covered a large number of questions for decision-making, haven't you?'

'In my view, Benedict, this is it. I think that all complexity can ultimately be reduced to a simple pattern, if we can identify the essence of what we seek. Once you get into the habit of using this process for self-assessment, it becomes simple. We routinely make decisions based on a frame of reference that is actually quite complex, but we find it effortless because we have internalised the steps. If you want to convert all my questions into two key ones, they would be, what the objective of my action is and will the likely response to my action make it more or less easy to achieve it. Also try and be positive in your approach.'

'To not be negative about others, even if they are not being good to us? That is a tall order, Francis,' Benedict said.

'It may help to recognise that someone's action being inappropriate is quite distinct from developing feelings of negativity about that action or person. This is an interesting feature of being positive because even when we consider whether an action is "good" or "bad", "correct" or "incorrect", we should do so without passing any value judgment about the person,' Francis said.

'But what if someone is aiming to harm us with negative action? Do we still keep the same perspective?'

'In that situation, your responsibility is to protect yourself through your own action, not to evaluate whether or not the other person's action is negative. Focus on the actions of that person and your own rather than assigning a value judgment on either. That would be an objective and positive way of dealing with the situation.'

'Very interesting. I will try to work on it. But how do we find the great strength, which you say is inside us?'

'Look around you, see the people who are really successful. They show immense energy and resolve because they have a clear sense of purpose that they have nurtured through discipline and resolve. By reaching our inner energy source, we too can augment our levels of energy and strength, higher than we can ever imagine. You must have read about the yogis in the Himalayas. Do you know how they are able to withstand extremely inhospitable conditions? It requires great inner strength. Likewise, the extraordinary feats performed by martial artists or others, be they ordinary or highly-placed individuals. Whenever we face major difficulties in life, we need to rely on exceptional strength that we normally do not access. Our effort should be to always be in touch with that inner strength and feel the quiet and peaceful self-assurance which comes with it.'

'But strength can be used for good purpose as well as for the assertion of ego. How do the two points you just mentioned, being objective and positive, play a role in this?' Benedict asked.

'Benedict, we are in life for the long term, with all its ups and downs, but always with the potential for improving ourselves. With each action, we build a base for ourselves, a base which is actually within us, but also extends beyond us, enhancing the scope of our presence. This base defines us, is our potential and the foundation for all that we achieve. A positive approach helps to build our strength, provides deep contentment in our heart and a growing feeling of completeness within,' Francis replied.

'Is this something new, or are there some books which also say the same thing?'

'Benedict, whatever we are discussing has been contemplated, discussed and acted upon for ages. Even in modern times, a large number of books exist that make similar or overlapping points, and suggest similar ways for making progress. So, the idea should be to try and understand these issues, from whichever perspective one finds easy to comprehend.'

'Is there any other book which talks about the importance of being in the present?'

'Yes, as I said, each point has been discussed in some form or other in various places. In fact, you may recall that even *The Power of Now* refers to earlier masters, such as the Buddha, who emphasised this concept.'

'Is there a book on metaphysics which talks about the importance of objective and rational analysis?'

'A good example is a book which discusses spiritual concepts relating to the teachings of Naropa.[5] Do you remember Naropa? He was one of the Buddhist monks David mentioned in his lecture.' Saying this, Francis got up to get a slim book from his shelf and flipped through it.

'This is a very interesting book, which also shows how limited our normal framework of logic and reasoning is,' Francis continued. 'It contains some of the ideas we were discussing in relation to objective and clear thinking. Here are some relevant bits to answer your question:

> From the Buddhist point of view, our basic being is fundamental intelligence and wakefulness that has been clouded over by all kinds of veils and obscurations. Intellect in the sense of *prajna* is a state of being logical and open, open to any information and willing to collect it, chew it, swallow it, digest it, work with it. (56, 72)

'The author makes other interesting points. For example, on the need to face situations and take action to deal with them, he says that it is "important to deal with a situation, rather than with what is right and what is wrong". When we go deeper into our other entity, he says that over time "the watcher dissolves". He emphasises the importance of meditation in a very special way—Practice of meditation is the only way one can step out of planting further karma.'

'This is very interesting and very useful to me.'

'Well, I am glad you are getting some useful ideas from our discussion. Think of consciousness as another deep level of your personal resources.'

'Francis, you have explained the mind and the thinking process in terms of two separate and different levels. I have read some other books too, some deeper than others. I think I should save those for later. Let me digest what you have explained today,' said Benedict.

Francis saw that Benedict was smiling at some new thought and raised an eyebrow to enquire. Benedict asked, 'Have you read the latest book by Stephen Hawking,[6] where he says that scientific advances now can adequately explain how life came about on Earth? He talks about the M-theory, or a collection of different theories that may overlap, saying these are enough to predict that many universes were created out of nothing. Their creation did not require intervention by any supernatural being or God. What do you think about this?'

'Why don't you save this for my Indian friend, Ananda, who will be with us soon? Let us see what he has to say. What about the other books you wanted to discuss with me?'

'Thank you, Francis. You have been most generous with your time and friendship. But I must confess, when I come across views such as those of Stephen Hawking that explain creation without recourse to self-analysis or spirituality, my enthusiasm for reading these books starts waning precipitously. It is perhaps also because there are so many books to read! Sometimes, I feel I should stop reading such books.'

'That can be one option. Especially after our extensive discussion today, where we have covered so much ground and dealt with so many concepts. I recall Ananda telling me several years ago how he had decided to do meditation and actually follow other practices rather than read more and more about them. He decided to give primacy to action over knowledge from books, which often remains only at the cerebral level. Better to incorporate our ideas in our behaviour than seek more of the same at a theoretical level alone. Give yourself a chance to act instead of asking questions.'

'That is a good idea, Francis. I will definitely do so. But I would like to question Ananda about the idea in Stephen Hawking's book.'

'Very good. You should definitely do so. On that good note, we end our discussion today.'

References

1. Tolle, Ekhart. *The Power of Now*. UK: Hodder, 1999.
2. Sharma, Robin S. *The Monk Who Sold His Ferrari*. India: Jaico Publishing House, 2003.
3. Brooks, David. Social Animal: How the new sciences of human nature can help make sense of a life. USA: *The New Yorker*, 17 January 2011.
4. Tolle, Eckhart. *Practising the Power of Now*. UK: Hodder, 2001.
5. Trungpa, Chogyam. *Illusion's Game: The Life and Teaching of Naropa*. USA and UK: Shambhala Publications, 1999.
6. Hawking, Stephen and Mladinow, Leonard. *The Grand Design: New Answers to the Ultimate Questions of Life*. UK: Bantam Press, 2010.

17

Trip to the Ashram in Varanasi

They were all safely seated in the plane for their ten o'clock flight from New Delhi to Varanasi. Vadya shared with Ananda all she had discussed with Marie and Nancy. Ananda realised that Vadya had extended some of his own ideas on small steps and concentric circles. The flight took off on time. Ananda looked at his group of six eager travellers. The air hostesses indulged Juhi and Joy, so the two girls were in a happy state of mind. As the plane landed, their excitement increased.

'Will Anil Baba be at the airport or would we see him at the ashram?' asked Juhi.

'I am sure he will be at the airport,' replied Joy before anyone else could respond.

She looked confident and fully in control, as if she was going home. Anil Baba, whose ashram they were going to visit, always indulged the children and made them feel like they were part of the management at the ashram. It amused Ananda to see the children mingling with everyone at the ashram, as if they were as much a part of the place as anyone else.

No wonder they were excited. Vadya and Ananda also closely identified with the ashram and could strongly feel the presence of their spiritual masters, their peaceful energy permeating the place. Though they had always felt close to that energy whether they lived in India or abroad, that abiding feeling was intensified each time the family visited the ashram. The place generated greater stability and sense of security within their hearts and made them more complete, as if they connected at a deeper level with themselves and those around them.

Marie and Nancy had greatly enjoyed their earlier visit to Varanasi with Guru Purna. Varanasi, a holy city of the Hindus, they learnt to their amazement, had existed several centuries before Christ. However, this visit was different. They were excited and looking forward to some interesting meetings and discussions.

Each one with a different motive but similar excitement got off the aeroplane and started walking towards the place where they would collect their luggage. It was a small airport and the distance from the plane to the luggage retrieval point was less than three hundred metres. Fifteen minutes later, they exited the building and saw Anil Baba, slender and straight, standing some distance away, waving to them. Juhi and Joy ran to hug him. The three of them looked an island of happiness, laughing together with gay abandon. Ananda and Vadya walked over to them and bent down to touch Anil Baba's feet. Ananda and Baba hugged each other like long-lost brothers. Ananda had an interesting relationship with Anil Baba. Whenever they met, Ananda first showed respect in the traditional Indian way by touching Anil Baba's feet and then hugged him as a brother.

Vadya introduced Marie and Nancy. All of them greeted Anil Baba and two others from the ashram who had come to meet them. The trip to the ashram took about half an hour. Beautiful devotional music was playing in the car, but all attention was on the excited chattering of Joy and Juhi, who were talking non-stop with Anil Baba.

When they reached the ashram, several people were waiting for them. The children from the ashram school were lounging around, holding some wild flowers in their hands. As soon as Juhi and Joy got off from the vehicle, these children rushed to welcome them with the flowers. The older people exchanged greetings; some of the regulars at the ashram greeted Vadya and Ananda in the traditional Indian way, showing their respect by bending low to touch their feet. Ananda and Vadya folded their hands and acknowledged their greetings with smiles of affection. Marie and Nancy were introduced and they too shyly acknowledged the greetings and the flowers of welcome. Together with their children, Ananda and Vadya went to the temple and spent a few minutes in prayer. For them, this always marked the starting point of their ashram visit and was also their last act before they left the place.

The luggage was already in the rooms prepared for the guests, who were taken to their respective rooms to rest before lunch. While the suitcases were getting unpacked, Juhi and Joy ran away to play at the primary school, which had over four hundred children, studying in grades ranging from one to five. These children came from very poor households, but felt liberated and carefree at the school, happily laughing away their difficulties. They were scampering around with Juhi and Joy, eager to show them their work in the classrooms. Even the school teachers had taken a break to welcome the young visitors from New Delhi. Anil Baba was watching them from a distance, not wanting to interfere but keeping an eye. The children from Varanasi and Delhi were oblivious of any such supervision. They mixed as easily as the confluence of waters from two different rivers, their adjustment looked seamless for they were completely comfortable with each other. Anil Baba gestured to one of the teachers, requested her to look after Juhi and Joy, then walked back to the main area where Ananda was waiting for him. They moved towards the open shed near the main temple, sat down on a couple of cots kept there and accepted the steaming cups of tea offered to them. Marie and Nancy too joined the group and were given some hot tea and roasted chickpeas. They sat on straight-back chairs and glanced around to take in the activity at the ashram.

'Would you like to walk around the ashram after you have rested a bit?' asked Anil Baba with a smile.

'That would be very good. Vadya has talked so much about the people here, but we do not know much about the various facilities. I can see a small temple. Which other buildings do you have here?' Nancy asked.

'The big building you see on the right in front of you is a small hospital. We have eight doctors sharing the work on different days of the week, addressing a variety of medical concerns. There are some rooms for patients who need to stay for a few days after treatment. We also have alternative medicine and naturopathy treatment in the building adjacent to the big one. Behind the hospital building, we have a small area where medicines are dispensed to patients at a token charge.'

'Do you provide health facilities only in the ashram or do you have some other centres too?' asked Marie showing her own interest.

'Outside the ashram, we hold eye camps for cataract operations and run programmes for immunising children against hepatitis. Otherwise, our health-related activities are all here,' replied Anil Baba. 'On your left, we have the kitchen which is very handy because we often provide meals for a large number of people, mostly our school children and the poor people in the area.'

'How many persons do you feed and how often?' Marie continued.

'On four special occasions each year, we have over two thousand people eating here. Whoever comes is welcome. On some other occasions, about seven to eight hundred people gather, half of whom are school children.'

'That is really a large number. How do you manage? Who does all the work?' Nancy asked with some hesitation.

'It is the grace of our guru. We have several volunteers who join in to help our regular employees,' explained Anil Baba.

'And Anil Baba works the hardest amongst all of them. People help in various ways but it is the commitment and dedication of a few which helps achieve such large tasks with facility,' explained Ananda.

Anil Baba continued, 'Beyond the fruit trees, behind the low wall you see on your left, there is a primary school for the children who are unable to go to regular schools here. Most of them are fishermen's children, very poor families. All this keeps us quite busy.'

Nancy looked around. She saw the softly flowing river Ganges behind her, various buildings, fruit trees and flowers before turning to Anil Baba, 'That is a lot of work for you. Must keep you very busy. I am a bit perplexed, Baba. I was thinking that an ashram is basically like a monastery, which should have more than just one building for spiritual activity. You have only the temple, and that too quite a small one compared to all these other buildings. Should you not have more dedicated space for spiritual activities?'

Anil Baba was silent for some time. He liked to focus on doing active work rather than talking about it. However, he was an excellent and most considerate host and that implied being fully responsive to any question from his guests. 'Nancy, spiritual activity is not limited to prayers, meditation, chanting or preaching to a congregation. Spiritual activities include working within the Divine Will, using our abilities to bring positive change, to wipe away a tear and bring hope and help to people, provide them with better opportunities in life, to try and bring joy to others. These are all spiritual activities. Therefore, every building in this ashram is for spiritual activity, every activity here is spiritual. The temple you see on your right is a place for formal spiritual activities, which we perform together or in small groups. We sing hymns to the Lord and our great guru, or perform prayers through our sacred fire ceremonies. But meditation, we do in our rooms or any place where we can sit alone undisturbed. People normally associate spiritual activities with prayer, ceremonies and meditation. But there is much more to it than just these formal activities.'

Nancy interrupted, 'Yes, but what about the other activities you have here, those related to health, education or feeding the poor?'

'Those too are spiritual activities because they are performed with love, concern for others and with an attitude of worship. You would have heard the phrase "Work is worship". By definition, this requires a particular attitude towards work, an attitude of worship. In the spiritual tradition of our great master, we believe that acts of worship include working with the poor to address their health, education or nutrition concerns. These are spiritual activities. Do you know that our spiritual master, the highest spiritually evolved person I have ever known, used to work with lepers, treating them with alternative medicine. He gave vocational training and helped them resettle in the society once they got cured. He established schools and dispensaries for the poor and provided facilities for their social upliftment. These were all a reflection of his spiritual behaviour, an expression of his love and compassion, which came from his spirituality. So, if you see the essential spiritual nature of these activities, you will understand that all we do here is spiritual and all the buildings at the ashram are for spiritual activities.'

'Who is this great master you are talking about?' asked Nancy.

Ananda intervened, 'He is the same person whose large photograph you saw in my living room. All that we do here reflects his spiritual focus. He encouraged people to focus on serving the poor in various ways. He used to emphasise that we should serve God through service to the poor, spending only the minimum time required for our daily meditation and formal spiritual activities. This implies using most of the time at the ashram to address the concerns of the poor.'

Nancy paused for a while, then said, 'Interesting concept. Based on this philosophy that work is worship, we can treat every bit of work we do as a spiritual act, as long as we do it with devotion.'

Anil Baba complimented her, 'Very well put indeed, Nancy. This is the philosophy we follow—all of us who are disciples of our great master or are influenced by his personality and work. All our work is done with reverence to the Divine—as a humble offering of love, thanking God for providing us the opportunity to be of service to our brothers and sisters in society. Sometimes the tasks can be joyous for all, such as a cultural programme or a special event that we all celebrate together. Other occasions involve dealing with specific concerns such as serious health problems or some other tensions in life. Each step we take in any of these situations should be taken with reverence and commitment.'

Marie, who was sitting quietly till now, asked softly, 'How do you manage to hold onto this attitude when you face major difficulties? Do you not get disturbed? Do you not find it difficult to address such situations with devotion? Is it not easier to have this devotional attitude only in good times?'

'The attitude of devotion develops over time. It is a journey. Ordinarily, such an attitude is missing, irrespective of whether the time is good or bad. In good times, people get self-absorbed and are lost in the moment. In bad times, the tension keeps a person away from any other thought except being preoccupied with the cause of the trouble. In each case, one has to develop an understanding of the larger reality. Some say that it is easier to remember God during difficult times, when we realise that only a far superior omnipotent power of the Divine can help us through. There is an interesting couplet by a saint who lived long ago in Varanasi. He said, "In difficult times, everyone remembers God; but no one remembers God in good times. If people remember God in good times, then why would they face bad times!"'

'Does this mean that we are more able to develop an attitude of devotion in bad times?' asked Nancy.

'This feeling of devotion should be generated when we work for others, not just for ourselves. We need to work towards developing a general attitude that treats work as worship. Such a feeling of devotion is not easy to develop; it takes time and dedicated effort. We need to move in that direction every day, with small steps. A beginning can be made in a simple way, using two concepts to change our perspective. One is to develop a positive attitude towards our experiences in life. Second, we should treat each experience as being there for teaching us something which helps us improve ourselves, while considering all experiences and persons as instruments of the Divine for this purpose.'

'These do not seem to be small steps,' said Nancy, and Marie nodded in agreement.

Baba reassured them, 'Once you start taking these steps, you will realise they are actually small steps. They need commitment and persistence. In fact, if you think about them, you will see that they are a special form of self-indulgence, one which allows us to keep improving with time.'

'What about those who do not believe in the Divine? How should they approach this?' continued Nancy.

'Those who do not believe in the Divine could focus only on using all the experiences as teaching them something to improve themselves. This is something we all should be doing in any case, with or without a spiritual attitude. The important point to bear in mind is that the concept of "improving ourselves" does not, on its own, have any specific spiritual content. Depending on our attitude, the steps we take could be towards developing negative capabilities that harm others or positive capabilities for helping people. The specific content, which we emphasise here, is given by a spiritual mindset. With this mindset, we improve to become more positive, caring and devotional.'

Marie finished her tea and kept the cup on the table. She raised her right hand to attract attention, 'Anil Baba, I have two questions. Why do you say we should see persons and situations as opportunities that have been provided to help us improve? Also, you emphasised the importance of working within the Divine Will. Can you please explain what you mean by that?'

'Yes, Marie. Please give me just a minute and I will address your questions.' Anil Baba turned to a disciple who was standing nearby and said, 'Murari, can you please check the houseboat? I think it has floated away downstream in the river and needs to be intercepted and brought back.'

Murari rushed away to check, without any question. Anil Baba turned to Marie and continued as if there had been no interruption. 'Marie, it is interesting that your two questions are linked. But let me take them one by one, and you will see the obvious links.'

Nancy asked, 'You have a houseboat, Anil Baba?'

'Yes, a very old one. It was my place of stay for five years, when I was living on the river Ganges, just in front of our present ashram. My spiritual brother and Ananda's spiritual guide, Guru Baba, gave it to me.'

'How was it, living on the boat?'

'Sometimes easy, sometimes very difficult. Just like our other experiences in life.'

'Marie, let us take your questions now and after that we should have some lunch. It is ready. We will continue our conversation later,' said Anil Baba and he looked at everyone sitting around him for agreement. There were nods from everyone. He then addressed Marie again.

'For someone like me, a monk and an ascetic, it is normal to see all that happens with me and around me as a Divine Play. All situations are opportunities created for each of us to make progress by developing our understanding and capabilities. Each situation provides us with more than one option for our response and we have to choose one amongst them. We have some control over the attitude we adopt and the kind of efforts we make to deal with each situation, and to subsequently learn from the evolving situation. Each situation gives us a possibility of going in a positive direction. Alternatively, we could choose other possibilities, which reflect our self-obsessed and limited horizons. With a positive attitude we can always see opportunities, even if they may suggest only ways to avoid errors in the future.'

Marie intervened, 'But, how are all situations and persons instruments of the Divine?'

Just then, Murari came back to inform Anil Baba that the houseboat had indeed drifted away from its place, going downstream with the flow of the river. He had sent two persons from the ashram down the river to locate the boat and bring it back.

The visitors were surprised how Anil Baba knew that the boat had lost its mooring and was now somewhere downstream, everyone except Murari and Ananda, because both of them had seen such prescience from Baba on several occasions. Anil Baba thanked Murari and continued talking to Marie.

'We are fundamentally linked to the Divine through our Life Force. The natural tendency of our ego or external force is to be self-obsessed and limited. I think of this as our external weakness. The Divine keeps providing us opportunities to reduce the external weaknesses and strengthen our internal forces, to overcome our limitations and move towards our larger presence and awareness.'

'And what if someone does not believe in the Divine?' asked Nancy once again.

'As I said earlier, the fundamental nature of our effort remains the same, which is to learn from each situation and improve ourselves. The interesting part of our journey in life is that whether we seek material objectives or spiritual, it calls for a similar mode of behaviour.'

'Isn't there any difference?'

'Yes, there is an important difference. With a material attitude, we focus on our limited and narrow self-oriented improvement. With a spiritual attitude, we focus instead on our larger existence and our linkages with all that is around us, while recognising that each situation is an opportunity provided for us to improve ourselves. An interesting part of the spiritual insight is also that positive achievements with a spiritual attitude build the basis for better achievement of the relevant material objectives.'

Nancy was quick to notice an important qualification regarding achievement of material objectives, 'Anil Baba, what do you mean by "relevant" material objectives?'

Anil Baba smiled and Ananda could sense the glow of joy Anil Baba would be feeling as he softly directed Nancy towards deeper concepts.

'Nancy, you have put your finger on a very important issue. By definition, "relevant" is not a specific and unchanging set of actions or emphasis. Relevance depends on the situation, on your needs and your objectives. Think about this in the various contexts of your life, first with a material frame of reference and then with a spiritual one. You will see for yourself what is relevant for your different circumstances. Interestingly, you will also notice the similarities and major overlaps of the steps required to improve yourself for achieving both material and spiritual objectives.'

Nancy made a mental note to conduct the exercise later. Marie was also nodding and she looked at Anil Baba to see if he was in any hurry to rise up for lunch. Baba was sitting patiently, so she reiterated her point, 'I see what you mean by instruments of the Divine. What happens when we move forward within the Divine Will?'

'Several positive effects take place. We become calmer and steadier and are able to evaluate situations more objectively, with a balanced perspective. We see more clearly the interlinkages between each one of us and our horizon expands beyond just ourselves. We are able to keep a distance from our failures and become more steadfast in our efforts to make positive contributions and improve ourselves. Over time, this process generates within us more understanding, love and compassion for others, and we start treating all actions, including our work, as offering to the Divine. Our work becomes worship.'

Marie was nodding as she looked at Nancy, who was thoughtful too. 'That is quite an achievement, Anil Baba.'

'Yes, it is so. We start small and keep building on it. It takes time for substantive progress but as we get more comfortable with these efforts, they become almost second nature. That is when we are able to strongly see the palpable conflict between positive and negative actions. Once we reach that stage, other doors start opening and we progress to greater achievements.'

Nancy smiled as she asked, 'Such as knowing whether a houseboat parked far away has lost its mooring and floated away with the flow of the river?'

Anil Baba did not respond. He just looked serenely at everyone and asked, 'Should we go for lunch now? There are some friends in the kitchen who are keen that we taste their culinary products. Simple food, but made with affection. They say that the taste of food is better if it is made with love.'

He got up and patted Ananda on his back, encouraging him to get up too. Ananda had enjoyed himself. He had rarely seen Anil Baba talk so much. Perhaps he felt that Vadya and Ananda's guests should be given special treatment. Or was it that they were all being treated as guests of Juhi and Joy, who so obviously were granted all kinds of privileges by Anil Baba. Ananda got up with a deep radiance in his heart. Soon, the aroma of food being served roused their appetite for lunch.

After lunch, the children and the foreign guests rested in their rooms while Vadya and Ananda spent some time with Anil Baba in his room. They discussed plans to acquire good books and some educational videos for the school children and the logistics for sending eye lenses from Delhi to be used in an eye-camp, which was planned for the next month. They talked about their great master and basked in his memories. Soon the topic changed to more mundane matters.

'Ananda Ji, it will be a good idea for all of you to take a boat ride on the river and show some of the important sights of Varanasi to Marie and Nancy. We will send Murari and Prakash with you. They know the city very well,' said Anil Baba. 'While you are busy with the sights, one of them can run across to your favourite sweet shop and get the sweet which you are so fond of, *kheerkadam*.'

Ananda was not surprised. Anil Baba always showed lot of care and concern for him and his family. Baba always said that they were his own family and he wanted to indulge himself by feeding them special sweets and savouries. Ananda also noted that Anil Baba always used the suffix *Ji* with his name, a Hindi word which showed respect. Ananda smiled to himself as he thought: This was another self-indulgence by Baba, perhaps. Amazing, how the spiritual persons get great pleasure when they make others happy.

Suddenly, Anil Baba changed the topic and spoke to Ananda in a serious tone. 'Ananda Ji, I need a favour from you.'

'Anything you need, Baba. What would you like me to do?'

'Tomorrow morning, we have a couple visiting us. They are Europeans going around the country, seeking answers to some spiritual questions. I want you to spend some time with them and address their concerns. Would you be willing to do that for me?'

'I will be happy to talk with the European couple tomorrow. But please explain to me how you get glimpses of likely events? For example, how were you able to know that the houseboat was floating away today?'

Anil Baba looked at Vadya and Ananda very calmly. Softly, he said, 'When I do my meditation in the morning and evening, I see what events are going to unfold. Based on that, I plan my day.'

Ananda made a mental note to keep doing his own meditation regularly. It was time for the boat ride and they all left the room. After some enjoyable but tiring hours in the city, they returned to the ashram for dinner. Another delicious meal was awaiting them. The children were quite tired and everyone retired to their respective rooms. Ananda and Vadya put the children to bed and spent an hour on their meditation before sleeping.

Early morning they woke up to the ringing of bells and singing of melodious hymns. Ananda went down to join the group at the temple singing the hymns. Soon he and Anil Baba were sitting down near the temple, with a mug of tea each, when a tourist car stopped at the gate and a couple entered the ashram, asking whether they could meet the person in charge. They were brought to Anil Baba, who offered tea and refreshments to them and also to their driver and the local guide.

'We have been travelling across India for the last three months, discussing our spiritual experiences with various people. Is it possible for us to do this here also?'

Anil Baba smiled and pointed to Ananda, 'This is Ananda Ji, a very experienced person in this area. He will be a very good choice for this discussion. He knows English very well and will be able to adequately explain issues to your satisfaction. Perhaps the three of you could go to the office room to discuss these matters. You will not have any disturbance there. If you need me, I will be nearby.'

As he said this, an old man came in with a child, looking very lost, 'I want to meet Dr Anil. I was told that he is a very good and kind doctor. Can you please tell me where I can find him?'

Baba folded his hands and got up from the chair, 'Sir, there is no Dr Anil. My name is Anil. I am the only Anil here, but I am not a doctor.'

The old man was not satisfied, 'I was told to find Dr Anil. I must meet him.'

Anil Baba moved towards the old man after indicating to Ananda that he should take the European guests to the office. He spoke softly to the old man, 'Please come with me. We will find out how to address your concern. I will take you to the doctors. Please come along.'

Ananda took the couple to the office, which was a small room with four chairs, a table with a phone and a laptop computer and some books in the small cupboard in the wall. Once they sat down, the couple introduced themselves, 'We are Hans and Gudrun. We feel very good here, a sense of peace and good energy. We are very happy that at this ashram, our driver and guide were given the same welcome as us, there was tea and refreshments for them too. This is the only place in the last three months where we have seen such non-discriminatory behaviour. This makes us feel very good about this place, it has good energy all around,' Hans said looking at Ananda with a broad smile.

'Thank you. It is interesting that you mention there is good energy in this place. This ashram is actually a place of high energy. In ancient times, some important mystics lived here, recognising the high energy emanating here.'

'We do feel it, and it encourages us to share our experiences with you. When we meditate, we both have strange experiences. We would like to discuss them with you. Is that okay?' asked Hans.

Ananda nodded and Hans continued, 'When we meditate, we feel as if some insects are crawling on the skin, sometimes our arms, sometimes on the face. When we open our eyes or touch the spot, it vanishes. What does this mean?'

'Does this happen only when you do meditation or on other occasions also? How long does this continue, whenever it occurs?'

'It happens only when we meditate. We never get such a sensation any other time. And even during meditation, if we stop meditating, this sensation stops,' Gudrun explained.

Ananda looked down and thought for some time on how to respond. The couple waited, fidgeting anxiously till Ananda started speaking, 'This kind of sensation can happen for various reasons, some of them medical. This also occurs at a certain stage during meditation. It is the stage when one has progressed to a level beyond which focused meditation can lead to more rapid spiritual growth. Your description seems to suggest that this sensation is linked to meditation. Have you ever consulted a doctor for this?'

'We have done that. The doctors have no idea about it.'

'I would say that this experience shows you are getting prepared for higher levels of meditative achievement. I used to get similar sensations about eight years ago, and they vanished as I kept on with my meditation. You could look at this as a good sign of progress. But if it occurs on a more regular basis, you should discuss it again with a medical practitioner.'

'Thank you,' said Gudrun. 'We were concerned about this. We feel relieved to know that this will go away as our meditation progresses. We have another question. We see certain colours when we meditate; I see red and Hans sees red or green. What does this mean?'

Ananda sat straight in his chair. He wished that Anil Baba was there to address this concern. Then he recalled Baba saying that Ananda was capable to handle the issues which would be raised. This gave him confidence and he responded with a smile, 'This is also a good sign. But it would again be important to get some more detail. Do you meditate with your eyes open or closed? How do you see these colours, as dots in front of your eyes or within your body? As more diffused colours within the body? If so, then which part of the body?'

So many questions, and so abstract, thought Ananda. I hope I have not discouraged these people. He looked at both Hans and Gudrun to judge their reaction.

Gudrun was smiling and looking at Hans with a pleased expression. She turned to Ananda and asked, 'Have you yourself also had such an experience? Your questions seem very focused and relevant.'

'Yes, I have,' answered Ananda and waited for more information.

Hans replied, 'We meditate with our eyes closed. We see the colours in a diffused way, within our body. Not in front of our eyes. They are seen either at the chest or the abdomen.'

'If you start getting spots in front of your eyes, do visit a doctor. From what you are telling me, again I think this is a good sign. Our body energies are able to generate such colours, though green appears to be unusual.'

'Can you explain this a bit more? Why do we see these colours?' asked Gudrun.

'There could be various reasons, generally linked with the fact that the subtle energies in different parts of your body start rising due to your spiritual practices. Ideally you should not be concerned with these phenomena and continue with your spiritual practices. On their own, these developments give you nothing substantive. They are only indicators of certain levels of progress. Take note of them, feel good about them and continue with your meditative practices.'

'Thank you again. Could you refer us any good books which explain these in detail?' Hans asked, looking around for a pen and paper.

'Yes, I can think of some, but I feel that you should not get into these books. As I said, use these experiences as indicators of progress, like milestones, and continue on your deeper spiritual journey. I hesitate to provide you with references because these books talk about practices which require an evolved spiritual master who is willing to provide special and careful guidance. If you do not have such a guide, then the books should not be relied upon. If you do have the guide, then these are relevant only if your spiritual master says so.'

'You are being very careful. Are you suggesting that we should think about getting a special spiritual guide?' enquired Hans.

'Perhaps. But speaking of Indian spiritual practices, the general view is that the guide finds you, rather than you finding the guide. However, it may be useful to request some elevated soul for this. That is up to you.'

'Will the head of this ashram or you agree to do this for us?' asked Hans looking outside towards the door.

'You can ask him. My experience is that he does not take on many disciples, if at all. Regarding myself, I apologise but I am not authorised. I am not special enough to guide you in these matters.'

Just then Anil Baba entered the room and sat on the vacant chair. When requested, he confirmed Ananda's assessment that he did not take disciples. He opened a box of sweets that he had brought along, and offered sweets and water to the visitors, including Ananda. The sweet was *kheerkadam*, Ananda's favourite. He could eat countless of these and had to impose special willpower to restrain himself.

Anil Baba smiled like a child and enquired, 'I hope your concerns have been addressed adequately. Do you have any more queries?'

Gudrun answered, 'Yes, thank you sir. We have had a very useful discussion. But may we ask one more question?'

'Please do so. Ananda will answer that too.' Ananda looked at Anil Baba with some concern, because he did not want to address such queries when Baba was himself available. Anil Baba simply kept smiling and said, 'You know, Ananda is almost a monk and can easily become a mystic if he follows a more disciplined regime.'

Gudrun looked at Ananda and asked, 'Sometimes, when we are meditating, we experience along our spine a strange sensation as if we are breathing in waves through the middle of our spine. As if there is air in there and that instead of our lungs, we are breathing along the spine. What is this?'

'This is an indicator of the potency of your spiritual experience. These are all parts of a common set of higher-level experiences. The colours and breathing sensations occur even more once the itching sensation has been controlled. You are perhaps in a transition phase. Similar to the subtle energies, there are subtle movements within our body, which are like the movement of the wind. May I suggest one easy exercise in your present situation? After your meditation, put your thumbs in your ears and use your fingers to close your eyes and nose, and try to listen to the internal sound of these subtle winds moving within. It can be very interesting. I want to compliment you for your progress in meditation. We wish you both the best in further progress and spiritual prosperity.'

Hans and Gudrun took this as a cue that the discussion was over. They nodded and got up to leave, saying, 'Thank you again for this very useful and reassuring discussion. We are grateful. We will be in touch through letter or email,' said Hans, sounding quite happy with the conversation.

Ananda wrote down the postal and email addresses to hand over. They folded their hands to bid each other goodbye.

Anil Baba turned towards Ananda and thanked him, and then asked, 'Would you like to do the havan now? There will not be much time later as you are leaving by the afternoon flight today. I have made preparations for all the visitors from Delhi to join in the havan.'

Havan was a fire ceremony for special prayers in which the participants made offerings to the Divine through a fire they lit up in the middle. Ananda nodded, but shared one concern, 'That will be very nice. However, will the children be able to sit for the time required? It will take almost three-quarters of an hour.'

'They were able to do it during your previous visit, when they were even younger. I think they will enjoy it, as will Marie and Nancy.'

'Okay. Then let us do it now so that we can have a relaxed lunch and leave in time for the airport.'

Anil Baba patted Ananda on the back, indicating that they should now move towards the temple. Seven places were set around the havan *kund*—the triangular structure established in the centre of the outer part of the temple. The *kund* was dug into the ground, which facilitated logs to burn for the hour or so required for this specific prayer ceremony. If required, more wood was available to keep the fire strong. Vadya, Marie, Nancy, Juhi and Joy joined them, the children very happy at having spent time with the school children. They started with some simple rituals, the guests copying Anil Baba's actions.

As Ananda performed the havan, he felt a golden glow envelop his heart, and at times, even engulf his whole body. Some other interesting experiences occurred before he finished the prayers. As they were going for lunch, Anil Baba asked him, 'Was it good? Did you have good experiences doing the havan?'

Ananda felt too overwhelmed to speak. He just nodded and sat down on a chair near the kitchen, pausing to savour this sense of radiant completeness before focusing on grosser tasks like lunch.

Anil Baba came with them to the airport. They had more luggage than they brought from Delhi, since they carried sweets, some fruits and even some special small-grain, fragrant rice which Anil Baba had packed for special occasions. They bid their emotional goodbyes, requested Baba to come to Delhi soon and boarded the plane.

They had spent only about a day in Varanasi, but it seemed as if they had been there for many days. They all wanted to linger back at the ashram. Ananda turned to Vadya and remarked, 'This was very short, wasn't it?'

Vadya was adjusting the seat belt around Joy, who was treating it like a toy. She asked Joy to sit still in her seat and looked up at Ananda, 'It is always a short visit to Varanasi, but it is always fulfilling. This is what people mean by "quality time", when each moment has special meaning. I am glad we made this trip.'

'So are we,' said Marie and Nancy together.

Joy and Juhi began giggling and Juhi said, 'Ah, ha! You both said the same thing together. Joy, this means it is time to make a wish.' The two girls locked their little fingers and made a wish. The children loved to follow this ritual of making a wish when two persons made the same statement. Vadya, the typical mother who wants to know all the thoughts of her children immediately asked, 'Girls, what did you wish for? Can you share it with us?'

Juhi, the elder one shook her head from side-to-side, refusing to divulge her thoughts. Joy, the younger one blurted out with a twinkle in her eye, 'I wished that Anil Baba should come to our house in Delhi and we should all do havan there together again.'

Ananda was taken aback. Here was a small child who he had assumed would find it difficult to stay connected to a prayer ceremony, which took almost an hour of focused attention. Yet, she wanted more of it in Delhi. Perhaps she too had some happy experiences which she wants to recapture, thought Ananda. It made him look at his children with a fresh perspective, lifting his spirits. That was when the plane took off, soaring into the clouds.

18

Milan—the Meeting, a Reunion

Ananda settled in his seat once again as the plane prepared for take-off for Milan. The pleasant glow of his trip to Varanasi was still with him. At home, when it was time to leave for the airport he had to go through the old family routine wherein his mother made him eat some sweets with yoghurt. She insisted that he should always do so before travelling. This tradition was a relic from the times when people travelled long distances on foot and perhaps needed such nutrition. Though he had repeatedly explained to his mother that such feeding was no longer relevant, but for her it was a necessary and almost auspicious act before any travel. So, Ananda kept his mother happy by quietly eating the yoghurt and sweets.

He had assured Vadya that he would pass on her regards to the spiritual master and his family. He smiled upon recalling how when he was leaving in the cab, his parents had almost shouted out that he should also give their regards to Guru Baba and Gururatnaji.

Ananda adjusted his seat and stretched a bit, recalling the time when he was younger and had not seen much of the world. Each trip was an exciting event—discovering new cultures, new people, new foods, building links and deepening his knowledge. As time had passed, he had visited many different parts of the world and his keenness to travel had dimmed.

This trip, however, was different. He would be meeting his spiritual guide after a long time, visiting him in his home near Milan. He softly whispered the word 'Milan' a few times, playing with the sound. He took out a piece of paper from his pocket and wrote the word 'Milan'. A Hindi-speaking person would have normally read 'Milan' as 'Milun'. In Hindi, it means 'the meeting' or 'the reunion'. Ananda lowered his seat further and leaned back with happiness. Indeed! He was going to a very special meeting. He closed his eyes and imagined himself at the house he was going to visit, sitting near his soft-spoken and affectionate spiritual guide, talking about their great master, recalling events and insights, exchanging experiences, Ananda asking all the questions that came to his mind for clarifications by his spiritual master, an Italian adept from an ancient Indian tradition. Those from the Tibetan Buddhist tradition would say he is a reincarnated divine soul. Guru Baba indulged him with information which one rarely finds in books. Such knowledge came only from direct experience.

He recalled an Indian sage telling him long back that in the metaphysical world, growth and real knowledge are based not on imagination, but on experience. There is a very strong link between 'knowing' and 'being', a link that was essential for bringing effective changes at the individual and collective levels in society. With such substantive experience, a person could actually empathise with others, an experience which helped in transition from a normal interaction towards a deeper interaction.

Ananda landed at Malpensa. Collecting his luggage, he went out through the green channel and saw his spiritual master waiting for him. His master first waved to him and then folded his hands in greeting.

Looking at his master, Ananda was once again struck by the thought how handsome his master was, with his bright eyes and a deep sense of peace.

No, thought Ananda, there is much more. It is not just peace but much more. Ananda could not think of an English word to describe this attribute. He thought of a Hindi word that came closest to describing this quality. It was *sthir*, which covered a wide span of meanings including being calm, still, stable, unchanging, firmly rooted and so much more. Ananda hurried forward with his luggage trolley and bent low to touch his spiritual master's feet in the Indian tradition to show respect. His master picked him up and hugged him, smiled and asked, 'How are you Ananda?'

In their traditional spiritual lineage, Ananda would be his 'spiritual son', or just 'Ananda'. His guru gave him so much love and respect; he treated him like a brother. Ananda walked with a bounce as they moved towards the parking lot.

They reached home and within a couple of hours, Ananda had met his guru's wife, Gururatnaji, and their two children and paid his respect at the shrine to the great master. He felt peaceful and energetic. His Guru Ma, Gururatnaji, was pampering him with all the nice things he liked to eat. Soon, some other spiritual acolytes joined them, having heard that Ananda would be visiting. It was like homecoming for Ananda. All of them took their tea or coffee and gathered in the living room. His guru was sitting on his regular couch, which he would turn into a bed at night. He lived a simple life amidst plenty. Ananda and his eight spiritual brothers gathered around Guru Baba, the person who had initiated them all into special spiritual practices. Ananda glanced around, perfectly comfortable, and smiled as he saw this gathering of an ancient Indian spiritual lineage, so far away from the origin of those traditions and he was the only Indian there. He was also aware that the others in the room were much more spiritually aware and advanced than him, more evolved, more *sthir*.

The conversation started with others asking after the welfare of Vadya, Juhi, Joy and Ananda's parents. Ananda conveyed his family's regards to Guru Baba, Guru Ma and others. The group brought Ananda up-to-date on their social service initiatives. This evidence of their compassion, emanating from their deeper spirituality, was what marked them as different. Otherwise, they all lived normal lives like any other person—as a doctor, an ambulance driver, a civil servant, a teacher, a grocer or a beautician. They did their jobs well, with commitment, honesty and compassion.

Welcoming Ananda again, Guru Baba said, 'Ananda, it is very good to have you with us. We would like to know about your experiences these last few months. You shared a lot with me during the drive from the airport—your ideas about small steps and concentric circles and addressing each issue in terms of its components or attributes in order to deal with them through manageable small steps. I think these ideas are important for progress in material life within a spiritual framework.'

Ananda then quickly summarised the main points of his evolving framework of small steps, concentric circles. He was relieved to see that everyone was taking him seriously.

Ignacio, one of the older people sitting close to Ananda spoke softly, 'There are some books which show how meditation can lead to interesting results and spiritual practices can affect the development of the human brain. Perhaps we could share them with you, Ananda.'

When Ananda nodded, the old man started, 'I have the books with me here. One is written by two neuroscientists who have studied how the brain changes if we meditate or focus on the Divine in any form. Another is written by an author of Indian origin.[1] There is yet another interesting book that offers deep insights into the human brain based on functional magnetic resonance imaging (fMRI).[2] Ananda, you can take these books and read them at your leisure.'

'Thank you, Ignacio,' said Ananda. 'I wonder how the book would help me achieve the objective of developing a simple spiritual framework for interacting with people.'

Ignacio nodded,'Ananda, perhaps I could read a part from the fMRI book on selflessness. These scientific insights reveal a very important aspect, saying that our brains are normally structured to feel pleasure when we are selfless and do positive acts to help others. This shows that we have a natural tendency for what you refer to as "extending our ego" and with effort we can enhance this attribute within us.'

Ignacio started reading,'Ananda, I will read certain parts from the relevant section:

> Using real-time fMRI imaging, we can watch brain activity that coincides with self-sacrificing and cooperative behaviour, and we are learning that our altruistic tendencies are just as much a part of our wiring, just as automatic and "natural" a part of our brain activity, as violence-provoking emotions like fear, lust and anger.'[3]

Ananda raised his hand, as if physically stopping the flow of words. 'This shows that altruism is as natural as fear, lust and anger.'

Ignacio responded, 'Yes. The important point that we overlook is that selflessness and doing good for others are a natural part of our personality, our brain. With time and orientation we can increase this selfless and altruistic tendency and even the pleasure we get from such actions.'

'But the same is true with fear, lust and anger too,' remarked Ananda.

'Yes, that is so,' said Ignacio. 'If we work on these aspects of our personality, then we will be building them instead. People often presume that since the ego is strong, the most natural part of our brain's structure is to have fear, lust and anger, rather than any positive attributes. But that is not so. Both aspects are natural. We actually build up on each attribute by working on it, making it more and more a part of our character.'

Ignacio nodded, 'Ananda, the book mentions a study at the University of Oregon in which fMRI is used to examine altruism and brain response. The result was as follows: "fMRI images showed that donating money to a local food bank and, to a lesser degree, paying an involuntary tax that would benefit the food bank, activated the brain's reward centres—the same areas that brighten when we eat yummy desserts, get paid or take recreational drugs."[4]

'Very interesting. This validates what I have always felt,' responded Ananda with excitement. 'On my flight, I finished reading a very interesting book which discusses this aspect, basing it on research and results derived from different subjects. Guru Baba, may I please read a particularly interesting part which I have marked in the book? It takes forward this message of altruism and positive interactions in a highly relevant way, though with a wider scope of reference.'

Guru Baba smiled and nodded. Ananda got his book and sat close to his spiritual guide. He read from two different parts of the book, slowly but loudly:

> 'Life exists because of a fundamental duality, a multiplicity of influence and being, a cooperative partnership. To the extent we ignore our natural impulses we work against our nature, which responds to the pull of wholeness. With every step away from the Bond, our natural birthright, we take another step towards separation and alienation, and away from what is best and truest about ourselves. We create more economic crises, more political struggle, more conflict, more calamitous ecological disaster. We erect higher and higher walls between ourselves and the rest of the world. In our real-life Public Goods games, we are now all refusing to play.'[5]

Everybody was listening seriously and nodding as Ananda finished reading. He looked at his spiritual guide and asked softly, 'What are your thoughts about the possibility of enhancing this feeling of altruism, Guru Baba?'

Guru Baba looked at Ignacio as if in silent communication. 'Yes, I will just read some more,' Ignacio said turning a page.

> 'Now that researchers know that these same areas are engaged in during altruistic behaviour, we might next explore whether altruism is as teachable as other rewarding behaviours. Recent discoveries about the flexibility of natural pathways involved in emotion, attention, memory and recovery from chronic pain and addiction are certainly suggestive of our potential to strengthen our "giving" circuits as well.'[6]

Guru Baba intervened, 'That there are beneficial effects of spiritual practices on the capacity of the brain is not a major insight for spiritual practitioners. All of you already know that and much more. But our experiences are personal and not always credible for those who seek more easily replicable evidence. This book and other similar works provide such scientific evidence, which makes it more credible and relevant for others. It also provides one more source for two interesting systemic insights about ourselves.

'One is the evidence that our mental capacity and capabilities are enhanced by various activities, including spiritual activities. Another is that spiritual activities are key for growth in those parts of the brain which lead to greater peace of mind, contentment and enhanced capabilities, illustrating, thus, the greater potency and hitherto scientifically unrecognised benefits of spiritual practices.'

'What are the deeper spiritual lessons from this, lessons which span also the material tasks we perform?' asked Mario, a slim, bearded disciple.

'A basic important lesson is that we can affect all our capacities, including mental capacities and peace of mind, through our actions. Thus, if a person wants to achieve any result, spiritual or material, physical or mental, that person can take specific positive action to achieve the desired result.'

Ananda wanted to know more, 'Guru Baba, this seems to be a logical conclusion, something straightforward and apparent. What other additional steps would be relevant?'

'Whenever we see any solution with which we agree, we consider it to be logical and apparent. However, the logical way of addressing situations is not always apparent. Do you remember Ananda, as a graduate student, you used to wonder what was so special about management studies, because to you the subject seemed to contain logical and straightforward solutions to various problems? Yet, management is a subject with specialised knowledge and people compete intensely to get this training. Perhaps, there is a message for us. What I have just shared with you may seem straightforward, but we tend to forget about it in our normal behaviour.'

Ananda was nodding slowly, wondering how his spiritual guide had pertinently recalled a statement that he had made more than two decades ago. Nonetheless, he persisted, 'Can you please explain how this is a spiritual result, or a spiritual insight?'

Guru Baba smiled and responded, 'Logical analysis and application, based on clear perception, is a fundamental part of a spiritual mindset. In fact, the link with spirituality is much more than that; it is a two-way link. As we achieve greater spiritual progress, we incrementally improve our intellect and clarity of perception. It is something like the capacity of the brain gets enhanced by spiritual actions. Also, if we consider spiritual practices from this perspective, we see that spirituality does not mean one cannot be active in the material world.'

After sipping some water, Guru Baba continued, 'The spiritual mindset acts to progressively improve our intellect, develop our perspective, positive attitude and wisdom, and we become more effective. After all, wisdom is the most appropriate and best possible application of the intellect, knowledge and relevant perspective to different situations in life.'

'Is this the link between material and spiritual?' asked Ignacio.

'The material and spiritual dimensions are two distinct yet connected parts of our existence. Since we are present in both these dimensions, our concerns, problems and sources of happiness also exist in each of them. Therefore, to improve our overall situation we normally need to address both these levels of our existence.'

Ananda was thoughtful as he asked, 'What is the difference in the progress we make in each of these two dimensions, that is material and spiritual dimensions?'

'In the material world, we seek results from our actions. We are actively seeking or looking for positive results. True spiritual pursuit is without such seeking of results. Instead, we take note of whatever we receive and move ahead with commitment and subsequent action. There is another important distinction. Material progress provides us with a better ambience to do whatever we wish, including spiritual pursuits, but it does not equip us to progress in the spiritual world. In contrast, spiritual progress actually equips us to move ahead in both the material and the spiritual world.'

'What do you mean by "true spiritual pursuit"?' asked Germano, suddenly participating in the conversation.

'When we normally walk the spiritual path, we may still have our aspirations and seek specific results from our actions. That state is a mixture of the spiritual and material. In true spiritual pursuit, we simply receive whatever we get because the result is a by-product of the road we walk on. We do not get caught up with the results because that would mean deviating towards the material mindset, which emphasises on results. This thought is strongly expressed in the statement: "God closes doors no human can open and God opens doors no human can close."'

'How is this relevant to the points you are explaining, Guru Baba?' asked Ananda.

'This shows that we really do not know which door is closed for us and which is open. In a material path, we have to keep testing this with our efforts. With a material mindset, we hope that the door is open and that we would be able to walk through that door. But with a spiritual mindset, we make our efforts and that act or effort itself is of value to us. The spiritual journey itself is our destination. Thus, we get detached from the results, acquire a sense of humility about our prowess and interact with others with a feeling of commonality, seeing them as similar to us.'

'This is very interesting,' said Ivano, a disciple with a smiling face. 'Guru Baba, can you please explain how we can achieve happiness in the material and spiritual dimensions.'

Guru Baba was listening with great attention, his face luminous and serene, his eyes bright and focused on the speaker. He waited to see if there were any more queries. 'There are various kinds of happiness,' he said. 'For example, happiness due to achieving our own limited objectives, or that derived from the happiness of others, including those we care for. Happiness may be linked to our ego, our mind or even the heart. A special kind of happiness is linked with our soul, in terms of deep internal happiness, which normally happens when we are happy on account of others, not just due to our self-oriented achievements. On the spiritual path, when our presence expands and strongly merges with a larger spiritual dimension, we experience a unique kind of happiness, often referred to as "bliss". Nothing in the material world approaches bliss under which we are so completely happy that we lose our identity. It is a state in which we are the source as well as the recipient of the happiness.'

'How can we go deeper towards happiness, or move away from what causes us grief?' asked Mario.

'We can do this in two linked ways. One is to learn to feel positively about others and to enjoy the happiness of others, thus, moving away from feelings of indifference, jealousy and envy. Second is to perform spiritual practices such as meditation so that the pathway to our deeper self is increasingly opened up,' Guru Baba replied.

'Are these sequential or can they be done together?' asked Ananda.

'That is your choice. It is better to do them together to enhance the effect of each. Spiritual practices develop within us an ability to view our own actions objectively, as if we are a distant observer. Ideally, we become the viewer and the performer of the action. This process however, takes time and patience.'

'You were saying that since we exist in both the material and spiritual dimensions, we should work in each of them to be really happy. Why is it important to work in both these dimensions?' asked Mario.

'I distinguished between the two dimensions for simplicity. In reality, they are seamlessly connected, even overlapping. We span them both. Therefore, if we have to feel happy in a sustained and complete manner, we need to work on our total existence.'

Mario intervened, 'What do you mean by saying that our material and spiritual existence are overlapping or seamlessly linked?'

'Let us take the Earth as an example. There is water and land on the surface, which we can see, and there are other submerged parts, which we do not see. The land and water on the surface is equivalent to our visible material existence, and all that is beneath the surface is akin to our spiritual existence. We think of the land as distinct and separate, but its existence and stability depends upon its submerged parts, which are distinct yet connected. In the same way, the spiritual and material world coexist, intermingling and interacting with each other.'

'Does our stability in the material world depend on the spiritual part?' asked Mario quizzically.

'Yes, that is so. Our unease, our insecurities, our composure and our sustained stability or peace of mind have a basis in the spiritual world. To address them substantively, we need to approach them through a spiritual mindset. Working on the spiritual part helps us connect with our larger self and takes us beyond the narrow emphasis on achievements that are limited to ourselves. This stability allows us to look at issues in a more objective manner and take better decisions when dealing with different aspects of our life. It lets us build a sense of contentment and inner peace, which arises from deep within us. Ananda, don't you think that your management techniques will also have greater effectiveness with such stability?'

Ananda was nodding in agreement, 'Guru Baba, could you please explain the spiritual metaphysical basis for these ideas?' he asked.

Guru Baba had a soft smile playing on his lips, a twinkle in his eyes. 'Ananda, since you ask, I will explain. Creation arises from the Original Life Force, which we also refer to as the Divine. Through its "will" or thought energy, the Original Life Force creates further dimensions of existence and is present in each of them in the form of Life Force and consciousness. You will notice that thought energy is the preserve of a living being; it is a unique attribute of the Life Force. In order to more strongly connect with the Life Force in its basic dimension, which is beyond the surface of our own dimension as in my example of the Earth, we need to get distant from our immediate situation. Applying a logical framework of thought, we can enhance our objectivity when looking at events around us. We can learn to do so as part of our normal decision-making process or we may take the help of spiritual methods.'

'Not only is our material world a manifest creation of such "will", each of us has a component of this Original Life Force, which gives us life and enables us to think and perform various actions. In essence, there is a continuum of the Original Life Force that connects each of us to the source in the original dimension, from which our existence is derived. Think of it like a tree, with different parts connected to each other, different levels of the tree representing different dimensions from which life continues to spring forth. Since the same Life Force is present in each dimension, we are in effect present in all these dimensions, which means that our presence in our own dimension is linked to our presence in the other, deeper dimensions.'

'However, most of us are usually preoccupied with our existence in this dimension and thus, focus only on a part of our whole existence. This leads us to a lack of balance in our existence, something I have already explained today. To have a greater balance, we need to grow towards our larger self in another dimension. In the more basic dimension of existence, we all have the same origin. Therefore, one way of achieving growth towards our larger self is through affection and empathy for others, treating them as ourselves. In effect then, we are in touch with the larger part of our own existence in another deeper dimension, where these others are basically the same as us.'

'Guru Baba, do you mean that in the material world, we are not in a normal situation and our objective should be to reach the normal situation?' asked Ivano.

'No, that is not so. Each situation we are in can arise in the normal course of events, and every situation we face should be treated as a normal situation. It does not help to start wondering whether our situation is the one we deserve, whether it is fair or unfair, normal or abnormal. We should stop focusing on the normality or abnormality of the situation. Instead, we should consider how to move to another, improved situation and focus on generating qualities that enable us to be more balanced and effective in life. In the framework of metaphysical linkages which I have shared with you, becoming more balanced requires increasing the extent to which we develop our links with the base of our existence and enhance the spiritual attributes within ourselves. Interestingly, with this we also improve our abilities to achieve more in the material world.'

'So, we identify the concept of a normal situation only to dismiss it?' asked Ignacio.

'No. It would help us to understand and accept the concept as a wide-ranging one, and then to move towards substantive matters. That way, we will not spend our energy unduly worrying about it. Understanding the large scope of a normal situation is important for another reason—each situation arises partly due to our own actions, so its solution also lies in us taking appropriate actions,' explained Guru Baba.

Ivano interrupted, 'How do we get more balance when we extend these links across our larger self? What gives us this stability?'

Guru Baba continued, 'Just like gravity pulls objects towards the centre of the Earth, the original base of our existence pulls us towards itself. This metaphysical pull does not physically take us to the other dimension. Rather it expresses itself through a feeling of our larger existence because our Life Force is strongly connected to its extended presence in other dimensions. This larger existence inspires us to take steps to convert the incipient awareness into an obvious awareness. Till we are not aware of this larger existence in an obvious or explicit way, we are in a sense, somewhat rootless and feel a sense of incompleteness. The pull we experience reflects our own desire to be in touch with our larger awareness.

'As we progress along the path, getting additional glimpses of the larger picture of our reality, we are better equipped to develop enhanced abilities, balance and peace of mind. In this sense, every situation we face is an instrument of the Divine, providing us an opportunity to improve ourselves and enhance our presence and awareness, across different dimensions of our existence. All this can take place only through spiritual growth. The more we grow spiritually, greater the control we have on our larger selves and better is our ability to achieve balance in life.'

Guru Ma came into the room to announce that dinner was ready. Only then did Ananda realise how late it had become for him, taking the jet lag into account. Good food, one of the material joys that never failed to make him happy, was beckoning him with its appetising smell.

References

1. Nataraja, Shanida. *The Blissful Brain: Neuroscience and Proof of the Power of Meditation.* UK: Gaia Thinking Publishers, 2008.
2. Boleyn-Fitzerald, Miriam. *Pictures of the Mind.* Pearson Education Ltd, 2010.
3. Ibid, p 85.
4. Ibid, p 85.
5. McTaggart, Lynne. *The Bond: Connecting Through the Space Between Us.* Australia: Hay House, 2011, pp 18, 241.
6. Boleyn-Fitzerald, Miriam. *Pictures of the Mind.* USA: Pearson Education Ltd, 2010, p 87.

19

Clarity in Combloux

Benedict was driving slowly up the mountain road to Combloux, enjoying the exceptional panoramic vista. Situated in the French Alps, Combloux had a perennial view of Mont Blanc—the highest mountain peak in Europe. Victor Hugo had called Combloux the 'Pearl of the Alps, nestled in a jewel box of glaciers'.

The drive took a couple of hours. It was longer than usual because of the snow that had gathered on stretches of the road. Both Ananda and Francis had felt uncertain about the route, and kept repeating to Benedict that they should take the motorway on their return journey. However, during the drive, whenever they looked at the snow-clad Alps and the valley to their left, they were charmed by its extraordinary beauty and exclaimed loudly with appreciation.

Reaching Combloux, they turned onto the main road going in the direction of the motorway. After a few hundred metres, they stopped at a place which had been specially developed as a picnic spot. Francis carried their hamper and a few bed sheets to this small hilltop, which had some benches and a permanent grill which could be used by visitors. No one was there. The sun was shining, but there was a chill in the air. They occupied a bench near the grill. Ananda was reluctant to sit down, as he stood taking deep breaths of the fresh air. On his right rose a string of snow-clad Alpine peaks, with Mont Blanc prominently towering over them all. On his left, valleys spread out a vast span of green with trees and grass covered intermittently with snow. It was ethereal, beyond imagination. Ananda was mesmerised.

Francis walked up to him and asked him to join Benedict who was opening the picnic basket. They ate in silence taking in the stunning surroundings. Francis was the first one to speak.

'I am glad you both like this place. It is among my favourite spots, it helps me feel closer to the immense unknown and combines great beauty with mystery. I think this is an ideal venue for carrying forward our conversation. Ananda, I feel you may be able to take Benedict further on the road to achieving greater internal calm and happiness.'

Ananda always felt happy talking about spiritual aspects. Amidst the astounding beauty at Combloux, he was even more inclined to do so. He felt a flower of light open up within his heart, expanding outwards, giving a sense of peace. He thought of Metatron's cube and the flower of life.[1] His thought went to how light is the result of electrons leaving their excited state and return to their state of lower excitement, or in terms of human feelings acquired greater calm.[2] He was feeling very calm, indeed! He enjoyed his own state of mind at that moment, as he felt the light in his heart fill his entire torso and generate a calmness that is very rare and deeply fulfilling.

Ananda closed his eyes to savour the feeling before re-engaging in the conversation. As he opened his eyes, he saw Francis gesturing to Benedict to be patient. Ananda smiled at Benedict, reflecting the happy energy that he was experiencing. 'Benedict, our conversation during the trip shows that Francis has already discussed a lot with you. Let us take this forward today?'

Benedict replied, 'Ananda, Francis has helped open my mind to a larger perspective. He has explained several spiritual concepts, showing how spirituality can be a basis for achieving the results I seek. However, I still do not find spirituality tangible. It seems to overreach, especially if I consider the advances in science, including the fact that science has now been able to create life artificially. In fact, Stephen Hawking also says in his book[3] that creation can be explained without recourse to self-analysis or spirituality. Another book I read shows that all the feelings of near-death experience and the vision with light and spiritual messages that we see, they all are from within our brain, a product of our brain[4]. When I consider these scientific insights, I feel uncertain about the validity of spiritual efforts to help me reach my objectives. That is what I would like you to address.'

'Thank you, Benedict. Francis had informed me of your interest, and I got some books along that illustrate such thoughts, including those which you just mentioned. I like them very much, indeed. It is heartening to see that science has progressed rapidly, way beyond what we imagined even two decades ago. Some of the answers lie in this continuing progress, for instance, in the area dealing with biophysics.' Ananda took out a book from his bag then and opened a page he had marked, 'I was reading a book recently which gives some fascinating accounts of such progress. Let me read out a passage to explain:

> 'Moreover, biophysicists have discovered that living organisms are permeated by quantum waveforms. Invisible quantum waves are spreading out from each of us and permeating into all other organisms. Neuroscience, quantum biology and quantum physics are now beginning to converge to reveal that our bodies are not only biochemical systems, but also resonating quantum systems. These new discoveries show that a form of non-local connected consciousness has a physical–scientific basis. Further, it demonstrates that certain spiritual or transcendental states of collective oneness have a valid basis within a new scientific paradigm.'[5]

'What is the significance of this quotation for me, Ananda?' Benedict asked.

'Three interlinked points. First, we must keep an open mind. Scientific exploration continues to give us better glimpses of a larger reality but we are still in the process of seeking a more complete and comprehensive picture. Even Stephen Hawking in the book you mention says that there is no single theory which explains different situations. While we may not recognise the validity of spiritual thought, it is interesting to note that the emerging scientific understanding about entanglement or interconnected nature of our existence was revealed by various spiritual insights too. They are but attempts to study and understand these aspects from a different approach. Over time, the insights from these two approaches may converge more and more. The basic difference in my view would be whether or not there exists a larger, outside force, which determines events in our lives. Thus, a fundamental difference would be with respect to the relevant cause and effect.'

'Yes, that is so. And that is what makes it difficult for me to easily accept spiritual concepts. That, along with the fact that I need some tangible results,' Benedict said.

Ananda took out another book from his bag. Benedict was surprised to see that it was the book by Stephen Hawking, which he had mentioned a few minutes ago. 'Benedict, you have relied on Hawking's book to make your point. It said that creation does not require the intervention of some supernormal being, because the multiple universes we now recognise in science arise due to physical law; they are predictions of science. I will now read another very interesting passage from that same book for you.

> Until the advent of modern physics it was generally thought that all knowledge of the world could be obtained through direct observation, that things are what they seem, as perceived through our senses. But the spectacular success of modern physics, which is based upon

> concepts such as Feynman's that clash with everyday experience, has shown that this is not the case. The naïve view of reality therefore is not compatible with modern physics. To deal with such paradox we shall adopt an approach that we call model-dependent realism. It is based on the idea that our brains interpret inputs from our sensory organs by making a model of the world. When such a model is successful at explaining events, we tend to attribute to it and the elements and concepts that constitute it, the quality of reality or absolute truth. But there may be different ways in which one could model the same physical situation, with each employing different fundamental elements and concepts. If two such physical theories or models accurately predict the same events, one cannot be said to be more real than the other, rather we are free to use whichever model is most convenient.'[6]

'Once again, how is this relevant for me in this context?' asked Benedict.

'The simple point I am making is that knowledge is evolving and reality is not always what you perceive. Rather, reality could be counter-intuitive, difficult to comprehend and may actually be beyond the tangibility that you see. However, while we have to progress and live in our "tangible" surroundings, within which we are comfortable, we should also consider more than one way of explaining reality. The work of the biophysicists that I have mentioned shows that now we have a "physical" theory which overlaps with a spiritual conceptualisation of a larger reality. So, we could treat the spiritual theories also as a possible model to rely on,' Ananda explained.

'But with the spiritual models, you are not able to accurately predict in every case. The scientific method does not apply if we use these theories,' interjected Benedict.

'I think the predictions occur at the level of experience, especially if the theories are too complex to easily understand in a straightforward way. Take, for example, the growing evidence on how meditation techniques help you expand your mental capacity, even change the brain interlinkages and provide you with a better ability to deal with daily issues. Francis told me about the books you have read on this. Likewise, experiments with telepathy increasingly reveal the extended scope of our understanding, whose basis is described better by spiritual insights. We see that in some cases, the prediction and replication may be more straightforward, such as seen in the effects of meditation, especially because now we can monitor the brain activity during meditative states. However, to apply the scientific method in other cases, we may need to first reach an adequate ability and preparatory state, which again requires sustained efforts to enhance our capability.'

Benedict was all attention. 'What do you mean by preparatory state?' he asked.

'Let me give you an example. One of the modern yogis, late Gopi Krishna says that our brain needs to be adequately stimulated through our internal spiritual energy in order to evolve and see the larger scheme described in a spiritual framework.[7] One way to prepare is to try and stimulate the relevant part of the brain. The yogis and mystics have talked about this and done it. However, this requires sustained and focused effort which is normally difficult for us.'

'Then what good is all my knowledge on this aspect?' asked Benedict.

'This brings me to my second point,' Ananda clarified. 'Often we seek the ultimate experience in the beginning itself, without having patience or willingness to make the relevant effort. We forget that all important insights need time, effort and focus. Take the progress in science itself. The scientific perspective you are mentioning has taken a long time to emerge as a part of knowledge, and it is still evolving. All our efforts are like a journey. From a spiritual perspective, the important part is not the result per se, but the journey itself. We need to keep moving onwards, taking whatever small steps we can take each day towards our objectives. Often, these steps may only deal with the necessities of life. The important part is to focus on the objectives that can be achieved and keep building on them cumulatively. We must focus on the relevant action that is required from us, and perform that action to move with small steps across the concentric circles of our objectives.'

'What is so spiritual about this? I see this as a method to live life in general. There is nothing other-worldly contained in this suggestion!' exclaimed Benedict.

'Spirituality is not necessarily other-worldly, Benedict. Spirituality is not the same as metaphysics, which may be considered other-worldly based on our usual criteria. Spirituality is an attitude, a way of going through life with methods that help us progress towards our objectives with a sense of calm and contentment. In a sense, our success at applying the relevant methods in themselves becomes a part of our achievement—our journey with small steps across consecutive concentric circles of achievement.'

Benedict was nodding, but he was still not comfortable, 'What do you mean by spirituality being an attitude? Moreover, as mentioned in Nelson's book,[8] if perceptions of metaphysics arise due to sensations in the most primitive part of our brain, it is more a figment of our imagination. Does this not complicate spirituality? Extending all this to metaphysics makes me uncomfortable.'

'Thanks, Benedict. I will take these two questions separately. First, the point you make about metaphysical experiences. It reflects a broader search within the topic of neurotheology,' Ananda started.

'What is neurotheology?' asked Benedict.

'It is a host of efforts to study the brain and theological aspects of our behaviour. There are a number of books on this subject. For instance, you could see this book by Nelson whom you have already read, namely, the author of the book on how God changes your brain.'[9]

'Well! The conclusion I mention does not negate the result propounded by Nelson,' asserted Benedict.

'True. It does not negate the result. However, the interpretation of the result could differ from his conclusion. I, for instance, interpreted it like this: Since these experiences arise in the most primitive part of the brain, then perhaps they have always been there, since the beginning of life. This aspect has, thus, been an integral part of our existence and internal prowess. I have already told you about Gopi Krishna's insights on how the capacity of the brain grows and extends our comprehensive reach and understanding. If you read books that narrate the life story of certain yogis, including some who are still alive, you will find that the energy for spiritual enhancement could pass through to us with a high-level adept touching our head. That could activate the centre of spiritual sensation in the head.[10] In fact, after that, the person receiving that energy changes forever.'

'But can the sensations still be limited within the body?' asked Benedict.

'The experiences I describe are not so limited. My own experiences with my spiritual master were way beyond physical limitations. Some of them can be verified by others who were with me when these events occurred. The spiritual people who reach this evolved state normally do not care about providing such proofs. One example of scientific proof that I am aware of is the experiments that were done on Swami Rama. He demonstrated his ability to control and affect events and operations, within and outside his body.[11] But such control is not the most important part of our journey in daily life. We should seek whatever progress we can make within the framework that we find suitable for us. That would be a positive attitude.'

'Yes, please explain how spirituality is about attitude and how does this fit in with your way of looking at spirituality,' Benedict requested.

'Regarding spirituality being an attitude, the simplest way is to consider spirituality as a combination of compassion and positive attitude towards each event in life.'

'Compassion, I understand. What exactly do you mean by a positive attitude?'

'It combines a number of aspects, starting with treating each event as a learning experience which provides us with opportunities, and then deciding to move ahead with a constructive approach. This would equip us to deal with difficult situations in our life. On my flight, I watched a movie, *The Best Exotic Marigold Hotel,* in which a character makes a very insightful statement, "The only real failure is the failure to try. And the measure of success is how we cope with disappointment."'

'Isn't this also the main point which Buddha is emphasising, namely the importance of dealing with *dukkha* or suffering?' intervened Benedict.

'There is an overlap, yes, that is so,' answered Ananda. 'We have to focus on both dealing with disappointments or sufferings and making the right kind of efforts to progress in life. The dialogue I just quoted from the film emphasises a very important aspect when it comes to applying a positive attitude to life. This also links up with my point, that life, in fact each of our initiatives, is part of our journey and we have to seek the most constructive way to keep moving ahead. The best way, in my view, is to travel with a positive attitude.'

'How does this play a part in your spiritual framework? Also, how does this become important for a happy journey in life?' asked Benedict.

'This brings me to my third point. Even though biophysicists and spiritual adepts suggest that we are interconnected, we go through life based on our own individual thoughts and actions. In each situation, we are the ones who must take the relevant actions and our own efforts are required to move towards that objective. In this context, if we manage to live in a manner that is consistent with the larger interlinkages amongst us, we will be able to take better or more suitable actions. That is the essence of spiritualism. That is the purpose of all the methods we have talked about, which you have read in various books and heard during the lecture by David that you attended with Francis.'

'Aren't you converting spiritual principles into very simplistic constructs? Is this not an extension of spirituality to managerial modes of behaviour, which are emphasised for success in everyday life? These ideas are, for instance, similar to the concepts in management books or those used by psychologists to make us more comfortable with ourselves.'

Ananda was smiling with a faraway look in his eyes. Something seemed to have clicked within him. He felt his presence had expanded and his multiple experiences with partial visions had all combined. The jigsaw puzzle was complete, all pieces in their appropriate place. He focused again on Benedict, his eyes showing a sense of gratitude, 'Thank you, Benedict. Your question is brilliant and contains the answer within it. Let me take a piece of paper and respond to your query.'

Saying this, he took a sheet from a notepad in his bag. He drew a long rectangle and then divided it into five parts and wrote something in them and then drew another diagram with five circles.

Logic, Objectivity, Detached Analysis, Prioritisation	Positive Approach	Meditation	Mantras, Chants	Metaphysics

'Spiritual activities and thoughts cover a wide spectrum, ranging from good, personal and social management at one end, different methods such as meditation, chanting and mantras in other parts and metaphysical aspects at the other end of the spectrum. We can think of all this as one common strand which has overlapping yet distinct and separate components.'

Francis and Benedict were looking at the diagram when Ananda followed his other thought, 'This idea will become clearer if we represent these concepts within a set of concentric circles. In such a picture, we have the option of considering all these as being part of one whole, with the outermost circles showing these aspects all together. Yet, each of these could also be seen in terms of the segmented parts or individual circles, depending on our focus at any moment.' Saying this, he wrote within the set of concentric circles that he had drawn earlier.

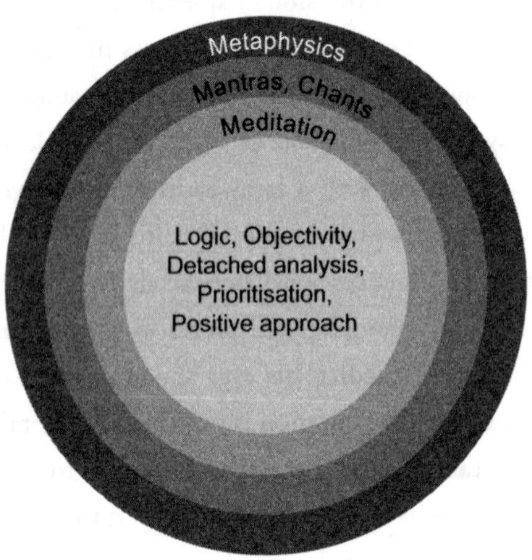

Ananda showed the paper to Francis and Benedict and continued speaking, 'Let us consider that spiritual insights span a spectrum of ideas and activities, which are all interconnected at one level, but can be seen as separate parts also. As shown by David's lecture that you went to with Francis, each concept can be approached from any point in this spectrum. Likewise, each of these circles is connected yet separate, and it is up to us to determine where we situate ourselves. The genius of Buddha was to identify a starting point which could be devoid of any doubt regarding what Benedict terms as "tangibility" or "reality" of spiritual experiences. This is the innermost circle in my diagram. Another aspect of his genius was that he recognised if we progress well within the spiritual context in terms of "good" thought and actions, then the spiritual principles also become our concluding point. Thus, it is interesting that the innermost circle contains both the starting point as well as the final point of our essential spiritual journey, but to manage this convergence our thoughts and actions must embody a positive approach. All the rest are either the means or methods to better accomplish the journey, or some byproducts of these methods. If the positive approach is missing, then our thoughts and actions will not have the basic ingredient of spirituality.'

'Thus, while you may begin the journey from the innermost circle, you will not end up performing your actions with calm and contentment, without this one important ingredient of spirituality. Looking at it in this simple way, one could say that a positive mindset defines the methods for applying spiritual behaviour in our daily interactions.'

'Is there a link between the positive approach and what Buddha emphasised?', asked Benedict.

'Yes, indeed. The term positive is not only with reference to how we should approach situations but also the "good thoughts and actions" emphasised by Buddha. Thus, with a positive approach, we are positive in terms of each situation, as well as in terms of the impact of our thoughts on ourselves and others.'

Ananda was looking carefully at the concentric circles and he started visualising each one merging into the other seamlessly. As he stared some more at the diagram, he saw the smaller ones rise, as if they were not circles but different levels of a pyramid. Just like different dimensions of creation, merged into one but still separate, he thought. How many messages were evident in this simple picture, if one saw it with a deeper vision!

Benedict's mind seemed to be working in overdrive. He had been deeply attentive and gave Ananda a piercing look, 'I know of these spiritual methods and principles through the lecture I attended and books I have read. Francis has described them to me during our discussions. It is indeed interesting if you consider the innermost circle as a starting point and the positive approach as the filter to strengthen the direction and content of your actions. A lot of the lessons start coming together in a coherent way. Francis has also taught me a simple form of meditation. Should I focus on only the innermost two circles and would that make me grow in the desired way, or should I also combine them with meditation?'

'It is up to you and depends on what you wish to emphasise. I think that people like us, those who live a life of intense material experiences could try and focus on at least the innermost circle. If you move ahead with a positive approach and then move on to meditation, that will improve your capability to effectively achieve the objectives that you aim for in terms of the innermost circle,' Ananda explained.

'I find it interesting that you are referring to these as spiritual principles. If I do detach myself adequately, in the way spiritual persons or monks are supposed to do, will I not be giving up on my other responsibilities in life—my family, my friends and my own work responsibilities?' asked Benedict.

'Detachment here means an ability to put yourself at a distance from the situation and assess your options in an objective manner, without involving personal bias in your decision-making. It will be even more interesting for you if I tell you that all these aspects are emphasised, in some way or the other, in self-help books that guide you with methods, based on which some people have achieved major success. Take for instance the book by Covey,[12] where he has summarised certain habits of highly effective people. You will see a major overlap with the principles I have mentioned and the points or habits that he emphasises. An interesting feature of spiritual evolution is that it actually combines both attachment and detachment. Attachment is through compassion and being concerned about others in need, and detachment through an improved ability to adopt a wider and more objective perspective reflecting this new-found attachment. These two help us, thus, to consider our own situation from a more balanced point of view.'

'Thank you. This is an important point for me. How should I increasingly embody these features in my behaviour?'

'The most straightforward way is to treat them as simple rules of daily behaviour. Since these are reasonably specific in what we should emphasise, they provide us with a tangible focus in our actions and attitude, as well as a clear direction and sense of purpose. In this way, they are a touchstone, in relation to which we can judge what should be our appropriate response under different situations, and thus, ascertain the type of effort we need to improve our situation. Combine this with the concept of small steps and concentric circles and we have the spiritual tools for our journey based on an increasingly more balanced and content mindset.'

Benedict nodded at Francis and then turned around to take in the stunning beauty of the mountains and the valleys. 'This place looks even more beautiful today, does it not, Francis?' he asked.

Ananda was happy that Benedict was exhibiting a sense of freedom as he let go of his doubts. How long before some other thoughts would come up to create further queries? Well, he now had a better perspective to deal with those situations. Ananda thought of the Chinese proverb: Give a man a fish and he will eat for a day. Teach a man to fish and he will eat for the rest of his life. Today, in a sense, Benedict had learnt to spiritually fish in the ocean of life rather than just receive fish from those who had answered his questions. With time and experience, he could sustain himself even better and his confidence would improve. Hopefully, he would even teach others.

'This is a beautiful place, Francis. Thank you for getting us all here,' Benedict said joyously. 'And thank you, Ananda. I find so much peace and beauty everywhere. I think I now know what David meant when he emphasised being content instead of being just happy. I feel a sense of calmness deep within.'

'Benedict, you had asked me to explain positive attitude. Well, your present state is another example of being positive,' Ananda said with a smile as all of them fell silent, gazing at the Alps.

In that quiet and peaceful moment, Ananda thought of Vadya. He took out his pen and scribbled on the piece of paper with his diagrams, 'For Vadya'.

He looked at the paper again and saw a beauty in it, which perhaps would be lost to others. The two diagrams were separate, a rectangle, a set of concentric circles, and then something interesting started happening before his eyes. He looked at the rectangles, and saw them become circles, five of them sometimes overlapping and sometimes next to each other. He smiled as he saw these circles creating the basis of some other geometrical shapes that had earlier come to his mind: "the flower of life" and "Metatron's cube". They were two diagrams used in spiritual geometry encapsulating both the beginning and continuity of creation, all entities, animate and inanimate, different expressions of a deeper energy, form and balance.

Ananda focused on Metatron's cube, and then on the five circles that he had drawn—each one connected with the others, while maintaining a separate identity as well. This was the essential ingredient for developing a perspective on what the wider reality encompasses, he thought. To understand ourselves as a whole, we need to better see the connections within our inner and outer structure, two levels of existence, apparently independent and yet connected in a deep integral way.

He looked at the five circles again. He recalled how Metatron's cube begins with five circles in one row, and then by repeating those circles to encompass the three dimensions, it resulted in all platonic solids being described by three sets of five circles. In this way, Metatron's cube begins as a picture simple to understand but as the links amongst the circles multiply, the initial simple structure evolves into more complex objects. The simple becomes complex because we focus on what we see, and not the simple structure that forms the basis of it all. We keep focusing on the overall complex structures that we embody with all the interlinkages amongst its individual components.

Simple yet complex! Complex yet simple! Our ability to understand each part individually or completely would depend on which way we examine a deeper reality about our existence. If we insist on beginning with the complex and staying at that level without understanding the relatively much simpler foundations of it all, we will never understand the way small structures have combined together to give us our whole. He quickly drew Metatron's cube on the piece of paper.

Metatron's Cube

Ananda looked at the three sets of five circles, and the lines that connected the different circles. He recalled how great spiritual masters had simplified this larger reality for humanity, and how each time we insist on making it complex because perhaps, we are not comfortable with the idea that the basic truth, i.e., what we are and what we can make ourselves to be, depends on some simple steps.

The various connections amongst these circles showed that for our inherent balance, stability and completeness, we need to better understand how each level of our being is linked to the other, and also, how each one can mutually enhance our combined presence and achievements provided that relevant steps are taken. The important point is that we need to identify the pertinent content of those steps to move in the direction of enhancing their impact. Small steps covering concentric circles of objectives.

The interlinkages show for instance, that to grow in the material world, we need to achieve inner clarity and growth, which itself becomes a foundation for outward growth. In turn, this outer growth provides a greater potential for inner growth, and in this way a positive cycle is initiated.

Ananda looked at Benedict again to help connect these thoughts with the diagrams he had drawn. 'Benedict, take a look. See how my five circles can be seen in terms of spiritual geometry. Consider the five circles I had mentioned to you and combine that thought with the set of circles in Metatron's cube.'

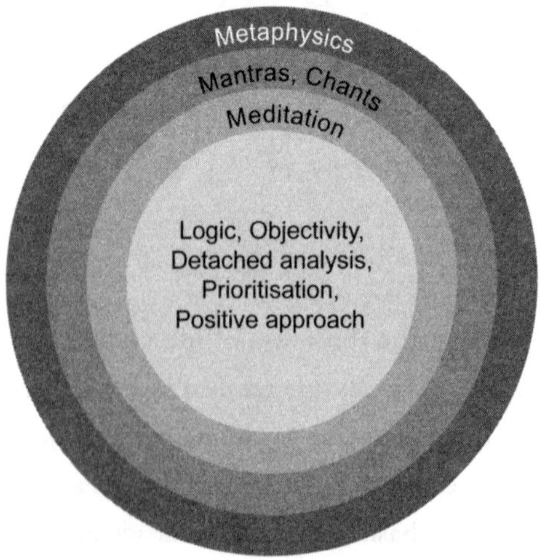

Putting the two diagrams next to each other, he started speaking almost as if he was explaining the concept to himself. 'Take a look at the five circles I have drawn. Place them individually next to each other, in the same way as three sets of five circles are placed in Metatron's cube. This is the basis of spiritual geometry to capture the essential structure of all creation.'

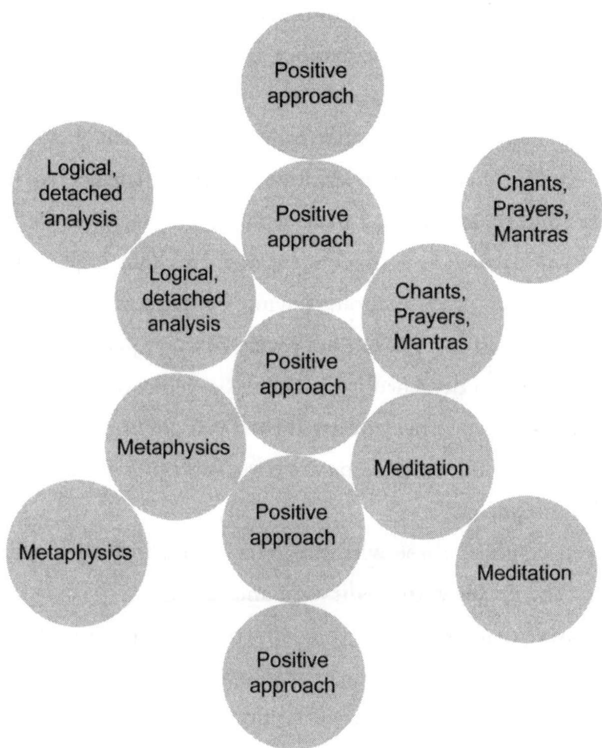

'Now place the concepts from my five circles within the circles of the Metatron cube. In the vertical set of five circles, write "positive approach". Pictorially, this is the spine in our body, essential for us to have balance in every situation, a balance which helps us bring our best potential to apply to any situation. Now consider the nearest four circles around the central spine in this diagram. Write the other four concepts in these circles, one concept in each. A complete spiritual spectrum would cover these five different concepts or circles. However, to be successful in life, while you do not need to experience all of them, you do need to apply some spiritual principles. The starting point amongst these principles would be to base your actions on detached logical analysis and using a positive approach in each situation.'

Benedict took the paper from Ananda and stared at it for some time. 'Is there a reason for the manner in which you have written these five different concepts in this picture?'

'Yes, Benedict', said Ananda. 'Since you have felt uncomfortable with the conventional way that spiritual actions are considered, in terms of prayers and metaphysics, I have separated them from the parts of our framework which are independent of them. Your logical, detached analysis can take place without relying on prayers or metaphysics. Or even meditation or a positive approach. You may just restrict yourself to actions based on detached logical analysis. However, if you combine such efforts with a positive approach then you are further empowered. In that situation, your small steps can cover more of a distance along the concentric circles.'

'If you combine these with meditation, you further expand your potential. The circles with meditation and logical analysis are separate. To give a spiritual content to your efforts with one or both of these concepts, you must connect them through a positive approach. With these three in one set of five circles, you have one part of your existence complete. You will have the ability to make progress in your life, step by step. No need to rely on any prayers or to have any so called metaphysical supernatural experience.'

'Then why draw the other circles and write in them the other concepts?' asked Benedict.

'Because the complete reality, or creation as it exists, includes these other methods as well. You may not wish to rely on them or experience them, but they are part of a larger reality as a lot of the substantive part of our conversation today suggests. Chants, mantras and prayers are today part of healing practices. Sound frequencies do impact our body. Prayers and chants have been shown to cause a change in the capacity of our brain. You may wish to rely on them or not, but they are methods or mechanisms to potentially empower you. It is important to note that even with these concepts, the appropriate content and direction is provided by a positive approach. It is this approach which generates the faith that enhances our positive actions and thoughts. You will recall that one of the books you read has shown faith to be amongst the strongest factors that provides you with peace of mind and reduces internal agitation. That is a good state to be in, if you wish to continue with logical detached analysis.'

Benedict looked uncomfortable and Ananda continued. 'Yes. I know that there is an apparent inconsistency in what I have just said. You are thinking that faith and logical analysis are opposite concepts, one does not overlap with the other. However, scientists who pray and have spiritual faith, and there are many like that, do not leave their logical thinking when applying themselves to any scientific issue. They have a sense of calm which prayers instil. That is one way of looking at it.'

'And metaphysics?' asked Benedict.

'Ah, yes. Metaphysics, the bane of all logic and objective thought. Consider, however, that even Buddha, whose teachings have no place or emphasis on God, at times performed metaphysical acts or miracles.[13] The existence of a larger presence is one which has been experienced. We may or may not wish to focus on these aspects. However, even with the metaphysical realm, a positive approach with compassion is essential to maintain stability. Otherwise, it only leads you away from a mainly spiritual mindset.'

'In this background, look at the drawing of Metatron's cube with its various circles and the lines which connect each of them. This is supposed to be the spiritual geometry of all creation, including the expanding universe. In our framework, consider these connecting lines as compassion. Then the diagram I have drawn gives you another way of looking at the entire creation or deeper basis of your own existence.' Saying this, Ananda picked up the paper with the drawing of Metatron's cube and showed it to Benedict.

'All of creation and the figures which are referred to as platonic solids, are contained in this diagram. Now think of these circles as representing the five different methods or aspects we have talked about. The fulcrum of the centre of this entire representation, as I have shown it, is a positive approach. Each of these methods connect with another through a line connecting the centres of the circles. Think of this line as compassion, i.e. feeling for another in the same way as we feel for ourselves. Without compassion, we cannot really connect. If we do not connect, then our capabilities are far reduced compared to their potential. In the diagram, each of the circles represents one aspect of spiritual thought or principle. Together, connected with compassion they enhance each other.'

'You can choose to function in the part of this diagram which has no link at all with the idea of the Divine. That does not mean an absence of the Divine in the entire construct, but you can be spiritual even without it, or alternatively you could be spiritually infused with the thought of the Divine. The choice is yours.'

Benedict was nodding, Francis was smiling and Ananda looked pleased with himself.

'Benedict, the choice you or I make does not show the limit of the overall spiritual framework, but the part of it we choose for our journey is that part of the spiritual principle or practice that we wish to use. Without using any of the spiritual methods or principles, our progress would be impeded, and we would not advance in a direction that provides us with stability and inner peace.'

Benedict continued nodding, lost in his thought. Carefully, Ananda folded the papers and kept them in his pocket, thinking of his flight back to Delhi. Lost in his world, he closed his eyes and felt a soothing light fill him with a strong loving presence in his heart. He softly called out to his spiritual master, 'Baba', as he was lost to others, totally self-contained and content. How far he had travelled to be so close to himself, walking with his small steps across so many concentric circles!

References

1. https://www.bibliotecapleyades.net/geometria_sagrada/esp_geometria_sagrada_4.htm https://www.bibliotecapleyades.net/geometria_sagrada/esp_geometria_sagrada_6.htm
2. http://www2.astro.psu.edu/users/rbc/a1/lec8n.html http://uhaweb.hartford.edu/nasa/basic/light_6.htm
3. Hawking, Stephen and Mlodinow, Leonard. *The Grand Design*. USA: Bantam Books, 2010.
4. Nelson, Kevin. *The God Impulse: Is Religion Hardwired Into the Brain?* UK: Simon & Schuster, 2011.
5. Dennis, Kingsley L. Quantum Consciousness: The way to Reconcile Science and Spirituality in Laszlo, Erwin and Dennis, Kingsley L (ed.). *The New Science and Spirituality Reader*. USA: Inner Traditions, 2012, p 39.
6. Hawking, Stephen and Mlodinow, Leonard. *The Grand Design*. USA: Bantam Books, 2010, p 7.
7. Krishna, Gopi. *The Real Nature of Mystical Experience*. Connecticut, USA: Bethel Publishers Incorporated, 1978.
8. Nelson, Kevin. *The God Impulse: Is Religion Hardwired Into the Brain?* UK: Simon & Schuster, 2011.
9. Newberg, Andrew B. *Principles of Neurotheology*. UK and USA: Ashgate, 2010.
10. M, Sri. *Apprenticed to a Himalayan Master: A Yogi's Autobiography*. India: Magenta Press, 2010.
11. Boyd, Doug. *Swami: Encounters with Modern Mystics*. India: The Himalayan Institute Press, 1995.
12. Covey, Stephen R. *The 7 Habits of Highly Effective People*. USA: Free Press, 1989.
13. https://www.thoughtco.com/the-buddhist-view-of-miracles-449528